The
Instructional
Leadership
Toolbox

A HANDBOOK
for Improving Practice

SECOND
EDITION

Sandra Lee Gupton

CORWIN
A SAGE Company

D1211522

Copyright © 2010 by Corwin

All rights reserved. When forms and sample documents are included, their use is authorized only by educators, local school sites, and/or noncommercial or nonprofit entities that have purchased the book. Except for that usage, no part of this book may be reproduced or utilized in any form or by any means, electronic or mechanical, including photocopying, recording, or by any information storage and retrieval system, without permission in writing from the publisher.

For information:

Corwin
A SAGE Company
2455 Teller Road
Thousand Oaks, California 91320
(800) 233-9936
Fax: (800) 417-2466
www.corwinpress.com

SAGE India Pvt. Ltd.
B 1/I 1 Mohan Cooperative
  Industrial Area
Mathura Road,
New Delhi 110 044
India

SAGE Ltd.
1 Oliver's Yard
55 City Road
London EC1Y 1SP
United Kingdom

SAGE Asia-Pacific Pte. Ltd.
33 Pekin Street #02–01
Far East Square
Singapore 048763

Printed in the United States of America

Library of Congress Cataloging-in-Publication Data

Gupton, Sandra Lee.
The instructional leadership toolbox: a handbook for improving practice/Sandra Lee Gupton. — 2nd ed.
   p. cm.
Includes bibliographical references and index.
ISBN 978-1-4129-7540-7 (pbk.)
   1. Educational leadership—United States. 2. School principals—United States. I. Title.

LB2831.92.G86 2010
371.2—dc22   2009028202

This book is printed on acid-free paper.

       10   11   12   13   10   9   8   7   6   5   4   3   2

Acquisitions Editor:	Arnis Burvikovs
Associate Editor:	Desiree Bartlett
Production Editor:	Amy Schroller
Copy Editor:	Susan Jarvis
Typesetter:	C&M Digitals (P) Ltd.
Proofreader:	Gail Fay
Indexer:	Judy Hunt
Cover Designer:	Anthony Paular

The
Instructional
Leadership
Toolbox

Contents

Preface

In a sense, leadership can be likened to a craft where knowledge, skills, and practices are of little use unless there is a functional purpose to one's work. However, one who aspires to a craft or to lead is at a loss if he/she has a functional purpose but lacks the knowledge, skills, or practices to work toward or to achieve that end.

—Carl D. Glickman (2008)

No role in school leadership's scope of responsibility today looms larger than that of providing instructional oversight and guidance. Principals—as CEOs of schools—are expected to ensure that good instruction and learning are taking place. Although the principal's desk still symbolizes the place where the buck stops, the principal is by no means the sole source of leadership in most schools today. A more integrated, democratic approach to today's principalship is not merely preferred; it is increasingly essential for dealing well with the nature of today's schools and students. Handling the complex nature of fast-paced change on many fronts and meeting the plurality of student needs demand more participation from stakeholders and the rich resources of multiple talent and skill that can only come from team-based leadership. This book deals most specifically with the principal's role in facilitating leadership that integrates multiple sources, including teachers, students, parents, and community members.

Although this toolbox text is written from the perspective that shared leadership is the preferred orientation for today's school leaders in all of a principal's domains of responsibility, it clearly focuses on instructional leadership and the principal's role in best fulfilling the responsibilities of this vital function. The job of the principal has evolved to one of mobilizer of these many leadership resources. When a principal is skilled in team building and empowering others, leadership can emerge from many of these stakeholder pools. Especially critical to the important function of instructional leadership is the role of teachers as instructional leaders and partners. Though this book is written expressly for principals, much of the information is rooted in the premise that principals and teachers work as partners to provide instructional leadership, with parents and students also involved appropriately in decisions impacting their education. Thus, a primary role for the principal is facilitating such partnerships.

Whether one thinks of school leadership as craft, art, or science, tools are basic to each field. This book offers the principal a compendium of skills, strategies, and information that should enhance (not prescribe) principals' work as craftspersons, artisans, and scientists, especially in the area of instructional leadership. The tools are drawn from the best that research and theory in school administration have to offer today. From this important, but often abstract and obscure knowledge base comes my attempt to organize, synthesize, and reframe the strategies into more practical, thought-provoking formats. Although the text is reader friendly, with frequent abbreviated lists and bulleted points for the principal, it is no monkey-see, monkey-do read. Instead of sure cures and formulas for success, this book offers a set of metaphorical, cognitive tools, which in the hands of reflective educators can help them grow professionally and hone their skills to facilitate better teaching and learning in their own unique settings.

This, the second edition of the book, includes the following revisions:

- It includes updated standards, research, and legislation that have emerged since the original 2003 publication. The latest National Association of Elementary School Principals' and the Interstate Leadership Licensure Consortium's standards are found in Chapters 1 and 2.
- New, exciting research that more specifically ties principals' behavior to student achievement is explained and referenced throughout the text.
- Discussion of the status and impact of the No Child Left Behind legislation is included.
- Quotes and examples of instructional leadership strategies given by practicing principals and veteran educators are featured, especially in the "Walking the Talk" sections added at the end of chapters.
- There is a special section at the end of the book titled "Additional Resources," which includes selected Web sites, workbooks, books, and articles relevant to the chapters.

Tools as Metaphors

The tool metaphor is used throughout this text, with each of the ten chapters presented as a tool having particular potential for helping school principals improve their leadership skill, and thus the school's capacity to help children learn.

Chapter 1 sets the stage for the entire text by helping the reader understand the importance of all educators—and most certainly principals as instructional leaders—to possess and strategically use an internal compass when making decisions, solving problems, and answering difficult professional questions in light of what is best for students and their learning. Glickman (1985) reminds us, "While research and experience help us see the connections between actions and outcomes, they cannot select our goals for us. In this regard, values and beliefs become central" (p. 342). School leaders' introspection and examination of their beliefs and values, and their assessment and awareness of their professional strengths and weaknesses, are the tools offered in this chapter as essential enablers for principals' providing instructional guidance at its best.

Chapter 2 deals with the nuts and bolts of school leadership, which include the importance of school leaders being reflective and well read about today's leadership issues; understanding accountability and standards for twenty-first century school principals; and being up to date and aware of a principal's key role in instructional leadership. These nuts-and-bolts understandings are fundamental tools of a school leader, regardless of the context or the leadership style.

Chapter 3 is about basic processes and products, the blueprints that guide the daily operation of the school and channel its energy most appropriately toward students and learning. The stakeholder-shared processes involved in creating a school's mission, vision, goals and objectives, and strategies (i.e., the blueprint documents) are as important as the products themselves. Only if the documents are living—that is, only if they truly guide the day-to-day operation of the stakeholders in the school—are they worthwhile. Thus, stakeholders must believe in these blueprints and share in their development if they are to be most passionate and enthusiastic about their roles in implementing them. The organization's blueprints are the processes and products essential to channeling the direction and energy of the various constituencies in schools, often characterized as loosely coupled organizations, inclined not to be well-centered or purposefully unified.

Chapter 4 is the superglue of a leader's toolbox. It provides insight into ensuring that the school's culture is positive, and centered on teaching and learning. The importance of and how to assess school climate and culture, the behaviors and skills most essential for creating and maintaining a positive school culture, and the importance of moving a school from a collection of classrooms and cubby holes, parents, and community members to school as a learning community are included in this chapter.

Chapter 5 adds the vital tool—communication conduits—to the principal's toolbox. Strategies for improving the school's communication include the importance of listening and understanding, facilitating dialogue and collaboration among the various school stakeholders, and connecting the school and educators with parents and community members as true partners in the village's shared enterprise of educating its young people.

Chapter 6 offers the leader a humble metaphor for powerful tools—whetstones for ensuring best practices from professional educators in the form of reflective practice, supportive supervision, and cooperative evaluation. These practices are key to professional educators' and schools' continued improvement. As healthy and sane as they may seem, these approaches to very fundamental leadership functions require a major shift in thinking about the roles and responsibilities of today's teacher and principal.

Chapter 7's tool, the instructional leadership lens, is to the principal what safety goggles are to the carpenter. It protects the leader from having his or her vision blurred or damaged by political and other extraneous debris. Using the research-based, learner-centered principles as the reliable lens for making decisions and guiding one's work facilitates leaders by keeping them focused and free from the barrage of distracters to clearheaded, student-centered thinking.

Chapter 8 contains the tools of accountability—tape measures, plumb lines, and common sense. For the principal, these tools are thoroughly understanding accountability issues; appropriately using well-designed standards to facilitate school improvement; and focusing on the classroom as the centerpiece for finding out just how well students are performing.

Chapter 9 adds the muscle tool to the leader's toolbox, the power saw of cutting-edge strategies, which include the important concept of proactive leadership, wherein school leaders make change work for, rather than impede, school improvement; the various processes for dealing responsibly and most productively with data to improve teaching and learning; and the power of technology to transform schools with large populations of students who are at risk of failing into learning communities where all adults and children are most likely to succeed.

Chapter 10 brings us full circle to focusing once again, as we did in the early chapters, on the leader as an individual, rounding out the points in Chapters 1 and 2, which deal with the importance of a principal's self-understanding and thorough examination of his or her beliefs and values, awareness of the standards and professional requirements of today's school leaders, and analysis of his or her strengths and weaknesses in light of those expectations. This chapter brings closure to the text by emphasizing the significance of attending to personal fitness, the undeniably ultimate tool for peak performance: physical stamina, intellectual prowess, social and emotional stability, and spiritual bounty. Sustained neglect in any of these facets of our humanity eventually leads to deficits that take their toll on other dimensions of our lives. Overemphasis on one area does not compensate for deficits in another. Balance is the key. Personal and professional lives are not lived separately; each impacts the other, for better or for worse. Achieving balance across all areas of our lives is challenging, but the better we manage this, the more wholesomely productive we become, at work and at home.

   This handbook for principals has much flexibility for individuals to put their own spin on leadership. Oversimplification of the complex work of leadership by reducing the content to recipes or formulas for success is avoided. Instead, readers are encouraged throughout the book to reflect on various sets of questions that can help a principal find direction most fitting to the situation and the school context. The text's tools are cognitive and work best for the reader who is reflective and sensitive to how the tools can best facilitate school improvement in one's particular situation. Good tools in the hands of a thoughtful, dedicated craftsperson are merely facilitators of the person's drive and passion to improve and to excel at leadership. My hope is that this book finds its way to those educators who have the stamina, ambition, intelligence, and disposition to want the best for our schools and our children, and that it helps them in finding their own way and achieving their dreams and mine for all students to grow up healthy, happy, and well educated. After eight years of focusing on "no child left behind," it seems a far more noble goal for the country to redirect its attention to ensuring that *no child's potential go untapped, unnoticed, under-nurtured or, worse yet, stifled* during his or her formative, developmental years. America's greatest achievement yet would be our ability to help each child be all that he or she can possibly be. My very best wishes to you as you seek to maximize your own potential in our mutual pursuit of making America's schools and the world a better place by investing our very best in children.

Acknowledgments

My special thanks to Corwin for their support of this book from its inception in 2002 to this, its second edition. Corwin's dedication to education and its longstanding commitment to providing top-quality books and media related to the field are exemplary. Special thanks to the Corwin editors who worked so cooperatively with me, Arnis Burvikovs and Desiree Bartlett, Amy Schroller, and Susan Jarvis.

I am deeply indebted and am proud to acknowledge the following outstanding educators who graciously gave feedback for this book's revision and examples of experiences they had as instructional leaders in schools. Their recommendations and contributions are used throughout this revised edition, many of them in the form of quoted pieces added at the end of chapters in the section titled "Walking the Talk"—voices of experience from the field—a new feature of this revised edition:

Dr. Nancy Adams is a veteran educator with many outstanding, award-winning years in the position of elementary school principal in Texas. She has recently moved to the position of Assistant Professor of Educational Leadership at Lamar State University in Beaumont, Texas.

Dr. Amy Lingren is a veteran educator and school principal. She has served in many capacities including, most recently, Chief Officer for Curriculum and Instructional Services for the Duval County Schools in Jacksonville, Florida, a position she has recently given up to move back to the school principalship. Amy has extensive experience as a school principal in three states—Wisconsin, Missouri, and now Florida.

Karen Sue Noble is a veteran educator and principal of Hillcrest Elementary School in Nederland, Texas, since 1992. Karen is the recipient of many prestigious principal awards. Her outstanding leadership seems best demonstrated, however, by the numerous awards bestowed upon the school during her stint at Hillcrest that include the school's recognition as a Title I Distinguished School for nine consecutive years (1998–2007).

Dr. Ricky P. Sahady is currently Curriculum Director of the Resiliency Preparatory School in Fall River, Massachusetts. He is a thirty-three-year veteran educator in the Fall River School District, where he was formerly the principal of John J. Doran Elementary School for twelve years.

Dr. Jan Walker is Associate Professor of Educational Leadership at Drake University in Iowa. Before coming to higher education, Jan served the Iowa public schools in various capacities including being an elementary school principal for many years, an assistant superintendent, curriculum coordinator, and a classroom teacher for twelve years with the honor of having been nominated twice for the Teacher of the Year Award.

Corwin gratefully acknowledges the contributions of the following individuals:

John W. Adamus, Assistant Professor
Rutgers, Graduate School of Education
New Brunswick, NJ

Barbara Gerard, Secretary
Alaska Charter School Association
Academy Charter School
Palmer, AK

Sharon Madsen Redfern, Principal
Highland Park Elementary
Lewistown, MT

About the Author

 **Sandra Lee Gupton**, EdD, is Professor of Educational Leadership at the University of North Florida in Jacksonville, Florida, where she has been serving for the past six years as Chairperson of the Department of Curriculum and Instruction. Before coming to UNF, she was Professor of Educational Leadership at the University of Southern Mississippi for eleven years. Her experiences before coming to higher education include more than twenty years in various positions in PreK–12 public schools, including English and reading teacher, high school principal, director of instruction, assistant superintendent for curriculum and instruction, and superintendent in Georgia and North Carolina schools.

Sandra's professional interests are centered on leadership issues related to PreK–12 and higher education leadership effectiveness, gender equity, program reform, and school improvement. Her early research on gender equity in educational leadership led to many presentations, the publication of several articles, and the 1996 Corwin publication *Highly Successful Women Administrators: The Inside Stories of How They Got There*, offering advice to prospective women administrators in education. Her research and writing in recent years have been focused on the role of academic chairpersons and leadership in higher education.

Sandra has two grown daughters who live near Denver, where she spends much of her free time these days—especially since the birth of her grandchild, Ryan, four years ago. She reports that nothing is much better these days than watching Ryan Parker grow and reveling in his marvelous companionship and passion for living, loving, and learning.

"in whose interest"
For Ryan, who has rekindled my life-long passion for and
dedication to helping schools and educators be their best at nurturing children,
helping them learn, and loving them for their individualities.

1

A School Leader's Compass

In Whose Interest?

Education is a deeply moral enterprise. How can the administration of such an enterprise be any the less moral?

—Christopher Hodgkinson (1991, p. 140)

Effective leaders continually ask questions, probing all levels of the organization for information, testing their own perceptions, and rechecking the facts.

—Warren Bennis and Joan Goldsmith (2003, p. 3)

To do what you say, you have to know what you want to say. To earn and sustain personal credibility, you must be able to clearly articulate deeply held beliefs.

—James Kouzes and Barry Posner (2008, p. 29)

The underlying beliefs that principals hold about teachers and learning determine the efficacy of their actions.

—Joanne Rooney (2008, p. 90)

Navigating successfully in the turbulent seas of today's school leadership requires that principals have a compass—an inner strength, derived from having examined carefully who they are, what they believe and value, and why they are in the business of education. Such self-assessment and reflection enable leaders to understand and thus better manage their emotions and the intense stress so often related to educational leadership positions. This chapter facilitates school leaders' examination of themselves so they can acquire a fundamental leadership tool: a compass that helps them maintain a level head and a moral purpose in doing what is best for students and student learning as they undertake the responsible position of school principal and their important role in instructional leadership. Regarding the power of having a moral compass, author and former school superintendent Larry Coble writes,

> The idea of the power of the moral compass for leaders is more far-reaching than our traditional views of morality. From my perspective, the axis on which the leader's moral compass spins is the leader's core values, the "deep stuff" of his or her make-up. Many would refer to this as executive character. Leaders must know the line that they will absolutely not cross. (Brubaker & Coble, 2005, p. 175)

INTROSPECTION

CLARIFYING CORE BELIEFS AND VALUES

A life lived well is earmarked by harmony between what a person holds dear and how one is able to practice those beliefs and values day in and day out. Outstanding leaders defy a concrete description. They come in all shapes and sizes, from all parts of the world, from across all of time, and may stand for good or evil causes. However, all are clearly alike in at least one distinguishing trait: Their values and beliefs are so well-defined and articulated, their sense of purpose so strong, that their values and resulting purposes become their passions. They feel so strongly about their beliefs and mission that they are willing to take great risks and perform with much courage to further them.

Underpinning all facets of an effective principal's many functions—even those that may not be so risky or require great courage—is what the principal believes in and values. If principals are to be more than managers, they must have at the center of their work and being a set of core values that will propel their work into the ranks of real leadership. Although managing may be interpreted as objectively performing one's duties, leading requires more. There is no value-free leadership; the term is an oxymoron because at the heart of leadership and its close companion—good decision making—are the values and beliefs that form the framework for guiding behaviors and action. Without a well-defined core of beliefs and values, there can be no true leadership. According to Christopher Hodgkinson (1991),

> The educational leader as practical idealist [acts] . . . according to personal ideals, to prevent the bad from being born and the good from dying too soon. The leader is not tossed upon the seas by every wave of political opinion, but feels the honor, and the obligations that go with that honor, to participate in an intensely moral vocation. (p. 165)

The education profession has increasingly focused attention in the past couple of decades on issues related to such moral and ethical leadership. The numerous sets of standards for today's school leaders more often than not include a dimension pertaining to *moral or ethical* expectations. Number five of six educational leadership standards first developed in 1996 by the Interstate School Leaders Licensure Consortium and updated this year (2008) pertains to this dimension of leadership: *An education leader promotes the success of every student by acting with integrity, fairness, and in an ethical manner.* This standard includes being accountable for each student's academic and social success, being a role model for reflective practice and moral behavior, safeguarding democratic values, making decisions that reflect moral and legal considerations, and promoting social justice and a "student-centered" perspective throughout the school's operation. In fact, the new set of standards replaces the term "all students" with "every student," which is repeated in each of the six standards, giving emphasis to the student's success and well-being as the core mission of the school and its personnel.

A number of well-known educational scholars (e.g., Kouzes Posner, 2008; Sergiovanni, 1996, 2006; Covey, 1991, 2004) have described what constitutes the moral imperatives of leadership that they espouse. Michael Fullan (2008), for example, offers "practicing fearlessness"—albeit selectively—as one of ten guiding principles for school leaders. "Effective principals," he asserts, "are men and women who take independent stances on matters of importance and in most cases, are all the more respected for it" (p. 31). Three criteria might be to be selective, to do it on a small scale, and to make your stand a positive rather than a negative act of courage.

Another of Fullan's (2008) guiding principles is for principals to "decide what you are *not* going to do" (p. 37). Fullan describes the hectic nature of a principal's routine day and makes a case for the absolute necessity of a principal setting priorities and not being swept up in the momentum of a school's constant stream of interruptions. In both of these principles set forth by Fullan, the principal's knowledge of his or her beliefs and willingness to stand up for them are key.

From extensive studies related to the principalship, William Greenfield (1985) concludes that a true leader "believe[s] in the worth of what [he or she] seeks to accomplish and exhibit[s] in . . . daily action a commitment to the realization of those." Similarly, Thomas Sergiovanni (2006), researcher and eloquent advocate of "moral leadership," contends that a "good principal needs to have some sense of what she or he values, something to be committed to, a compass to help navigate the way—a personal vision" (p. 334). Without such commitment and vision, researcher and contemporary author Roland Barth (1990) suggests that "our behavior becomes reflexive, inconsistent, and shortsighted as we seek the action that will most quickly put out the fire so we can get on with putting out the next one" (p. 211).

And finally, yet another example of the current focus on values, commitments, beliefs, and the way good leaders demonstrate such moral strength comes from Schwahn and Spady (1998), who claim that "total leaders reflect deeply on their values and principles, are open to their organization and the public about them, and consistently model them" (p. 73). In their fifteen performance roles of a total leader, two directly relate to the leader's personal integrity, which is derived from having and demonstrating a clear set of core values and beliefs: (1) creating and sustaining a compelling personal and organizational purpose and (2) modeling core organizational values and personal principles.

Principals must reflect deeply on their own value systems, particularly as they relate to their role as school leaders, and must be able to articulate their strongest beliefs and values regarding key aspects of schools. Joanne Rooney (2008) offers these suggestions for principals who are so busy "doing" that they find it difficult to have time for thinking and "digging" deeper to find out who they are and what they really believe:

- Seize times for reflection, such as while driving in a quiet car or while sleepless. The saying "the unexamined life is not worth living" is as true for principals as it was for the Greek philosophers.
- Network with other practitioners. Blogs, chat rooms, and e-mail can connect us without formal meetings. A quick lunch to brainstorm with a colleague often offers insights not discovered in isolation.
- Take risks! Few great leaders have played it safe. Let teachers know you are venturing into new territory. It encourages them to do likewise. (p. 88)

Stephen Covey (2004) suggests that all good planning begins by identifying what one believes in and values most dearly. Certainly, identifying one's core beliefs and values, particularly about teaching, learning, and schools, is a fundamental tool for enabling the leadership potential of a principal. Thomas Sergiovanni (2007) encourages all educators to clarify their educational beliefs by articulating them in an educational platform, which he describes as the assumptions or beliefs that deal with the way children and youth grow, with the purposes of schooling, with the nature of learning, with pedagogy and teaching, with educational programs, and with school climate.

Developing an educational platform is not easy. Even veteran educators sometimes find it difficult to describe succinctly what they believe about these important dimensions of school. Developing an educational platform requires a great deal of reflection, introspection, and clarification. The process can be facilitated by reading to learn more about the issues of schooling and education in this country in order to clarify your own thinking about your beliefs and position on issues. But the process of deliberation will surely make you a stronger educator, and one without which you will surely not succeed as a school leader and principal. As Kouzes and Posner (2008) so aptly put it, "To do what you say, you have to know what you want to say. To earn and sustain personal credibility, you must be able to clearly articulate deeply held beliefs" (p. 29).

If you have not engaged in deliberate clarification and articulation of such a platform, the questions in Box 1.1, based on the work of Sergiovanni and Starratt (2007), should be helpful in developing this fundamental piece so critical to effective leadership in general, but even more critical to effective instructional leadership.

BOX 1.1

My Educational Leadership Platform

1. What are the purposes of education?

2. What should the major achievements of students be?

3. What is the role of schools in students' education process?

4. What is the role of the learner in schools?

5. What is the purpose of the curriculum? Who should develop it?

6. What is my concept of an effective teacher?

7. What kind of pedagogy do I favor? Why do I favor this form of pedagogy?

8. What kind of teacher–student relationship is best to support learning?

9. What kind of school climate is best for learning?

10. How do I perceive school leadership?

11. What is the principal's role in school leadership? How do I see myself in this role?

12. What roles should parents, community members, business leaders, teachers, staff, and students play in school leadership?

PERSONAL SKILLS ASSESSMENT

A major part of understanding oneself is identifying "what makes you tick" and identifying your strengths and weaknesses—both personal and professional. Reflecting on and articulating an educational platform as proposed in this chapter are major steps toward self-appraisal and understanding. Done well, such a platform provides the grounding essential for evaluating and making tough decisions and taking action. "Without such a reference point," admonish Razik and Swanson (2001), "the administrator drifts like a rudderless ship on a stormy sea" (p. 351).

Although learning to be a reflective practitioner is probably the best, most reliable form of self-assessment, a host of assessment inventories and instruments are available—usually at a cost—to help individuals clarify their thinking and understand themselves better, both personally and professionally. The keener an individual's awareness is of his/her personal makeup (i.e., likes and dislikes, emotional and social skills, biases, personality, aptitudes, and character traits), the better able he or she is to apply that knowledge objectively and thus effectively in the workplace. Strategically gathering data about oneself is often the first step recommended in career planning. Yet many experienced, practicing principals have done very little to explore their own proclivities in a systematic, objective way.

Dale Brubaker writes about the "power of wanting to be there," a concept that is especially important for educators to understand about themselves—preferably when they first choose to enter a career. "The secret to 'wanting to be there,'" explains Brubaker, "is to know that what you are doing is an extension of what you really value" (Brubaker & Coble, 2005, p. 75). It is no secret that finding work that you are passionate about and really enjoy is often the key to success in it. But in the education profession, the risks of damages to others caused by a person being in a profession he or she does not enjoy—and perhaps even detests—is particularly heinous. As Brubaker aptly puts it, "Teachers probably look to administrators, and children look to teachers, with the same question in mind: *Do you want to be here with me?*" (p. 75). The best favor you could give yourself, your peers, and your students is to find other work if you are not happy being in education, even if it means having to re-tool to make a career change.

It is never too late to make a conscious effort to learn more about oneself. Ideally, this is a lifelong pursuit because, as we continue to learn and grow, we change. Remaining cognizant of how we change as individuals is essential to being our best . . . at home or in the workplace.

PROFESSIONAL SKILLS ASSESSMENT

In addition to self-analysis of personality, personality traits, and personal skills, further deliberate exploration of your leadership style, skills, and behavior can add significantly to understanding yourself and how others may perceive you. Although there are many instruments that are quite good and are appropriately designed to help with leadership analysis, be careful to choose instruments that are based on current research and knowledge about school leadership and that are well normed with subjects that reflect the diversity of today's professional leadership population. Unfortunately, some of the available instruments lack reliability and relevance for today's school leaders because they rely heavily on constructs and models of leadership from more than thirty years ago. The characteristics and behaviors of more recently recognized leadership styles labeled as transformative and integrative are fundamental to reflect the models of leadership needed in today's schools. In addition, the exclusion of minority and female subjects in the norming processes of the older instruments used to measure leadership renders them useless now. With the current literature that widely substantiates and acknowledges gender-as-a-class differences that exist in leadership styles, it is inexcusable to continue to measure leadership with instruments that have not been validated by a representative norming population that includes minorities and women.

The leading educational administration organizations have well-developed, frequently updated, easily accessed, free sets of standards for school principals that can easily be adapted to self-instruments. In addition, literature outlining the skills, behaviors, knowledge, and dispositions principals need to provide for sufficient leadership are also readily available. There is no dearth of standards for school leadership; the key is to find the ones that have most authenticity for today's school leader, and for you to study and use in assessing your own professional attributes.

The standards established for principals by the Interstate School Leaders Licensure Consortium (ISLLC) have had a major impact on principal licensure. As of 2006, forty-three of forty-nine states with administrator certification and leadership standards reported having based their standards on or aligned them with the ISLLC standards. A number of states have also contracted with the Educational Testing Service (ETS) to develop a licensure assessment based on the ISLLC standards, which many of them now use as the required principals licensure examination. Thus, the ISLLC standards, with their supportive functions, provide an excellent source to use as a trustworthy, relevant set of standards by which to undertake self-examination and reflection of one's professional strengths and weaknesses for school leadership today. School principals and leaders should certainly be familiar with this nationally endorsed set of standards since it has such widespread influence on today's policy makers. Each of the current six ISLLC school leadership standards (listed in Chapter 2) is illustrated with a set of exemplary functions. The complete version of these standards (ISLLC, 2008) is quite lengthy but easily accessed from the Council of Chief State School Officers' Web site (www.ccsso.org/ISLLC2008Research).

In its 2008 edition of *Leading Learning Communities: Standards for What Principals Should Know and Be Able to Do*, the National Association of

Elementary School Principals (NAESP) offers its six standards for "effective principals," followed by sample behaviors that demonstrate each standard. In addition, each standard is illustrated by what NAESP titles "Inside a School: A Focus on Practice," a real-world example of the standard from a practicing principal. These standards and illustrations can be found on NAESP's Web site (www.naesp.org).

More specific than "standards" are "proficiencies." One excellent resource to assist a principal in a more skill-specific self-assessment process is Daresh's (2006) handbook for principals, *Beginning the Principalship: A Practical Guide for New School Leaders.* This handbook offers a personal leadership checkup complete with summaries of several credible lists of principal proficiencies. Daresh suggests that the list of leadership skills developed by the NAESP in 1991 is a user-friendly tool for self-assessing one's leadership strengths and those areas in need of improvement or refinement.

Being reflective and analytical about yourself and what you believe is essential to being at your personal or professional best. Keeping abreast of the ever-changing standards for leaders developed by the profession and seeking honestly to assess oneself with these standards is one way to stay tuned in and sensitive to the areas needed for professional growth as a leader. Of course, the real usefulness of such personal and professional examination and clarification depends on what is done with it. To this end, Larry Coble contends, "Tapping the power of your moral compass will be a way of guaranteeing that you are being true to yourself and the people you lead. Using this power means that you must act. You can talk the talk and you can commit volumes of your philosophy to writing, but unless you live out what you believe, you are a fake" (Brubaker & Coble, 2005, p. 182). Once areas of personal and professional strength and weaknesses are identified, it is important to develop a plan of action with goals, specific strategies, and a timeline for accomplishing them. Personal and professional development should be an ongoing part of every educator's life. Outstanding educational leaders are exemplary lifelong learners who continue to grow personally and professionally, and hone their professional skills as long as they remain active in the profession. Such leadership will occur only with deliberate attention to and reflection about oneself and one's job performance and professional disposition. The time spent in self-assessment and reflection usually reaps rich dividends in the long run by increasing skill level and heightening a sense of enthusiasm and energy that is so essential to the work of good leadership.

Indisputably, routine clarification of one's personal beliefs, values, moral compass, and leadership skills can facilitate a person's ability to function well and to continue to grow and develop as a leader. The process is never complete, of course—what better model is there for teachers, parents, and students than school leaders who themselves demonstrate the power and benefits of lifelong learning, remain open to new ideas, and continually seek feedback, reflect, and then act on it for improvement? Writing on the importance of leaders' moral foundations, Schwahn and Spady (1998) assert, "quality leaders openly endorse, consistently model, and clearly exemplify the core values of excellence and productivity and the professional principles of accountability and improvement. Together, these four moral elements define and shape their commitment to continuous improvement—of themselves, their employees, and their organization's processes and products" (p. 91). School leaders could benefit from asking "In whose interest?" which acts as a compass to guide their daily work in schools. If decisions are not made and action is not clearly taken in the best interests of students and their learning, how can it be justified? *Nuff* said!

SAMPLING OF PUBLISHED ASSESSMENT INSTRUMENTS

Leader Behavior Questionnaire (LBQ), Revised (1988–1996). Authored by Marshall Sashkin. Published by Human Resource Development Press. Can be used by the principal to self-assess or to get feedback from faculty on leadership skills.

Leadership Competency Inventory. Authored by Stephen P. Kelner. Published by Hay/McBer. Can be used to self-assess or to get feedback from faculty on leadership skills.

The FIRO Awareness Scale (1957–1996). Authored by Will Schutz and Marilyn Wood. Published by Consulting Psychologists Press, Inc. Can be used to evaluate interpersonal relations by the individual or as feedback from a group.

Gregorc Style Delineator (1982–1998). Authored by Anthony F. Gregorc. Published by Gregorc Associates, Inc. Can be used by the individual as a means of self-assessment or to enable members of a group to understand each other and their varied approaches as individual to dealing with information.

Myers-Briggs Type Indicator, Form M (MBTI; 1943–1998). Authored by Katharine Briggs, Isabel Briggs Myers, Mary McCaulley, Naomi Quenk, and Allen Hammer. Published by Consulting Psychologists Press, Inc. Can be used for self-assessment by an individual for understanding her own personality type or with a group to enable the group members to understand each other's varied personalities.

School Principal Job Functions Inventory (SP-JFI). Authored by Melany Baehr, Frances M. Burns, R. Bruce McPherson, and Columbus Salley. Published by London House, Inc. Can be used by the principal and/or faculty to rate the leader's ability to perform various functions. Different forms are available for individual self-assessment and group assessment.

Walking the Talk

An example of introspection and continuous improvement from the field

I have found that surveys are a great way to get information (for assessing the school's progress). Although principals do need to have conversations and meetings with our teachers, surveys enable us to question a wider audience and get thoughtful and candid perceptions. I regularly survey staff members and parents. I always ask parents to agree or disagree with the statement "My child's individual needs have been met." That's an intimidating measure, but we need to hear parents' responses. I always ask teachers if I have been helpful to their growth. It's important to end all surveys with an open-ended invitation for the respondent to share thoughts on any issue. Eliciting others' perceptions in this way is an important first step in creating a team.

As we review the year, principals need to reflect on personal performance. What did we accomplish? In which areas were we successful, in which areas do we feel frustrated, and in which areas do we wish we could have a "do-over"? What practices should we continue and what should we change? . . . As we look ahead to the re-opening of school, we need to think about preparing *ourselves*. What can we do this summer to refresh ourselves as people, not just educators? (Hoerr, 2008, pp. 88–89)

Thomas R. Hoerr is head of school at the New City School in St. Louis, Missouri, and a frequent contributor to Educational Leadership Journal's *department, The Principal Connection, from which this excerpt is taken.*

POINTERS FOR THE PRINCIPAL

- Develop your educational leadership platform.
  - Clarify by putting in writing your most basic beliefs about students, teaching, learning, and leading.
  - Differentiate between your core beliefs and values and those open to change.
  - Look for inconsistencies in your actions and your stated beliefs.
  - Try daily to behave in concert with your beliefs about what is in the best interest of students.

- Know thyself.
  - Take routine, objective stock of yourself—personal characteristics, biases, personality.
  - Find out how others perceive you (the good, the bad, and the ugly)!
  - Act on the results to make a personal plan to improve.
  - Always consider yourself a "work in progress."

- Know thyself as a leader too.
  - Take stock of your leadership skills.
  - Do self-assessments and actively seek anonymous input from relevant others (i.e., supervisors, faculty, students, staff, parents).
  - Be objective and open to the feedback, then act on it to become a better principal.

2

The Nuts and Bolts of School Leadership

It would be easier if effective leadership were simply a skill set to be learned . . . Truly effective leadership demands a thoughtful examination of who we are as human beings, professionals, and leaders.

—Joanne Rooney (2008, p. 90)

The future of American education can be no brighter than the future of the . . . school principalship.

—National Association of Elementary School Principals (1990, p. 45)

As basic as nuts and bolts are to the handyperson's toolbox is the principal's understanding of the literature base related to organizations and leadership skills needed to be an effective leader. Too often, the importance of studying and understanding relevant research and theory is dismissed by the school practitioner as being too "ivory tower" and unrelated to the real world—the day-to-day operation of schools. Indeed, over the last decade, the national push for accountable programs to prepare school leaders has set in motion a trend toward mandatory internships and strong problem-based curricula to address what is perceived as a lack of relevancy in the preparation of principals.

Although scant research exists to support any one form of administrator preparation, the need for more practical applications of this knowledge and theory base as part of integrated administrator-preparation programs has been widely accepted and supported by numerous nationally recognized leaders, accreditation councils, and professional organizations in the field (e.g., National Council of Accreditation of Teacher Education, American Association of School Administrators, National Association of Secondary School Principals, National Council of Professors of Educational Administration, Interstate School Leaders Licensure Consortium). This widespread acceptance and endorsement of such hands-on, field-based preparation experiences may now have tilted the theory-versus-practice scales so far to the right that leadership preparation programs' treatment of the extant literature and theory base could be in jeopardy. Jacques (1989) warns,

> If you dislike theory and seek only "practical action," that is unfortunate . . . Anything you do is founded upon a theory of some sort, and eschewing theory merely means that your decisions are being misdirected by some bad theory which you do not know about. (p. 3)

The more an administrator reads and reflects upon the research and theory base in the profession, the more likely the leader is to be able to draw from that well of understanding to make sound decisions, rather than react in knee-jerk fashion. Daresh and Playko (1995) assert the following:

> When our perspectives are rooted in theory, we also have access to a way of guiding our behaviors in everyday problems and situations. As a consequence, our actions will be based on something other than the same tired answers to the same tired questions. (p. 71)

Being professionally well read and keeping abreast of the growing knowledge base on effective leadership, reflecting on your practice and the relationship between it and the literature, embracing the concept of accountability as a responsible professional person and as a fundamental part of the school's everyday operation, being aware of and using national standards for the school and for yourself as a means of evaluation and professional development, and understanding the critical role of instructional leadership as the pervasive, over-arching fabric of the school leadership umbrella are the nuts and bolts of the contemporary principal's trade and the tools with which you hone professional skill and increase your understanding of the complexities of good leadership and accountability. This chapter deals briefly with each of these four basic areas of concern, which today's principals must know and understand to maximize their leadership potential in the position.

LEADERSHIP FOR TODAY'S SCHOOLS

WHAT THE LITERATURE SAYS

Without question, the role of the principal has evolved into a very different job from the principalship most often associated with the first half of the twentieth century. Even since the writing of this book's first edition (2003), the role has morphed further. Increasingly, scholars and researches are linking better defined leadership practices to the ultimate variable in educational research: *student achievement.*

The role of today's principal as "instructional leader" is giving way to such terms as "leader of learning" or the "learning leader" (Reeves, 2006). These latter terms suggest what has become clearer and better documented in the research in recent years: there is a definite link (although it is more indirect than direct) between principals' performance and student achievement (Hallinger & Heck, 1998; Leithwood, Jantzi, & Steinbach, 1999; Marzano, Waters, & McNulty, 2005). Simultaneously, there is a growing emergence and increasing emphasis on *distributed leadership*, which is not solely posited in the principalship nor seen as hierarchal and top-down, but rather is shared among others in the stakeholder pool.

Synthetic reviews of the many research studies on effective school leadership (i.e., in schools where students' academic achievement is not consistently predicted by their parents' income levels or their ethnic origins) are increasingly indicating the vital role of the principal in the success of the school (e.g., Cotton, 2003; Goodlad, 1994; Leithwood, Louis, Andersen, & Wahlstrom, 2004; Marzano et al., 2005). One of these reviews, Kent Peterson's (1999) review of research on what effective principals do to help students achieve success, yielded the following condensed behavior patterns:

1. Principals provide instructional leadership and nurture it in others.
2. Principals shape the school culture and climate.
3. Principals manage and administer complex organizational processes.
4. Principals build and maintain positive relations with parents and community.
5. Principals lead and support school improvement and change.

Examination of today's effective principal literature reveals that the most conceptually critical role shift has been from a focus on the managerial orientation to the leadership orientation. However, it is important to note that sound management continues to be a major part of effective leadership. Its role is an important one for effective, efficient leadership of any organization. Peterson's above summary of five dimensions of principals' responsibility illustrates the varied areas of expertise demonstrated by principals deemed successful in their roles, with number three of the five dimensions referencing "management" responsibilities. The issue of manager versus leader should not be one of "either–or." Effective leaders are also good managers. The issue is more about where the focus should be for today's school principals, and without question the focus in today's accountability-laden education landscape must be on providing learning leadership.

Even though management is a key part of leadership, the distinction between administrators as "managers or leaders" is often made in post-1980s research related to school leadership. "A manager does the thing right," offer Bennis and Nanus (1985) in their book on leaders, but "a leader does the right thing" (p. 4). Research has identified two primary dimensions operating simultaneously in organizations: organizational concerns and people concerns. Managers are more typically perceived as being focused on the organization's tasks. However, understanding and motivating workers in an organization to achieve its mission is more often ascribed to the role of leaders. Make no mistake, today's school administrators must concern themselves with both dimensions, both to be effective and to facilitate the mission and goals of the organization. Today's principal must embrace both organizational and human concerns—be a manager *and* a leader—in order to maximize the school's effectiveness. In its 1990 report entitled *Principals for Our Changing Schools*, the National Commission for the Principalship succinctly described the contemporary principal's dual role of managing and leading:

> Principals provide leadership to schools along two dimensions. Exercising broad leadership, they influence school cultures by building a vision, stimulating innovation, and encouraging performance. Principals also exercise initiative in a more technical sense by the daily practice of functional leadership. They "make things happen" and ensure that the organization's tasks are accomplished. (p. 21)

Understanding all one possibly can about these two complex dimensions of leadership—organizations and people, managing and leading—is at the heart of a school principal's work. To diminish the importance of or to ignore the research and increasingly enlightening literature on these topics is to seal a principal's mediocrity—or, worse, one's doom.

There is no shortage of literature on leadership and the evolution of the school principal's primary function from one of managing to one of leading (Blase & Blase, 2004; Lieberman, 1995; Schlechty, 1990). In its 1990 report, the National Commission for the Principalship states,

> As demands grow upon schools for improved quality and broader services, a new principalship emerges . . . No longer [solely] a manager of routines, principals need increasingly to take initiatives . . . All this requires more knowledge. It requires leadership. Not ordinary leadership but astute leadership. (p. 11)

Leadership has been studied and conceptualized from numerous perspectives (e.g., personality, emotions, skills, behaviors, styles). Lunenburg and Ornstein's most recent textbook (2008) is representative of synoptic texts on educational administration that often include a chapter on leadership. Lunenburg and Ornstein summarize the state of the art on leadership studies in their opening paragraph in the leadership chapter of their text:

> Since the beginning of the twentieth century, the topic of leadership has been the object of extensive study. During this time, both researchers and practitioners have sought to analyze and define leadership. Today there are almost as many definitions of effective leadership as there are researchers who have studied the concept. More than 3000 empirical investigations have examined leadership. More recently, Kenneth Leithwood and Daniel Duke reviewed the literature dealing with leadership in educational administration over the past decade. The results suggest 6 major categories of leadership [which are] instructional, transformational, moral, participative, contingency, and managerial. (p. 114)

In addition to the importance of today's principal being more accountable for and focused on "learning," increasing emphasis is also put on the principal's role in facilitation of more democratic processes that engage relevant people in leadership throughout the school (distributive leadership); such facilitation creates a learning, collaborative community rather than a unilateral, autocratic environment complete with top-down authoritarian commands. Almost two decades ago, the National Commission for the Principalship (1990) posited that true leadership is exercised when "leaders nurture in their constituents a capacity to engage in the leadership task. Since autocracy undermines initiative, building this capacity requires leaders who consult and listen and who respect and develop the human potentiality" (p. 13). The principal's role in the distributed nature of today's school leadership has also been described as the creation of a safe environment for teachers, using dialogue rather than dictates to keep the focus on core instructional issues. However, such democratic processes at the school level require systemic support systems to be successful. Community expectations and district-level leadership can either facilitate or impede this democratic, participatory approach to the principalship. Although this movement is prevalent in the literature, its widespread application in today's schools remains disputable for a number of reasons— some of which are beyond the control of the principal.

Although definitions of leadership are numerous and vary widely, and models of leadership abound, one thing emerges loud and clear: No one leadership model, style, trait profile, or set of skills works best in all schools. However, that having been acknowledged, the work of a number of today's educational leadership scholars has produced better results in ferreting out from the research findings about what can be most useful in helping today's school leaders to be successful (Leithwood et al., 1999; Marzano, Waters, & McNulty with the Mid-Continental Research on Education Laboratory, 2003; Reeves, 2006). Despite the complexity of leadership and the profound impact that situation or context most surely makes on what constitutes appropriate leadership behaviors, the literature today is increasingly linking leadership behaviors to student achievement and offering more concrete suggestions to enable today's educator leaders to be more strategic in their approaches to leadership.

Researcher Kenneth Leithwood, for example, attempts to make sense of the profundity of research on the topic in order to give much-needed direction to school leaders regarding what leadership practices impact student achievement most positively. From an extensive review of research on this topic, Kenneth Leithwood and Carolyn Riehl (2005) conclude most emphatically that leadership makes a difference in student achievement. Their conclusions, drawn from the review, are framed in what they call "claims" (rather than certainties) about what the research indicates—for a "rational model" of leadership—about school leadership. These claims are valuable for today's school leaders because they are backed by a strong research base, which is not typical of much of the literature on leadership:

1. Successful school leadership makes important contributions to the improvement of student learning.

2. The primary sources of successful leadership in schools are principals and teachers.

3. In addition to principals and teachers, leadership is and ought to be distributed to others in the school and school community.

4. A core set of basic leadership practices is valuable in almost all contexts.

5. In addition to engaging in a core set of leadership practices, successful leaders must act in ways that acknowledge the accountability-oriented policy context in which almost all work.

6. Many successful leaders in schools serving highly diverse student populations enact practices to promote school quality, equity, and social justice. (pp. 12–27)

To facilitate even better use of the research, Leithwood's work offers school principals three categories of practices that cut across time, organization, and context as being behaviors indicative of successful leadership: Setting Direction, Developing People, and Redesigning the Organization. This study further describes what particular practices pertain to each of the larger categories of practices of successful leaders (Leithwood & Riehl, 2005).

Effective principals are, indeed, only part of the school leadership of highly successful schools today. Research on effective principals is overwhelmingly supportive of the principal as a facilitator and team builder, rather than the buck-stops-here boss and autocrat. Ann Lieberman (1995) asserts

> The 1990s view of leadership calls for principals to act as partners with teachers, involved in a collaborative quest to examine practices and improve schools . . . Principals are not expected to control teachers but to support them and to create opportunities for them to grow and develop. (p. 55)

Just how this is accomplished, however, defies specific prescription. Each school is unique and may require the use of varied, less than ideal, stop-gap leadership measures in progressing to the point at which the school community (i.e., teachers, parents, students, community members) is ready, willing, and able to embrace and participate in what is generally accepted as today's most ideal organizational state, which is school-as-community, with strong systems of collaboration and shared decision making.

Even though there is exciting new evidence to give better direction to leaders for making changes and using strategies that have a record of impacting student achievement most favorably, effective school leadership—much like effective teaching—remains highly individual, situational, and contextually sensitive (Lunenburg & Ornstein, 2008; Razik & Swanson, 2008). Acting expediently and effectively may indeed be facilitated by improving the interpretation and analysis of the profession's research base on leadership and by understanding general recommendations, but what will or won't work in a particular situation will never be "cut and dried." Leadership and teaching are true professions. The work is complex and will always necessitate more than overly simplified, prescribed formulas or sets of failproof how-tos. Most of the research referenced in this chapter stipulates just that. In Leithwood and his colleagues' research synthesis, they draw conclusions about leadership behaviors they term "claims"; and ISLLC's (Interstate School Leaders Licensure Consortium's) standards are called "policy standards" because they are not intended to be *overly applied*. More often than not, findings in the literature on effective leadership do not conclude step-by-step behaviors, but rather offer less-concrete guiding principles.

For example, in their 2005 meta-analysis of sixty-nine studies on leadership, researchers Marzano, Waters, and McNulty list *flexibility* as one of twenty-one "responsibilities" that correlate to student achievement. They define *flexibility* as the "extent to which leaders adapt their leadership behavior to the needs of the current situation and are comfortable with dissent." The ultimate test of leaders' expertise will continue to be how well they know and understand themselves and the context—both the organizational and people dimensions—in which they work, and how well they keep abreast of and apply the best of what is offered by the ever-changing literature and research base in education. Only then can a leader be expected to make the best judgment about what approach or practice is likely to be successful in any situation in terms of helping an organization and its people to improve—or, better yet, excel. Fortunately, the literature is offering more help to school leaders than ever before by synthesizing and analyzing the extensive research on effective schools that has accumulated over the past forty years.

To be sure, the work of contemporary school leaders is infinitely more complex than simply acquiring particular skills, knowledge, or style. Although all of these are important, the toughest challenge is knowing when and how to use and adjust one's skills and knowledge to meet the demands of the situation, which is often unique and may indeed have little precedence in the literature. Delicate work? Ah, yes indeed! One might even call it professional prowess, this craft of school principals. But impossible? Certainly not. Based on a well-developed set of professional and personal values and practices that give life to one's school vision—both clearly student-centered— a principal's course has sufficient internal compass and steadfastness to guide him or her. Skills, knowledge, and style are the important tools that help principals to adjust and tweak their role to meet the needs of the situation. With such grounding, understanding, and adaptability, a principal is more likely to be successful in leading the school toward realizing its shared vision and meeting its mission of educating *every child* in its charge.

ACCOUNTABILITY AND THE PRINCIPALSHIP

MAKING THE GRADE

No principal today can expect to survive, much less excel, without a good understanding, keen appreciation, and philosophical acceptance of (without being overwhelmed by) the need for schools and educators to be accountable. Accountability is indisputably fundamental to any profession. The early 1980s, with the nationally commissioned report *A Nation at Risk*, ushered in a decade of similar accusatory reports condemning America's schools for their mediocrity and shameless waste of the almighty tax dollar. These reports resulted in a nationwide push for more accountability from public schools in the United States and a flurry of reform efforts that continue today—most notably the No Child Left Behind legislation of 2001. Various analyses have been made of the accountability movement during the last two decades; these are similar to the following position taken by the National Commission for the Principalship (1990):

> Major environmental transformations [in the 1980s] created new expectations for schools as well as generated requirements for new organizational processes and structures. Among these expectations were demands that student achievement match international standards, that schools assume responsibility for graduating higher

percentages of students, and that operational structures be decentralized. Many principals were unprepared for these new circumstances. (p. xxi)

Essentially, the movement has progressed from demanding more of students by increasing graduation requirements and raising curriculum standards, by seeking more accountability from teachers and teacher preparation programs, to today's greater emphasis on accountability from principals and programs preparing school administrators. In response to the reports, to the public's growing discontent with their children's education, and to what legislators perceive as their constitutional responsibility, state legislatures have for the past twenty years spouted forth a nonstop stream of mandates and initiatives aimed at making schools more accountable for student achievement. The frantic search for the key to improving the nation's schools has led to a litany of ill-conceived, poorly implemented initiatives that for the most part have been woefully lacking in the substance, research base, funding, or commitment sufficient for successful implementation. Just as prepackaged kits and teacher-proof curricula were no panaceas to improving our schools' science and math curricula in the 1960s and 1970s, when the successful launching of the Soviet Union's *Sputnik* created the race to space, neither are today's legislated standards for schools and districts the cure for the ills of today's schools. Prescriptive or mandated approaches to school reform have never worked, nor are they likely to now. Such approaches defy a fundamental principle of change and improvement: *Significant, lasting change must come from within people and organizations.*

In the wake of the failure of most of these top-down reform efforts, the tide has most recently turned to individual school-based accountability. Required state standardized testing and the issuance of report cards on individual schools, Goals 2000, and the No Child Left Behind (NCLB) Act, are the most recent pieces of legislation to have a significant impact on the functioning of educators today. For example, the statewide report card issued annually by many of the states well before the enactment of NCLB originally reported its results by school districts, and then moved to reporting "grades" for individual schools. The "grade" is generated by using a formula to assess a school's effectiveness, which includes a number of criteria in addition to standardized test results. Depending on the state, the measures to help those schools that fall below a certain grade vary. Underperforming schools are usually targeted for special assistance and given a stipulated time in which they must show improvement or suffer a variety of consequences (e.g., replacement of the principal, replacement of the principal and underperforming teachers, takeover by a community parenting council, loss of certain funding, or state takeover). The hotly debated, highly controversial NCLB Act has heightened the school-based accountability movement and elevated the use of standardized testing results to an unprecedented level of importance in determining accountability. This act is now in a state of suspended "reauthorization" as the nation undergoes transitioning to a new president, and the schools brace for what will most likely be a new or significantly revised set of federal approaches to school reform.

States still have oversight of how schools and districts must comply with NCLB and other federal legislation. The states vary, however, in how they use tests to hold schools and districts accountable, even under the directions of NCLB. Heeding the pleas of teachers and school administrators, some states had already worked out—well before the NCLB's enactment—quite sophisticated grading formulas to level the playing field for schools and districts with large numbers of students who came from low socioeconomic homes and whose parents had little formal education. For example, certain states offered rewards for their districts and schools that exceeded their expected performance levels; some states had made good progress in focusing on student improvement (i.e., how much students gained during the year) as the primary measure for grading the school rather than looking only at students' test scores at the close of the year. Still, most principals and teachers find the standardized testing craze more of a liability to their work than an effective, useful way of determining accountability. The major educational organizations have reacted strongly to the problems they see with NCLB, and have been quite vocal in what needs to be changed, especially the way Adequate Yearly Progress (AYP) is determined under the federal guidelines.

Although many of the grading adjustments that some states devised do seem fairer and more sensitive to the realities of varying school populations, what has yet to happen on a large scale is the creation of more *accountable systems* for determining educational accountability. Authentic accountability for children's academic performance rests on much more than test scores and includes all parties who are responsible for children—schools, districts, board members, parents, churches, communities, social services, state and federal agencies, and legislators. Unfortunately, the emphasis on testing as a means of holding schools accountable shortchanges the schools' important role in dealing with the "whole child," and unfairly ignores or marginalizes the vital roles of other stakeholders in children's academic achievement.

If students are most effectively to be helped to achieve, all stakeholders should be recognized and included in the "accountability pie." After all, most folks understand—at some level—that a child's success or failure at school is not a sole function of how well the school is doing . . . that a child's chances for school success or failure begin long before the child gets to school and are impacted by a host of people, experiences, and circumstances outside the school's domain. Still, schools need not shirk, but indeed should embrace, finding better ways to account for students' wellbeing, successes, and failures. Indeed, schools are in the pivotal position to provide leadership in establishing more authentic systems of accounting for what is happening to students academically, but that does not mean that schools are sole proprietors of the "pie."

It is virtually impossible to ferret out the complex, multiple variables that influence students' achievement or to assign individual responsibility to each contributing force. What does *not* follow, however, is the other extreme: having no one accountable for anything! Until buck passing, finger pointing, and grading school performance primarily via standardized testing are replaced by sincere attempts to share responsibility and accountability for children's well-being through strong partnerships in the complex tasks of raising and educating them, little progress is likely to be made by holding any one constituency of the child's support system disproportionately accountable. Good principals and teachers know this. That is why the outstanding ones, though not ignoring the various accountability initiatives requiring their attention and feedback, clearly do not rely or dwell on such negative, shallow measures of accountability. Instead, effective leaders focus their mental energy and the bulk of their study, time, and attention on making good things happen for children. They do not waste their precious time and energy casting blame or making excuses. They choose instead to spend their time looking for ways to make children's lives better, and often take the initiative to coordinate and engage the efforts of various people, agencies, and groups that make up their students' support systems. They are true leaders and advocates for children, and as such realize the importance of extending their leadership beyond the boundaries of their school campus to ensure that children in their schools get the resources and nurturing essential for their good health and well-being—the bedrock of children's academic successes at school.

STANDARDS FOR TODAY'S SCHOOL LEADERS

MEASURING UP!

An outgrowth of the accountability movement is the trend toward developing national standards pertaining to all aspects of public schools—the curriculum, student performance, teacher preparation programs and state licensing, teacher performance, administrator preparation programs and licensing, and administrator performance.

America 2000, commissioned by the U.S. Department of Education, and its companion reform plan, Goals 2000, fueled the fire for developing standards initiated in the late 1980s. A number of national subject-area professional groups responded to the report by developing national curriculum goals and objectives for students at all grade levels (e.g., National Council of Teachers of Mathematics, American Association for the Advancement of Science). Although having no official authority unless adopted by states or school districts, these standards nevertheless have created a flurry of attention. Some states have either adopted the standards wholesale or adapted them for use as their required statewide curriculum.

Using national tests for licensing educators based on national standards continues to be an issue, since states have constitutional authority over the educational system—including the licensing of educators—in their own state. Most states have their own examination and process for licensing educators. The National Board for Professional Teaching Standards has now established standards for all areas of teaching. Although this board serves in no official capacity, its influence is indisputably strong as states struggle to develop professional licensing standards and examinations that meet the public's growing thirst for proof of teachers' competence.

Similar to the teachers' national standards, standards for the preparation of school principals have been developed by the National Policy Board for Educational Administration. Universities continue to undergo major reforms of their preparation programs to conform to the standards set in motion by this national board, which is supported by prestigious professional organizations such as the National Association of Secondary School Principals and the National Association of Elementary School Principals.

The most recent set of nationally recognized standards, less comprehensive and detailed (by design) than those stipulated by the National Commission for the Principalship, is titled *Educational Leadership Policy Standards: ISLLC 2008 as Adopted by the National Policy Board for Educational Administration.* These standards (referenced in Chapter 1) were developed by the ISSLC, a consortium of thirty-two educational agencies and thirteen educational administration associations that have established an education policy framework for school leadership. The first set of standards from this group was developed in 1996, and the standards have recently undergone review and revision. This group of professionals, known as the ISLLC, operates under the auspices of the Council of Chief State School Officers (CCSSO), which describes the new set of standards as "represent[ing] the latest set of high-level policy standards for education leadership" and "reflect[ing] the wealth of new information and lessons learned about education leadership over the past decade" (CCSSO, 2008, p. 1).

This 2008 set of school leadership standards clearly stipulates that these are *policy standards* designed to be discussed at the policy-making level, not to be rigidly interpreted or used to dictate practice or program content. Thus, these new policy standards do not have accompanying indicators as the first set of standards they developed did, lest they be overly applied rather than used to set overall guidance and vision. The new set of six standards replaces the former knowledge, skills, and dispositions of the original ISLLC standards with empirically researched "functions" that define each standard. The standards are similar but not identical to the original standards. The 2008 ISLLC standards summarized below emphasize school leaders' overriding responsibility to students by repeating the following introduction to each of the standards:

An education leader should promote the success of *every student* by

1. Setting a widely shared vision for learning

2. Developing a school culture and instructional program conducive to student learning and staff professional growth

3. Ensuring effective management of the organization, operation, and resources for a safe, efficient, and effective learning environment

4. Collaborating with faculty and community members, responding to diverse community interests and needs, and mobilizing community resources

5. Acting with integrity, fairness, and in an ethical manner and

6. Understanding, responding to, and influencing the political, social, legal, and cultural contexts

(Adaptation of ISLLC 2008 standards from the Web site of the CCSSO)

To date, forty-three states have either adopted or adapted the ISLLC standards in the reform of their educational leadership programs and licensing. Examination of a dozen or more sets of leadership standards that proliferate in the educational leadership landscape reveals much similarity among them. Knowing and understanding standards for principals is fundamental to being a responsible, effective school leader. That brings us full circle, back to the introduction of this chapter, where a number of research-based studies on leadership effectiveness were cited, including Kent Peterson's list of behaviors typical of effective contemporary principals, which contains both leadership and management competencies and stipulates the importance of "providing for instructional leadership" as a major function of today's principal.

DEFINING INSTRUCTIONAL LEADERSHIP

The progress made in finding out more about what leadership can do to improve teaching and learning is encouraging. There has been much muddled thinking about what constitutes instructional leadership, how it is distinguished from leadership in general, and what leadership behaviors are most closely linked to improving teaching and learning.

In 1995, Daresh and Playko wrote the following about "instructional leadership":

Despite the amount of discussion about, as well as support for, the concept of instructional leadership, little has been done to define the concept operationally . . . [W]e now recognize that individuals other than principals might engage in instructional leadership behaviors. Second, we have increasingly realized that instructional leadership can take forms that go well beyond direct intervention in classroom activities. (p. 132)

Although lacking specific behaviors or a prescriptive orientation, the definition of instructional leadership rendered by Daresh and Playko clearly puts the focus on student learning: "Instructional leadership consists of direct or indirect behaviors that significantly affect teacher instruction and, as result, student learning" (p. 33).

Douglas Reeves, in *The Learning Leader* (2006), offers a framework of "leadership for learning" to "encourage those who are discouraged because it provides specific guidance for the most difficult school, and it will challenge complacent schools to differentiate between being effective and being lucky" (p. xix). Reeves draws the following conclusions about leadership that support student and teacher learning based on some of the most significant and widely recognized studies in the field (e.g., John Goodlad, 1994):

1. Leadership, teaching, and adult actions matter.

2. There are particular leadership actions that show demonstrable links to improved student achievement and educational equity. These actions are

   o Inquiry
   o Implementation
   o Mentoring

3. Leadership is neither a unitary skill set nor a solitary activity. (pp. xxiii–xxiv)

Leithwood and Riehl (2005) make a very valid point in their study on school leadership and its impact on learning: The technological advances made in assessing student outcomes in recent years have resulted in more sophisticated data than in the past. These researchers explain that, while it has not always been easy to measure student outcomes, and especially not to connect those outcomes to teacher or school leader performance, today's technological capacity for analyzing and reporting outcomes makes these connections easier. The most important of their defensible claims about effective leadership listed earlier in this chapter is that successful school leadership most certainly makes contributions to the improvement of students' learning. In their elaboration of this claim, they quote the extensive sources of research on which the claim is made and conclude that, despite the fact that leadership's effects on student achievement are indirect, they are nonetheless demonstrable. Variables through which this effect seems most significant appear to be school mission and variables related to classroom curriculum and instruction.

Even with the newer links between leadership and student achievement, the recommendations for leadership are far from being prescriptive; the practices coming from the research base on leadership can be enacted in different ways, with many styles, and with various philosophies. They are patterns of behavior, not specifically defined behaviors. They give direction, not specification. Very different leadership personalities can be accommodated in these broad-stroke recommendations. Thus, I reiterate, this toolbox text is not intended to provide overly simplistic, step-by-step instructions to successful school leadership. Instead, my intention as author is to assist principals—given their own special styles and settings—to find their own way and make the most of their unique talents, abilities, resources, and circumstances in furthering the central mission of all leadership in schools: the education and well-being of young people. The research base is stronger than ever for giving principals and other school leaders direction. Still, there is no point-to-point road map to student success. A leader's internal compass and conscientious awareness and treatment of the profession's research and findings are great enablers, but they are not recipes. They are, however, excellent tools to assist the principal and other school leaders to make their best professional judgments day in and day out about what—under their control—is most likely to impact positively their particular faculty and their students' achievement and well-being.

Walking the Talk

An example from the field of dealing with task (manager) and people (leader) dimensions of a school

You have to develop a balance between tasks and relationship concerns of the organization. A good principal should be able to shift when the climate signals a need to re-focus on an area. For example, at the beginning of the school year, I am really big into tasks. There are so many organizational needs that must be attended for the year to kick off well . . . orientation, goals, committees, establishing ground rules for the year. However, come about November, morale usually starts to go down a little bit. Teachers start to get a little tired and discipline issues are picking up. Faculty get a little grumpy with each other. So I have to ratchet up the relationship piece. I do little things for faculty such as have an ice cream social after school one day for fun. You must be able to read where your faculty is and make adjustments accordingly. There are times I can really push the faculty in accomplishing school goals such as instructional improvement, and then there are times where I have to stand back and nurture them because it is a time that they need that nurturing. So, I think the balance between task and relationship is key. If you cannot read your staff like that, you are probably not going to be as successful as you could be. (Interview with Dr. Amy Lingren, June 2008)

Dr. Lingren is an elementary principal in Duval County School System in Jacksonville, Florida. Dr. Lingren has twenty-three years of experience as an elementary school principal in three states and just recently returned to the principalship after serving as Duval County Schools chief academic officer for four years.

POINTERS FOR THE PRINCIPAL

- Understand the principal's evolving role.
  - o Manage as a part of leading.
  - o Facilitate leadership at large; abandon chief in charge.
  - o Expand your style/skill repertoire; forget one-size-fits-all leadership models.
  - o Keep abreast of the increasingly insightful research on leadership that most positively impacts learning among students and faculty.
- Deal responsibly with accountability.
  - o Develop the school community's vision of student success.
  - o Encourage accountability among all stakeholders.
  - o Mobilize community resources on children's behalf.
  - o Fearlessly forge ways to help children succeed.
  - o Avoid excuse-making orientations to thinking and behaving.
- Be professionally fit.
  - o Read and reflect often.
  - o Seek ways to improve yourself, mentor others, and contribute to your profession.
  - o Embrace change as your friend—it will keep you active, alert, and growing.
  - o Be the number one model of lifelong learner . . . the "leading learner" in your school.
- Hone your role in instructional leadership.
  - o Visit classrooms daily.
  - o Communicate your passion for the success of teachers and students in word and deed.
  - o Operationalize the school's vision in your day-to-day functioning.
  - o Facilitate team-based instructional leadership.
- Persevere.
  - o Be guided by the school's goals.
  - o Be visibly supportive.
  - o View mistakes as opportunities to learn.
  - o Enjoy your work!

3

Blueprints for Success

In the absence of organizational purpose, leadership does not exist. And if the purpose is not compelling, why would anyone want to follow?

— Chuck Schwahn and William Spady (1998, p. 45)

A leader does the right things, which implies a goal, a direction, an objective, a vision, a dream, a path, a reach.

— Warren Bennis (1997, p. 95)

The importance of direction to the work of any organization is obvious. Various expressions are used to reflect this regard for direction: "If you don't know where you're going, how will you know when you've arrived?"; "So what have you accomplished if you're driving the bus and arrive safely at your chosen destination only to discover you left your passengers at the gate?"; or "Our reach should exceed our grasp, else what's a Heaven for?"

Accordingly, much has been written about the importance of providing direction as a major role of leadership, especially in times and contexts of extreme flux and change. The newer models of leadership call on contemporary principals and CEOs to shift from an old paradigm of "teller" to one of facilitator of an organization's direction and operation as one way of helping people deal with change in less hostile, nonresistant ways. The importance, inevitability, and desirability of change in an organization and its people are frequent issues in current literature on effective schools and leadership. Principals labeled as change agents, visionaries, and strategic planners are all indicative of the very basic expectation of today's school leader as a key player in providing direction to the organization.

A casual look at the various professional standards proliferating the landscape of school leadership bears witness to the importance of principals being able not only to articulate clearly their own guiding principles and personal visions of school excellence but also to lead others (i.e., parents, students, teachers, staff, community) in the organization to the ultimate shared development and articulation of the school's and district's operational blueprints—that is, a mission, a vision, goals and objectives, and strategies for accomplishing the organization's mission. In fact, the processes whereby stakeholders engage in the creation of these documents are deemed more critical and valuable than the actual documents themselves.

This chapter is included as an essential part of the instructional leader's toolbox. It contains suggestions to facilitate the work of leaders in providing direction to the school. It strategically follows the chapters dealing with the important tools of self-analysis, with the focus on what the leader as an individual believes and values. Such an examination of values and beliefs by the leader and the school community provides the framework, or compass, for setting in motion, and guiding, the organization's working directional documents, its blueprints for excellence—mission, vision, goals, objectives, and strategies.

MISSION

A mission addresses an organization's fundamental purpose. It answers the following question: Why do we exist as an organization?

Although often referred to as a statement, the mission may actually be several statements, even a paragraph in length. However, the central target of the mission of any school organization—the improvement of students' educational experiences and achievement—should clearly be evident. A distinction is made here between school slogans and school missions. Frequently, slogans are confused with missions, but each is useful and each serves a different purpose. Missions are more in-depth treatments of a school's purposes than are slogans. Ideally, slogans stem from visions and the mission and are symbolic, catchy statements that help the school and community bond together and remind a school community of its shared vision and mission for the school. As an example of the role an effectively used slogan can serve, Newman and Simmons (2000) share one high school principal's experience:

> Part of the work of [leadership] is to develop a shared vision with clear goals that focus on increasing student achievement. The leaders' responsibilities are to provide direction and guidance for the implementation of that vision, to keep it constantly evident in their

own words and actions, and to help the school community remain faithful to the vision in its daily practice . . . In the hallway at Fenway High School in Boston is a poster that reads: *Work hard. Be yourself. Do the right thing.* Principal Larry Myatt first used these phrases several years ago . . . with a class of incoming students . . . The motto now serves as a persistent reminder of what the school community stands for. It is effective, unlike many mere slogans, because it clearly encapsulates Fenway's shared strategic vision, with its focus on high achievement and high expectations for everyone—students, teachers, parents, and staff members alike. (p. 11)

Of their identified fifteen performance roles of a leader, Schwahn and Spady (1998) place "creating a compelling purpose which they involve all stakeholders in creating and maintaining" (p. 45) as the top priority. Schwahn and Spady contend that a major component in creating a compelling purpose is the development of a clear, concise, easy-to-remember mission statement that "answers the questions of why the organization exists and its fundamental business" (p. 45):

> To be effective, mission statements must be brief, discriminating, challenging, and exciting. If the mission statement isn't driving all decision making throughout the district (or the school), it simply isn't having the impact that it should. One true test of a mission statement's influence is to realize that if organizational members can't easily state the mission, then the organization doesn't have one. (pp. 45–46)

A word of caution: It is more important that the mission be genuine, shared, and well thought out, rather than catchy and easy to recite word for word. Without question, however, members of the organization should be able to define easily and in their own words the school's mission, and their individual renditions should vary only in semantics, not in content. Slogans are helpful in bonding the organization's members and reminding them of its greater vision and mission, but rarely do slogans have the substance worthy of being labeled a mission.

Stephen Covey (1991) gets at this same issue—mission statements versus platitudes. He emphasizes the importance of the process in developing among the school's stakeholders a shared mission statement:

> I don't mean a mission statement that was cranked out over a weekend at an executive retreat, but one that is the product of effort and input from every level of the organization. Most organizational mission statements are no more than a bunch of lovely PR platitudes framed on a wall. However, a mission statement has the potential of being a living constitution—something that embodies deeply held values and that is based on timeless principles. (pp. 184–185)

Warren Bennis (1997) agrees: "Companies are great at printing mission statements on 3 x 5 laminated plaques along with elaborate lists of company vision and values. Dazzling documents like these are useless" (p. 160). Useless, that is, if these fancy documents lack the vested interest that results from the broad-based involvement of all of the stakeholders in the organization in their development.

Covey (1991) and others saliently advise that the real power of developing a shared mission in an organization lies more in the process than in the actual document. This is precisely why it cannot be a top-down directive, generated by a few and disseminated to the masses; without the process of dialogue among the various constituencies of an organization (i.e., exploration of values and beliefs, genuine sharing of differences of opinion, earnest pursuits of common ground and mutually shared purposes), no common mission can be reached. Without the process's by-products—enhanced appreciation for and understanding of each other and how the group thinks about education, children, and learning—the chances of having the group focused enough to improve teaching and learning significantly throughout the school is not likely. Thus, attempts to preempt the rather messy, time-consuming, often emotionally charged and intellectually challenging processes involved in broad-based development of an organization's (ideally at the district level) commitment to a mission document in the long run impede the school community's ability to function as a team characterized by a passion and drive associated with a clear sense of mutually derived purpose for the district's schools.

VISION

Everybody talks about vision, but how many educators can readily, passionately, and with sufficient detail describe their visions of an excellent school? Bennis and Goldsmith (1997) claim "vision can be *pictured*—it has substance, form, and color. By vision we mean a picture that can be seen with the mind's eye" (p. 105). Although all of the blueprints discussed in this chapter are useful and work in tandem to give direction to a school community's work, vision is the most emotionally charged and intellectually challenging to produce. Kouzes and Posner (2007) include it as one of the five practices of exemplary leadership and explain, "To inspire a shared vision, you envision the future by imagining exciting and ennobling possibilities, and you enlist others in the dreams by appealing to shared aspirations" (p. 43).

The leadership framework designed by Brown and Irby (2001) and proposed in Chapter 1 requires reflection and clarification about the vital aspects of school, which all educational leaders should have thought about and be able to describe with some degree of specificity. Educational leaders should be passionate about these aspects and persistent in fulfilling them in their daily work.

The first step in the important work of creating a school vision is determining its community's individual, personal visions of what an excellent school looks like and how the people in it function. In excellent schools, principals and school leaders are not the sole proprietors of personal visions of school excellence; the more visionary, reflective, and passionate are all stakeholders of the school, the more likely the school's performance will improve and move to exceptionality. However, leaders must assume the role of exemplar and standard bearer in visioning and passionately pursuing a better state of school operation to facilitate the entire school community's creation of a vision.

Peter Senge (1990) saliently warns of the short-sightedness of an outmoded, traditional perception of top-down, top-heavy leadership that assumes an organization's members are "powerless, lack personal vision, and are incapable of mastering the dynamics of change" (p. 45). Michael Fullan (1997) similarly asserts, "As stewards, leaders continually seek and oversee the broader purpose and direction of the organization . . . The challenge is to improve education in the only way it can be—through the day-to-day actions of empowered individuals" (pp. 13, 47). It is only when the individuals—all of the individuals—in an organization are able to dream and envision more ideal states of existence and operation that the collective voice's vision—the shared vision—is likely to be developed with the sincerity, vested interest, and rigor needed for it to be meaningful and truly operational each day within the school.

Although visions are by nature grand, optimistic, and abstract, as they evolve the more concrete and specific they become. Fullan (1997), referring to Block's (1987) *The Empowered Manager*, describes the attributes of a good vision:

> The dialogue about vision, according to Block, should strive to achieve three qualities: depth, clarity, and responsibility relative to the vision. Depth is the degree to which the vision statement is personally held. Clarity comes from insisting on specific images. Vagueness . . . "is a way of not making a commitment to a vision." Responsibility involves moving from helplessness to active ownership: " . . . the primary reason we demand that people create a vision statement is to reinforce the belief that all of us are engaged in the process of creating this organization." (Block, 1987, p. 124, as quoted in Fullan, 1997, p. 35)

Douglas Reeves (2006) cautions about grandiose visions that come straight from the executive suite without involving the various other school constituencies:

> By definition, vision contemplates the future, and the future inevitability involves uncertainty, change, and fear. Therefore,

visions that are fuzzy and described in a haze of mystic reassurance have a counterproductive effect.

He goes on to say that it need not be this way, however. Trust can be built if leaders reduce the rhetoric and clarify the vision so that it becomes a working document, "a blueprint rather than public relations baloney . . . Equipped with an effective vision, the leader can respond in a consistent and coherent way to these questions":

1. Where are we headed as an organization this year?
2. Where will we be three to five years from now?
3. What parts of our organization will be the same, and what will change?

4. Will there still be a place for me in the future?
5. How will my work change?
6. What will I need to learn in order to be more valuable to the organization in the future?
7. Why will I still want to be a part of this organization in the future? (p. 36)

Until the vision is derived from the involvement of all interested stakeholders in the school or district, these questions will likely remain unanswered to many of the school's audiences. Thus, the vision is likely to lack the credibility, clarity, and allegiance needed to make it a true living document manifested in myriad ways throughout the school and district's operation—the litmus test of good visionary leadership.

Ultimately, through the subsequent development of goals, objectives, and strategies, the schoolwide, *shared vision* is realized in part, revisited often, and revamped as needed to meet the ever-changing needs of the students and the often-changing levels of sophistication and skill of the dreamers. Fullan (1997) discusses the complexity of bringing together multiple personal visions in trying to arrive at one shared, schoolwide vision: "Visions will tend to converge . . . This will sometimes result in sharper differences, but the more serious problem seems to be the absence of clearly articulated visions rather than a multiplicity of them" (p. 35).

Creating a common vision is a process, not an event. Not only is it ongoing, but it also takes time to come to any degree of fruition in the first place. According to Jo and Joseph Blase (1997), "Defining a vision, working toward it, and sustaining related efforts is a profound challenge" (p. 103). Depending on the situation and the people involved, the vision's initial creation may take several years of reflective dialogue and emotional and intellectual rigor. Then, of course, a vision is never final. The evolutionary nature of a vision is what ensures its continued relevancy and the regeneration of the school's and community's enthusiasm and commitment to the work and resources necessary for the school to operate routinely as an improving organization. Amy Lingren shared her insights into vision building from her experiences as principal:

> As far as building a vision and mission in a school is concerned, it is not something you go in and you spend two hours brainstorming with your faculty and you come up with something and it goes on a banner and that's about it. I never do a vision or mission statement until I have had a least a year with faculty. You have to observe what they believe not just hear it out of there mouths, and then putting it into terminology is really important. I think an example of this would be when I was at North Shore Elementary. I heard a lot of those kids say that their parents are not involved how can we expect to do x, y, z when they don't come with prerequisite skills and so out of the first couple of months what really started to come apparent to me was their was a lot of excuse and blame being spread different places and what this allows is people not to take ownership. So by the end of the year when we got together and talked about what we needed to do to turn the school around we decided we needed to get rid of that. There was nothing we could do to control a lot of that stuff. The teachers came up with our mission statement, two words: NO EXCUSES. No excuses went everywhere. People made banners and signs; it just was what we felt we had to do. Once you got off people's backs they knew that they were accountable and so they knew that it was their responsibility and everyone knew that in any conversations we could not put blame, we just had to look for solutions. (Interview with Dr. Amy Lingren, July 2008)

Unless a school community engages in the personal visioning and the reflective dialoguing essential to the development and articulation of a meaningful, shared vision of what excellent instruction and teaching mean to them, the quality of education afforded their children is likely to remain mediocre at best. Without leaders who recognize the important role they play in facilitating this work, such processes rarely if ever occur. "An ethic of care," asserts Lynn Beck (1994), "would compel school leaders to work to move visions, hopes, and plans beyond the conceptual stage into practice" (p. 82).

At the center of a comprehensive vision of an excellent school, principals and other school leaders should have clear notions of what constitutes excellent teaching and learning, and the role they should play in providing excellent instructional leadership. "Schools' guiding statements," espouses Lew Allen (2001), "are more likely to lead to action when they address in very specific ways the type of teaching and learning experiences that people believe will help their students realize the stated purposes and desired results found in the statements" (p. 291).

BOX 3.1

Instructional Leadership Vision Quotient Assessment

How's your ILVQ (instructional leadership vision quotient)? How much have you reflected on and how readily can you articulate responses to the following statements, which effective instructional leadership entails? Earnestly completing the following statements should help you to focus your thinking and decide if you need to clarify any areas. These statements will also help you develop a more complete vision to improve your leadership impact, especially in the area of instruction.

In my vision of an ideal school . . .

• Students are learning (what?)

_____

_____

• Students are learning by (how?)

_____

_____

• The school climate reflects the importance of teaching and learning (how?)

_____

_____

• Decisions about curriculum and instruction are made by (whom and how?)

_____

_____

• Instruction looks like (describe the things you envision in a school where teaching and learning are happening as you think they ideally should)

_____

_____

• Teachers believe (about children and learning)

_____

_____

- Parents participate in their child's learning (how?)

  _____

  _____

- The principal spends the majority of his or her time (where in the building?)

  _____

  _____

- The principal is (doing what?)

  _____

  _____

- The assistant principal spends the majority of his or her time (where in the building?)

  _____

  _____

- The assistant principal is (doing what?)

  _____

  _____

- Student achievement is assessed (how and by whom?)

  _____

  _____

- Faculty meetings' agendas primarily consist of (what?)

  _____

  _____

- Faculty meetings are conducted (how?)

  _____

  _____

(Continued)

(Continued)

- The content and nature of staff development is determined (how?)

    ○ (by whom?) ——————————————————————————————
    ○ (for whom?) ——————————————————————————————
    ○ (assessed how?) ——————————————————————————

- Teacher performance evaluation processes consist of (how?)

    _____

    _____

- The criteria for teacher evaluation come from (what?)

    _____

    _____

- Teacher evaluations are performed by (whom?)

    _____

    _____

- They are performed for (what key purposes?)

    _____

    _____

- Student achievement is tied to teacher evaluation (how?)

    _____

    _____

- The school schedule and organization reflect a focus on optimizing students' learning (how?)

    _____

    _____

- The process used to determine the schedule and organization (what?)

  _____

  _____

- Decisions made to implement new programs, do away with programs, or update and revise programs are made by (whom?)

  _____

  _____

GOALS AND OBJECTIVES

Having a clearly established purpose and a well-articulated vision of an ideal school, the next logical directional piece essential for moving an organization to a higher level of operation—for moving a vision from concept to practice—is the formulation of the day-to-day working documents: the school's instructional goals and objectives. The goals and objectives should emerge from and further direct the energy of the organization toward fulfilling the school community's stated mission and vision. Goals and objectives provide the specificity essential each day to guide the work of the organization. Those school goals that particularly relate to what is taught and how it is taught are usually referred to as instructional goals. However, if a goal cannot be tied ultimately to what happens in the classroom, to teaching and learning, then its appropriateness as a goal is questionable. The litmus test for the appropriateness of any school goal or objective—indeed, any expenditure or decision—is asking "in whose interest" each was made. If students' welfare and achievement are not the answer to the litmus test question, where is the legitimacy of the goal, expenditure, or decision?

The role of the leader is to facilitate, not dictate, these important directional documents. In fact, the work of defining and tailoring instructional goals and objectives for the individual school site should be developed primarily by those most involved in their delivery—the classroom teachers. The work should reflect a team effort among the school's stakeholders (teachers and administrators primarily, but with appropriate input from parents, students, and staff), with teachers taking a lead partnership role with the principal in breaking the larger vision and mission blueprints into more concrete, obtainable parts.

If the vision and mission documents of a school have credibility, they clearly reflect the central importance of students and learning to the work of educational institutions. The more the school's instructional goals and objectives are tailored to meet the unique needs of the school's specific population of children, the more likely students' academic success will be. Although most states have legislated, mandated curricula—and though some school districts have developed their own elaborated versions of these curricula—the most instructionally effective schools are those that have taken those state- and system-level curricula (which are generally open to a good deal of interpretation) as umbrella documents to guide the work of their own more specifically defined, school-based curricula. Although it is not in their purview to change the mandated curricula, individual school teams can make it more personalized for their specific population of students and teachers by answering the questions in Box 3.2.

BOX 3.2

School-Based Curriculum and Teaching Decisions

- How can national-, state-, and system-level goals and objectives best be taught to our students and in what order?
- What will the curriculum emphases be?
- What teaching strategies, materials, and resources should we employ?
- How will students be assessed?
- What timeframe is recommended for teaching the various goals and objectives?

"Faculty, administration, students, and parents should be aware of the instructional goals and assessment procedures for the school and for specific grade levels," asserts Rossow (2000, p. 9). In writing about the importance of focus and direction in a school, Rossow further contends,

the principal should be able to answer the following question: What are the curriculum goals for each grade, and what is the management plan for carrying out these goals? If the faculty in a school building were polled, their answers to the following three questions should be very similar: What business are you in? How is business going? What evidence do you have for your answers? (p. 9)

The best curriculum guides are those that provide a school-based dimension and detail for teachers, not in a prescriptive manner but rather in a spirit of support, coordination, and a sharing of resources and expertise. Novice teachers, weak teachers, and teachers new to a system stand to benefit most from such curriculum assistance but, more important, the participative process of developing these teaching aides engenders among the school community a can-do team spirit. The result of such shared processes for dealing with instructional goals and objectives at the school level is far more than a document—a directional set of goals and objectives. The most important results of such a process is the professional empowerment that results from ownership in the design and control of the essence of school enterprise—the teaching and learning that goes on in classrooms.

STRATEGIES

Strategies are about action and professional know-how. The most eloquently written mission and vision, the most clearly constructed goals and objectives all lie limp without well-designed strategies to bring them to life. Instructional goals and objectives have little power without accompanying strategies for their attainment. The important work of developing strategies for teaching can and most often should be developed at many levels:

- By a single teacher or a teacher and a mentor (usually in the form of weekly and daily lesson plans)
- Between teams of teachers—grade-level, vertical, or subject-area teams (in the form of units, field trips, shared projects)
- Between a curriculum leadership team representative of all the teachers, and with representative, appropriate input from parents and community leaders as well as students (in the form of curriculum guides or handbooks, which frequently offer suggestions for sequencing goals and objectives, pacing and making appropriate time allowances, using textbooks and software, designating state test items, and assessing and evaluating students' level of mastery of the goals and objectives)

Of all the directional documents addressed thus far in this chapter, strategies are the ones most often left up to teachers to develop on their own. Teachers, as professionals, must be allowed to make these ultimate strategic teaching decisions for their unique group of students. Dictating how a teacher instructs is clearly inappropriate and far too prescriptive; however, as a standard part of the school's operation, having routine opportunities and provisions for teachers to share their expertise in developing and improving their own teaching strategies is not only appropriate but also absolutely essential to providing good instructional leadership.

Such routine opportunities—which become characteristic of a school's culture—designated specifically for teachers to engage in professional dialogue about their work help to ensure that teaching and learning are the school's focus. As Allen (2001) emphasizes, "Principals play a key role in helping people find the time to write statements and to bring them to life. It is imperative that principals give this work a high priority and help direct the appropriate resources to it" (p. 292). A principal's leadership in making it possible for teachers to meet, talk, and plan—with the principal often participating—within and across grade levels and subject areas sends a powerful message: Classroom instruction and student achievement are expected to be continually analyzed and reflected upon—as well as to evolve—as a routine part of the school day.

The complexity of teaching and meeting the diverse needs of today's students, especially, requires that teachers pool their energy, resources, and expertise to do the job most effectively. The teaching support systems, level of professionalism, program coordination, and curriculum articulation among teachers that result from reflective dialogue about their work (especially regarding their shared beliefs, values, mission, vision, and instructional goals and objectives) greatly enhance a school's total performance and its quality as a true learning community, wherein the adults exemplify the importance of continued learning, growth, and development.

Walking the Talk

An example from the field of a principal's personal school vision and her process for developing shared organizational blueprints among the school's many stakeholders

My vision for my school is to provide an opportunity for every member of my student body, faculty, and staff to achieve a level of success that they never believed they were capable of. I have high expectations for my teachers and they have high expectations for their students. I support them in any way I can to ensure their success and ask them to provide the same support for their students. Our expectations are high regardless of the background of our students. The student population of our school is very diverse. We have students who speak sixteen different languages. Almost 20 percent of our students are from the Middle East and Mexico including several recent immigrants. Almost 60 percent of our students are children of poverty who do not understand education is their way out of that cycle. My goal is to show them there is another way of life and that they can enjoy a safe, productive life through education. Social skills are also a priority at our school. It is my vision that all of my students will have the social skills as well as the academic skills to be successful students and productive citizens. We practice making right choices, the Ron Clark 55 Essential Skills, and Ron Clark's rules of etiquette. We model the social skills we expect of our students. We recognize and reward students when they make good choices and display good social skills.

I use a campus committee made up of elected and appointed members to set goals and priorities. The elected members are teachers, paraprofessionals, and staff who are chosen by their peers to represent them. The appointed members are parent representatives, community members, and business representatives. All grade level chair people are ad hoc members of the committee and all special services are represented on the committee. Every member of the faculty and staff is represented and their input is invited. Parents are represented at and welcome to attend any meeting. The committee meets each month to set goals for student achievement, campus culture, budget considerations, and activities to meet the goals and objectives. Everyone has ownership of our goals.

Results are communicated through the Campus Performance Objectives Committee, the state report card sent home to each parent, news letters, and news paper articles. Campus wide celebrations are held each year when we achieve an Exemplary rating from the Texas Accountability System. We tell our students that we see how smart they are every day and that these tests are their opportunity to show others how smart they are. We tell them every day that they are the smartest kids in Texas and they live up to it! In 2005–2006 when our school was chosen as one of the two National Title I Schools for Texas we told them that they were the smartest kids in the United States. They decided that they wanted to be the smartest kids in the Universe. We fly our National Title I flag and Exemplary flag every day. We have six banners on our outside wall showcasing our six consecutive years as a Texas Honor Roll School and one that shows we have been chose by *Texas Monthly* magazine as one of the best schools in Texas. We have twelve plaques in our hall for each of the consecutive years we have received an Exemplary rating by the state and one for being chosen as a National Title I school. My vision is to for my school is its continued growth and continued success as a community of learners! (Karen Sue Noble, Author's Feedback Request Form, September 2008)

Karen Sue Noble is the principal of Hillcrest Elementary School in the Nederland Independent School District in Texas, a position she has held for sixteen years. Prior to this position, she served as assistant principal of Highland Park Elementary School in the same district for eight years.

POINTERS FOR THE PRINCIPAL

- Mission gives purpose to an organization and its people.
  - Involve stakeholders in a process to develop the mission.
  - Differentiate between catchy slogans and authentic mission statements.
  - Use the mission as a unifying theme.
- Visions are dreams of how best to accomplish the mission.
  - Help all stakeholders create a vision of what their ideal school is like.
  - Develop one collective vision from the sharing of individual visions.

- o Revisit visions often and facilitate their revision to reflect the school's improving, evolving status.
- o Encourage frequent visioning about teaching and learning.

- Goals and objectives are the vision's operational blueprints.
  - o Break the vision up into manageable parts with supportive goals and objectives.
  - o Tailor national-state- and system-level goals and objectives to fit your school and students.
  - o Create school-based curriculum documents with teachers taking the lead.

- Strategies specify how to accomplish goals and objectives.
  - o Provide a role model, support, and time for teachers to read, reflect, and dialogue about improving instruction.
  - o Formalize mentoring of new teachers to mediate their entry into teaching.
  - o Focus professional development on teacher collaboration, so they can hone their teaching skills and strategize to help children succeed in school.

4

A School's Organizational Superglue

Value

> School climate may be one of the most important ingredients of a success-
> ful instructional program. It is the school's "personality." Without a cli-
> mate that creates a harmonious and well-functioning school, a high degree
> of academic achievement is difficult, if not downright impossible, to obtain.
>
> —John Hoyle, Fenwick English, and Betty Steffy (1994, p. 15)

> Proficient principals lead the way toward creating a learning environ-
> ment in which teachers truly teach and students truly learn. The result
> is a productive, caring atmosphere in which every student can experience
> success.
>
> —National Association of Elementary School Principals (1991, p. 11)

You can't see it, touch it, hear it, or smell it, but you certainly can sense it. In fact, it's so real that you are immediately aware of it when you enter a school. What is it? Smircich (1983, cited in Snowden & Gorton, 1998) refers to it as an organization's glue, what holds it all together. It's the "way we do things around here," not necessarily what's written in the handbook. It's that nebulous, illusive, invisible, but utterly pervasive and powerful, school quality referred to as culture.

Often, the terms *culture* and *climate* are used interchangeably. Lunenburg and Ornstein (2000), for example, give their interpretation of the terms as follows:

> Over the past dozen or more years, the terms climate, ethos, and culture have been used to capture or describe the norms, values, behaviors, and rituals of the school organization, what the authors would simply call the significant features or personality of the organization. Here we are talking about everything that goes on in a school: how teachers interact and dress, what they talk about, what goes on at meetings, their expectations of students, how students behave, how parents interact with the staff, and what type of leadership behavior is exhibited by the principal. (pp. 329–330)

In their most recent edition of this synoptic text on educational administration (Lunenburg and Ornstein, 2008), these authors go into more detail in differentiating between culture and climate. They make the point that, technically, "culture has its roots in sociology and anthropology whereas organizational climate is rooted in psychology" and has a much stronger research base than does organizational culture. Ultimately they conclude, however, that the two concepts overlap in many ways. In this book, the two terms are used interchangeably—as they frequently are in the literature pertaining to schools.

The abundance of writing on the topic of organizational culture reflects its importance in the study of leadership. Even though little research exists that directly ties principals' behavior to student achievement, a leader's impact on the school's culture has clearly been established in the literature on organizational leadership and administration (e.g., Austin & Holowenzak, 1985; Deal & Peterson, 1999; Hallinger, Bickman, & Davis, 1990; Larsen, 1987; Peters & Waterman, 2004). If climate and culture are impacted by leadership, then it follows that student achievement is also impacted. Thus, educational researchers' efforts are increasingly focusing on finding out more specifically just how school culture is tied to leadership behaviors (e.g., Leithwood, Louis, Andersen, & Wahlstrom, 2004; Marzano, Waters, & McNulty, 2005).

What makes up school culture? Lunenburg and Ornstein (2008) say it is characterized by its heroes, rites and rituals, and communication networks (pp. 71–72). Allan Glatthorn (1993) describes a culture's content as its belief system (core values and guiding beliefs about the schools, students, and learning that inform action), norms (shared standards of behavior that derive from that belief system), and traditions (valued ways of the past). Of these, the one Glatthorn speculates is most critical is the belief system, the earlier content focus in Chapter 2. Indeed, beliefs form the guiding compass for human behavior. Culture is characterized by core beliefs shared by the members of the larger organizational community. These beliefs impact the values and behaviors of the people, which give shape to the culture. That is why it is essential to begin at the beginning—for people to examine their beliefs and come to terms with their differences in establishing a community of shared beliefs on the basis of which the organization can function with the least friction and with the most enthusiasm and passion.

Are there identifiable beliefs that characterize the more effective schools? Glatthorn (1993) defines five beliefs that he (based on his and a number of other researchers' work) feels are characteristic of a school culture that nurtures student achievement and healthy school improvement. These essential core beliefs are that

1. The school is a cooperative community
2. There is a belief in common goals
3. School improvement can be achieved through problem solving orientation
4. All those in the school—administrators, teachers, and students—can achieve
5. Instruction is the highest priority (pp. 63–64)

An interesting caution regarding culture building is noteworthy. Not all cultures are positive. Both positive and negative school cultures exist, and both can be equally strong and resilient. In fact, many new principals encounter the resistant forces created by negative cultures as they try to establish new norms and beliefs that are essential to facilitating school improvement and enacting change. Thomas Sergiovanni (1991) warns of the dangers inherent in shaping a school's culture:

> Cultural leadership can provide principals with levers to manipulate others that are more powerful than the levers associated with bureaucratic and psychological authority . . . Further, cultural leadership can become a powerful weapon for masking the many problems of diversity, justice, and equality that confront schools. (pp. 330–331)

Although a school community has strong, shared beliefs, visions, and values as well as democratic processes for making decisions, this does not guarantee that those shared values and decisions will be good ones. On this negative potential of strong cultures, Weick (1985) adds,

> A coherent statement of who we are makes it harder for us to become something else. Strong cultures are tenacious cultures. Because a tenacious culture can be a rigid culture that is slow to detect changes and opportunities and slow to change once opportunities are sensed, strong cultures can be backward, conservative instruments of adaptation. (p. 385)

Research on academically effective schools emphasizes the high priority given by staff in these schools to student effort and achievement. This priority is usually manifested in the beliefs (usually in the form of a philosophy of teaching and learning), mission, vision, goals, objectives, and strategies created by the school as a team. According to Snowden and Gorton (1998), the major elements of the culture of an effective school include

1. A clear set of schoolwide norms that emphasize the values of academic effort and achievement

2. A consistently applied set of expectations that stresses the importance of staff members striving for excellence and students performing to their potential

3. A system of symbolic activity and sanctions that encourages and rewards effort, improvement, and accomplishment, while discouraging disorder and complacency (p. 110)

In their review of ten years of research on exemplary schools, Austin and Holowenzak (1985) reinforce the importance of culture, or what they refer to as a school's ethos. They state that the single most important "cornerstone assumption" underlying their conclusions is that

expectations about achievement and social behavior held by the principal, other administrators, and teachers strongly affect student achievement and social behavior . . . Teachers, administrators, and others involved in the school social system communicate their perception of appropriate and proper achievement and their expectations and assessments of students through informal interaction with students and with each other . . . This interactive process significantly affects the nature of student achievement. (p. 69)

Summarizing their findings, Austin and Holowenzak (1985) speak of the hallmarks of those schools most successful in facilitating their students' achievement:

We would say that great schools are being run as opposed to running. Exceptional schools have a purpose as opposed to being purposeless. If a school is purposeless, it doesn't mean that the people aren't working hard; it does mean that they have not gotten together and agreed, "This is the way we do it in our school." It is a creation of a sense of fellowship. There is a sense of being a member of a warm, supportive family that is the hallmark of exemplary or unusually successful schools. (p. 70)

The work of building a positive school culture supportive of student achievement is multifaceted and complex, but it is an essential, fundamental part of instructional leadership. The compass formed by a strong belief system and the subsequent creation of shared blueprints for the school's operation discussed in earlier chapters of this book are indicators of the school community's willingness to come together and set in motion a shared sense of purpose and direction. These essential foundations help to create the organization's glue—its people's customs, norms, and values—otherwise known as school culture. Tools for working with culture, to help shape and make it most supportive of student learning, are (1) being able to assess and analyze it, (2) knowing how to operate in a participatory fashion as a key agent in facilitating positive changes in culture, and (3) understanding the importance of building community in the school.

ASSESSING SCHOOL CLIMATE AND CULTURE

"The first step in promoting good school climate," assert Hoyle et al. (1994), "is to create an awareness of climate and to assess the climate of your school or school district" (p. 20). That awareness, however, must begin with you. New principals in particular should carefully observe their new surroundings to learn about their school's unique culture, most of which is neither written in any handbook nor obvious in written documents. In John Daresh's (2006) handbook for new principals, he refers to the importance of becoming familiar with the culture:

> When a newcomer first arrives, it is critical that he or she spends time looking very carefully at the whole environment to see what story is being told . . . The importance of seeing a school and not simply looking at it is similar to taking time to listen to what is happening in a school [for] subtle indications of the culture, climate, and informal organization in which you now work. (pp. 120–121)

Personally assessing a school's climate can be done quite informally at first by carefully observing, not just looking; listening, rather than just hearing; and being empathetic to the school's past and how things were before the new principal's arrival. Daresh (2006) recommends developing an action plan based on a new principal's careful analysis of the present culture by answering the following questions:

1. Describe the most important aspects of the school culture that you inherited as the new principal—that is, the kinds of things you must understand as you step in as the new leader.

2. Which elements of the culture are you most uncomfortable with as the new principal? Why?

3. What practices appear to have been least popular with faculty, students, and parents? Why were they so unpopular?

4. How do you plan to move away from those practices without creating distrust or alienation among the people in your school and community?

5. How will you go about creating new practices to replace the ones you find most troubling? Why are these better practices than the ones they replace?

6. Which features of the old culture will you want to nurture and keep? Why?

(Adaptation of Daresh's original questions, pp. 124–125)

To answer these questions, the new principal must look, listen, ask questions, and rummage through the school's artifacts to learn more about the history of the school (i.e., events, people, activities, and processes that have given shape to the school's culture and have special meaning to students, staff, and parents). Assessing and shaping the culture are ongoing processes, however, and are an important function for veteran as well as new leaders. Although cultures are often resistant to change, change is nonetheless inevitable. Culture and climate are particularly impacted by the attrition rate of faculty, staff, and administration in a school and district. The mobility of the students and the community is also a key factor in the stability potential of a school's culture. Therefore, principals must continually keep their fingers on the pulse of what is happening with regard to the values, beliefs, and perceptions of a school's varied stakeholder populations. It is through such awareness that a principal can begin to find opportunities to shape a culture and strengthen it around a central vision and mission that are more conducive to teaching and learning.

In addition to assessing personally (through looking, listening, analyzing, reading) and being cognizant of and sensitive to what makes up a school's culture, there are also many instruments specifically designed to help gather data and assist with the assessment of the strengths and weaknesses of a school's culture and climate. Some of the instruments are used as observation guides and checklists for trained observers; other instruments are designed to get perceptual feedback from students, parents, community members, faculty, and staff. Many instruments are available, with much variation in the degrees of complexity in administering, scoring, and reporting results. It pays to do your homework and check out the many available instruments on the market. Some of them are quite expensive; others are nominally priced or even free for the asking. Scoring of some is complex and must be done by the publisher, whereas others are easy to hand score.

Andrew Halpin and Don Croft's Organizational Climate Description Questionnaire (OCDQ) is one of the most well-known among the climate inventories. It measures the climate along an open-to-closed continuum and has undergone several revisions to increase its relevancy since it was first published in the 1960s (Halpin & Croft, 1963). Yet another popular instrument, the Organizational Health Inventory (OHI), examines the quality of interpersonal relationships among students, teachers, administrators, and community members (Hoy & Tarter, 1997).

Among the plethora of available climate assessment instruments are those with forms designed to assess the perceptions of school climate factors among varied, specific school populations—administrator, teacher, student, parent, and community. In their book, *Skills for Successful School Leaders*, Hoyle et al. (1994) describe a number of climate assessment instruments. They contend that teacher self-report instruments are the most reliable in evaluating a school's climate:

> Teachers are the principal agents of climate because the way they perceive their situation affects their behavior and effectiveness . . . No matter how we define or characterize good and bad teaching, it is difficult to see how an unfulfilled, dissatisfied teacher could have a positive effect on students. Thus valid, reliable, teacher self-report instruments are important in evaluating learning climate. (p. 30)

Among the instruments described by these authors is Hoyle's own instrument for assessing school climate, a teacher self-report instrument known as the Learning Climate Inventory (LCI) (Hoyle et al., 1994). This instrument is versatile; it is applicable to both elementary and secondary levels and is easy to complete and much briefer than most of the other instruments. The LCI is designed to gather teachers' perceptions about their administrators, peers, and teaching situation.

Because the types and contents of tools for assessing school climate vary widely, it is important to decide first what elements of the school climate are deemed most critical to assess in your situation and then choose an instrument that best serves your purposes. You can design your own instrument if what is needed is feedback on particular issues that are unique, context specific, and not adequately handled on any of the ready-made instruments. In addition to the host of standardized and non-standardized self-reporting perceptual instruments and the more objective observation instruments designed to assess various aspects of school climate, instruments designed to measure the perceptions of the principal's leadership (discussed in Chapter 1) also contribute to developing a more complete profile of the school's climate.

Bottom line, the principal (new or veteran) must be a skilled observer and information seeker to operate most effectively. Assessing the culture involves dip-sticking into all areas of the school's operation to learn how its stakeholders feel about the school, students, colleagues, and their leader. The more information you can acquire about how and why the school operates and people's perceptions of various factors that impact the school climate, the more able you as leader will be to make good decisions and guide the school team in its efforts to grow and improve. By isolating and assessing selected climate factors provided on good instruments and observation guides, a principal and his or her leadership team can more readily discern which aspects of the climate need to be altered, eliminated, or reinforced to make it stronger, more student centered, and open. Hoyle et al. (1994) explain,

> Since the relationship between a learning climate and learner outcomes is global and complex, a combination of observation, self-report instruments, and common sense is the recommended strategy for evaluating the climate of the district and each school. Skills in measuring and maintaining a positive school climate are second to none in importance to good school management. (p. 36)

LEADERSHIP ESSENTIAL TO POSITIVE SCHOOL CULTURES

In addition to providing leadership in bringing the school community together to define its shared belief system on which mission, vision, goals, and objectives are grounded, what do we know about more specific behaviors characteristic of leadership that facilitates building a cohesive, student-centered school culture—one in which students' academic achievement is the clear focus of the school's entire operation?

Researcher Terry J. Larsen (1987) found that principals in high-achieving schools were perceived by their faculties to perform six functions significantly more often than principals in lower achieving schools. These six functions—goal setting, coordination, supervision and evaluation, staff development, school climate, and school/community relations—were then further defined in the study by specific behaviors that contributed most to each function. With regard to the school climate function, the following principal behaviors were most often identified by teachers from the higher achieving schools in the study:

1. Communicates high expectations for student academic performance to staff
2. Protects faculty from undue pressures, so primary focus is on instruction
3. Personally recognizes the professional accomplishments of faculty including basic goal attainment
4. Assesses faculty morale
5. Establishes a safe/orderly school environment with a clear discipline code (p. 15)

The Northwest Regional Educational Laboratory's (1995) research on effective schooling practices drawn from an extensive research synthesis includes a listing of leadership behaviors that best guide the instructional program (Cotton, 1995). According to the Laboratory's synthesis, administrators and other instructional leaders' behaviors are key contributors to effective instruction in a school.

What emerges from most of the research and studies on the behaviors most characteristic of outstanding instructional leaders is the constancy with which they act on behalf of what is best for students throughout the many functions they perform, day in and day out. Principals cannot accomplish the work alone, but it is certain they set the tone that directly impacts the school culture. To profess beliefs, mission, and vision is much easier than to live them. It isn't enough to be able to articulate the importance of teaching and learning being at the center of the school's operation. You must be able to "walk the talk." A true leader not only clearly articulates the school's primary purpose for being but also demonstrates that deeply held sense of purpose throughout his or her interaction with students, teachers, staff, central office staff, parents, and the community. The degree of consistency between what leaders profess to believe and how they demonstrate those beliefs through their myriad actions is the truest measure of their leadership integrity. It is such integrity that will ultimately have the strongest impact on others in the school community and will be the best tool the principal has in helping to create a healthy, productive culture that will best serve students' needs.

FROM CLASSROOMS AND CUBBYHOLES TO SCHOOL COMMUNITY

Without such integrity, leaders can never earn the respect and trust of others fundamental to a healthy culture and true school community. In their perspectives on what they call the "trust factor" so essential to good leadership, Bennis and Goldsmith (1997) write,

> You must create an environment where people feel free to voice dissent. You do this through behavior. You do not fire people because they goofed, and you actually encourage dissent. You have to reward people disagreeing, to reward innovation, and to tolerate failure. All these are connected with creating a trusting atmosphere— but most of trust comes not from a particular technique, but from the character of the leader . . . If you are an effective leader, what you say is congruent with what you do, and that is congruent with what you feel, and that is congruent with your vision. (p. 5)

Wholesome school communities are built on a culture of mutual trust and respect among members—students, classified staff, teachers, administrators, parents, and community members. This paves the way for internal harmony, cooperation, and smooth functioning, which enable the best instruction and learning to take place.

Although opportunities occur in many unique and unpredictable ways throughout the school day for a principal to capitalize on the moment to reinforce and thus shape a school's culture, the key community-building opportunities in Box 4.1 are available to any principal in any context to some degree.

BOX 4.1

Shaping School Culture

- Careful recruitment, screening, selection, orientation, and mentoring of new faculty and staff to create a family of philosophical kinship and shared passion for students' success
- Identification of teacher, parent, and community leaders and appropriate delegation of responsibilities to those whose beliefs and visions most closely approximate the leader's and are focused on students' learning
- Planning (with staff) for and being an active participant with staff in well-designed, meaningful staff development that is guided by student performance indicators, focused on improving instruction, and evaluated by one primary criterion regarding its impact on classroom teaching and learning
- Developing (with staff) and implementing a process of supervision and evaluation that is supportive and team based rather than competitive and punitive in its orientation; includes teachers, administrators, and classified staff, and clearly operates for the primary purpose of improving employees' performance and student learning
- Making and taking time to celebrate and reward students' and staff's accomplishments, outstanding efforts, and performance among the entire school community and calculated risk taking to improve teaching and learning
- Looking for ways to practice what you preach and reward those who do likewise

It is critical for leaders to recognize that strong, democratic school cultures must include processes to ensure that people are involved, focused on students' learning, and open to taking risks, making mistakes, changing, adapting, and improving. Despite the potential that organizational culture has to be stubbornly resistant to change, schools will not be effective without a resilient, unifying ethos of caring and commitment to the important work of educating students. This ethos of caring, however, must extend beyond the school walls. Schools do not exist in a vacuum. They are embedded in a variety of larger systems as well as subcultures that are complex and multifaceted. There are increasing pressures on educators to become more politically active and vocal as advocates of students' education and well-being. To be able to most ably deal with the external environments in which the school is embedded, school leaders must understand how systems work and how the school is both impacted by and impacts other contexts. Playing the part of victim to societies' harmful mores and policies does little to make a positive difference in the quality of education and students' learning. Educators have a tremendous opportunity and a growing responsibility to make certain that policy makers and fellow citizens understand critical issues that relate to teaching and learning. "Leaders who succeed," state Leithwood and Riehl (2003) in their article on research-based behaviors of successful leaders, "aggressively pursue positive relationships with their external environment, with the goals of fostering shared meanings and earned legitimacy, garnering resources and support, and establishing formal interorganizational relationships" (p. 18). Parents and educators working as a team have the potential to be formidable spokespersons for students and education in the larger political and governmental arenas where policies are often set that have tremendous impact on schools' operation, and thus on teaching and learning.

Walking the Talk

An example from the field of strategies that one veteran elementary school principal used to shape a strong, positive student-centered school culture and climate

The school's climate is the foundation upon which the house will be built. During my twelve-year tenure as the principal of a 500-student PreK–5 elementary school, I utilized many strategies that would facilitate the establishment of a positive school climate, but perhaps the most effective one was making a conscious effort to ensure that each and every staff member had a meaningful role to play in the overall success of the school, and each member understood his/her role. From the principal to the custodian, I felt that everyone must play a vital role if we were to have any hope whatsoever of fostering a positive school climate.

During recess and lunch, I would make a conscious effort to watch the students' interaction with custodians, paraprofessionals, and teachers, and make mental notes of which students seemed to have relationships with which adults, and would then utilize this information when establishing roles. For instance, if I noticed that a student seemed to have a particularly close relationship with a custodian, and the student was sent to my office for a disciplinary infraction, I would actually bring this student to the custodian, explain the situation, and allow the custodian to deal with it. To me, this tactic accomplished several things simultaneously: it allowed the custodian a meaningful role in the success of the school, it allowed the mutual relationship between the custodian and the student to be further cultivated, and it established another block in fostering a positive school climate, as well as facilitating mutual respect between the custodian and me.

Similarly, I quite often referred students who were experiencing difficulties to teachers and paraprofessionals who did not have the particular students in class, but nevertheless had an established relationship with the students. Principals who believe they are capable of fostering a positive and effective school climate without meaningfully involving every member of the staff, and having each member clearly understand and accept his/her role, are fooling themselves, and the folly of this thinking will soon manifest itself in several undesirable and counterproductive ways. At times, it may be difficult and very

(Continued)

(Continued)

challenging to find a meaningful role for each and every staff member, but this challenge actually becomes an opportunity for principals to demonstrate both their leadership qualities and their creativity. (Dr. Ricky P. Sahady, Author's Feedback Request Form, August 2008)

Dr. Ricky P. Sahady is a thirty-three-year veteran educator in the Fall River Public Schools of Massachusetts. He has been a teacher, director of the Fall River Teacher Center, and principal of John J. Doran Elementary School from 1993–2005. He currently serves as director of curriculum for the Resiliency Preparatory School, which provides alternative education to approximately 250 students in the district.

POINTERS FOR THE PRINCIPAL

- Be an avid, objective information seeker.
  - o Maintain a grip on the culture of the school—what people think, how they behave, and what they believe.
  - o "Dip-stick" regularly by wandering around, looking, listening, and talking to people.
  - o Really get to know teachers, students, parents, and the community.
  - o Ask questions, administer surveys, and plunder through old school documents and artifacts to learn about the school and its past.

- Thicken the cultural glue with issues of teaching and learning.
  - o Although resistant to change, culture is always changing.
  - o Capitalize on inevitable change events to improve the existing culture by strengthening the focus on teaching and learning.
  - o Communicate consistently through word and deed your high expectations for everyone's performance and success.
  - o Identify and enlist the help of student-centered change agents.
  - o Be a politically active and informed advocate for children and education in the larger contexts of society, where policy and legislation are set that frequently impact education and students' well-being.

- Nurture a sense of community and trust.
  - o Carefully recruit, screen, orient, and mentor new employees.
  - o Deal honestly and respectfully with others.
  - o Encourage openness and shared problem solving.
  - o Reward innovation and risk taking on behalf of students.
  - o Celebrate students' and staff's accomplishments.

5

Organizational Conduits

Communication Strategies for Effective Instructional Leadership

People communicate most eloquently through their actions, not their words.

—Association of Supervision and Curriculum Development (1998, p. 83)

To share learning and knowledge across the learning community, effective leaders create information and administrative systems that align schedules, budgets, facilities, communications, transportation, and human resources functions to instruction.

—National Association of Elementary School Principals (2008, p. 5)

More frequently than not, failures in communication lie at the heart of problems in organization, goal setting, productivity and evaluation.

—Jerome P. Lysaught (1984, p. 104)

Barriers [to communication] can be removed by managing the use of power, eliminating fear, encouraging feedback, and establishing a climate of openness and trust.

—Reginald Leon Green (2001, p. 126)

Quality leaders know that feedback loops are the backbone of continuous improvement.

—Charles Schwahn and William Spady (1998, p. 101)

Never more than today has the communication role of school principals been so vital to their success. If principals today are to be effective leaders—as distinguished from managers—they must be masters of the "crucial Cs"—the processes that, according to Paul Houston (2001), executive director of the American Association of School Administrators, support the work and get it done: connection, communication, collaboration, community building, child advocacy, and curricular choices. In today's organizational leadership, the degree of effectiveness of a leader is tied more directly to his or her effectiveness as a communicator more often than it is to any other skills and functions fundamental to being chief administrator. "The image principals project—verbally, nonverbally, and in written communication—forms the dominant perception of the school on the part of the students, staff, parents, and community" (National Association of Elementary School Principals, 1991, p. 7). Regardless of the principal's skill and prowess in understanding curriculum, analyzing teaching, budgeting, being visionary, or accomplishing the numerous other important requirements of the position, all is moot if the principal is unable to communicate well, and thus connect well, with the school's various constituencies.

If the job is being done well, one might ask, shouldn't that speak for itself? Well, yes and no. Undoubtedly, when a principal is taking care of business (i.e., is clearly focused on student achievement and welfare and performs the job with care, commitment, and competency), the proof will be evident in a number of dimensions. However, folks' perceptions of how well a school is running and how well a principal is leading can be a tricky thing, even within the school. The external stakeholders—parents and people in the community—are often privy to distorted or incomplete versions of what is happening in a school, and thus frequently make erroneous or premature judgments about the school, its teachers, its administration—or all three—based on such flawed information. Doing the right things and doing them right simply isn't enough for principals to be successful if these right things do not include the vital role of communicating well with people and involving them appropriately. Connecting both internally and externally to all stakeholders requires the establishment of multifaceted communication loops for keeping people well informed and updated on what's happening in the school and, in turn, for getting vital feedback and input as well. Open, multidirectional channels of communication are essential to a healthy school culture.

Covey (1992) refers to such channels—or conduits—as "stakeholder information systems," which he explains are ways to "put teeth into a mission statement, turning it into a constitution, the supreme law of the land, because you are gathering data on it, looking at it regularly, problem-solving and action planning around it, and rewarding people on the basis of it" (p. 235).

Effective leadership requires ensuring people's input in all aspects of the school's operation, from defining its mission and goals to supporting their attainment. An ongoing responsibility of leaders is to provide the various stakeholders (internal and external) with systematic ways of giving input and feedback to the school and with conduits for getting accurate, reliable information from the principal and staff. Leaders too frequently fail to realize how important it is to lay the groundwork, the communication conduits, essential for this multifaceted exchange of information to occur. Such access is vital if people are to understand the principal's and staff's motives for taking certain actions, for leaders to understand what others are thinking and get vital input in making decisions and shaping the school culture to ensure a good fit with the community, and for involving key stakeholders in appropriate ways in the operation and decision-making processes that pave the way—with least resistance—for improvement and necessary change in the school. Such a multidirectional flow of communication is essential to the health of the organization. Without it, an organization—much like the human body—will atrophy.

This chapter deals with issues and strategies related to communication—those related to the principals themselves and those related to their role in facilitating communication among the organization's stakeholders. Three essential aspects of the principal's role as instructional leader and chief expeditor of the flow of information (internally and externally) are (1) seeking first to understand, (2) facilitating collaboration within the school, and (3) connecting with parents and community as partners.

SEEKING FIRST TO UNDERSTAND

Leadership style itself is very much determined by communication style, which consists of a unique blend of how a person listens, speaks, writes, and uses body language. Although there are fundamental skills involved in communication, each of us has our unique approach to it, which forms the essence of our personality. Because of our wonderful uniqueness and individuality as human beings, there is no one best way to be a good communicator, any more than there is one best leadership style. Each of us must come to know ourselves well enough to identify our communication strengths, weaknesses, and how we as individuals can use our unique set of communication skills to enhance our personal power, to interact best with others in our own special environments.

As with all of this book's interrelated tools for leaders, no single recipe or how-to-communicate-best formula exists that can ignore the fundamental leadership issues of self-awareness and understanding dealt with in the first couple of chapters of this book. Who we are as people, our genuineness of purpose as school leaders, the moral compass formed by this purpose, and the related core values each of us as leaders should identify and stand up for lay the foundation for any other leadership strategy or skill, including this chapter's focus—being an effective communicator. No communication skill or strategy will compensate for internal hollowness that results from shallow thinking and insufficient investments in self-awareness and reflection. Assuming these fundamental nuts and bolts are intact, however, there are external strategies that can then be used as tools to hone a school leader's communication effectiveness—to ensure that the leader is well connected to his or her broad array of audiences. These audiences include students, staff, faculty, parents, and central office, but extend well beyond this more traditional group to include other important stakeholders in the community (i.e., businesses, governmental and social agencies, civic organizations, senior citizens, and advocacy groups). Established mechanisms for multidimensional flows of information among and between these audiences and the school are vital to the health of the organization. With the technology available today (i.e., Internet venues such as chat rooms, Web sites and pages, e-mail correspondence, blasts and blogs, and telephone access via palm pilots and cell phones), there is no excuse for not having fast, easily accessed flows of communication among and between the various and numerous school stakeholders. The bigger issue is managing this plethora of communication media to ensure that they are assets, not liabilities, to good communication.

In their description of the communication roles of the principal, Snowden and Gorton (1998) include not only the dissemination or sender role but also the principal as receiver, monitor, and seeker of communication. Too often, the communication responsibilities of the principal are interpreted too narrowly as primarily a role of disseminator of information; in reality, that is only one of a principal's many communication roles, most of which hinge on understanding what others are saying and feeling. "Perhaps the most powerful principle of all human interaction," asserts Stephen Covey (1992), "[is] genuinely seeking to understand another deeply before being understood in return" (p. 272).

Studies have shown repeatedly that the communication skill most often needed by administrators is listening. "Much of the communication that administrators receive is oral; therefore, empathetic, accurate listening is necessary for a valid understanding of what is being communicated" (Snowden & Gorton, 1998, p. 39). In the communication role of receiver, hearing is distinguished from listening: Actively listening to others involves understanding what they are saying as well as attempting to understand what they are feeling and, furthermore, genuinely caring about those feelings. Covey (1992) calls this kind of listening empathic listening—listening carefully to what a person is saying while simultaneously trying to understand what the person is thinking and feeling:

> Giving full attention, being completely present, striving to transcend one's autobiography, and seeking to see things from another's point of view takes courage, patience, and inner sources of security. It means moving into the minds and hearts of others to see the world as they see it . . . [I]t means that you understand how they feel based on how they see the world. That is empathy. (p. 116)

Often, accurately assessing what a person is feeling is more crucial to understanding that person than listening to what he or she is saying. The tone, pitch, and pace of the voice, the facial expressions and body language, are all excellent indicators of what a person is really feeling.

Like Covey and many others, Snowden and Gorton (1998) assert that good listeners are made, not born, and that effective listening must be developed and cultivated. "In part," these authors espouse, "[effective listening] involves an attitude that indicates the administrator is interested in and cares about what the other party has to communicate. It is an attitude that cannot be easily fabricated without self-betrayal, and to be effective, it must be sincerely felt and communicated nonverbally, as well as verbally" (p. 39). Covey (1992) describes what he calls empathic listening.

As discussed in the preceding chapter on the importance of assessing school culture, listening and observing, making a deliberate effort to take in all the sounds and sights around you, are important processes in preparing a new principal for being an effective leader by learning "how things are around here" before launching major change initiatives. These skills also serve the veteran leader well for staying informed and remaining mindful of what is being communicated by the school's daily sights and sounds. Daresh (2006) admonishes,

> Listen carefully to the words that teachers use to describe the students. Are they indicative of a feeling of warmth and support? Or is there an indication of some kind of constant battling between "us" and "them"? Do the "war stories" shared in the teachers' lounge reflect instances of adults controlling kids, or are the stories shared about successes in achieving positive results? (p. 121)

The sounds emanating from the classrooms are important indicators of the kinds of learning activities (active or passive) going on and the interaction quality among students and teachers. The tone of the language used by the staff, classified and professional employees, when interacting among themselves or with those outside the school sends distinct messages that can typecast the school (e.g., friendly and inviting, disorganized and confusing, cold and indifferent). Taking objective stock of these visual and auditory clues should be a routine part of a leader's day and can be a key tool for gathering useful information.

As *monitor,* a principal must do more than simply remain open to what others have to say and listen empathically. Monitoring the quality of communication in the school is sometimes a skill referred to as with-it-ness—that is, being open and receptive to what is being said and the messages sent by the behaviors of people. In addition to such openness, with-it-ness requires taking deliberate action to stay informed about what is being said to whom, by whom, when, where, and in what manner. Effective principals are always vigilant and reaching out for such information in their efforts to understand.

Principal as *seeker of information* implies even more assertive action than monitoring and with-it-ness require. In addition to information the principal can acquire by being vigilant and a good listener, she or he must strategically set in motion mechanisms for gathering information that otherwise would be elusive. No leader can single-handedly (or "ear-edly") cover all the bases in ferreting out what is being communicated—and how well—among the many stakeholders in a school.

One means of facilitating a principal's search for information is to identify what Snowden and Gorton (1998) call key communicators in the school and community, establish open lines of communication with them, and regularly interact with them. These key communicators are people the principal identifies (by being with-it) who have more direct, frequent interaction with varied stakeholders and are ready-made conduits of information about the school and community: usually secretaries, parent leaders, community leaders, student leaders, and teacher and staff leaders. Key communicators—either because of their positional or their personal power—are major players in the communication networks of the school or community, or both. Their position may be the source of their power, or it may come from less-formal, more personal leadership qualities. Whatever their source of legitimacy as key communicators, they are important people for a principal to get to know, to observe, and to recognize as valuable conduits of information—as facilitators of messages being sent to others from the principal and as reliable sources of information, feedback, and perspectives of those school stakeholders who may not be directly accessible to the principal.

The role of communicator in school leadership is multifaceted, and highly dependent on the leader's attitude. Viewing communication as a people process, rather than a language skill, may help you focus on the importance of understanding others as a prerequisite to being understood. Principals must be receptive communicators—seekers of understanding—first, by developing and routinely using well-developed communication skills of active listening, observing, and learning from others as a major part of their role, if they are to be effective leaders and set a healthy tone for the entire school.

FACILITATING COLLABORATION WITHIN THE SCHOOL

Value

A climate of trust and mutual respect in a school is both essential to and simultaneously facilitated by a spirit of collaboration among faculty, staff, and administration. Site-based management, shared decision making, integrative leadership, teacher empowerment, and schools as communities of learners are a few of the many concepts that have emerged in the last decade amid a flurry of failed attempts (primarily legislated, mandated reform initiatives) to improve the public schools in this nation since the early 1980s. The common thread among many of these more recent concepts has been redirecting reform efforts away from the failed top-down approaches to a bottom-up, grassroots orientation. This redirection of reform efforts requires a new form of leadership as well. No longer does an autocratic style of leadership meet the needs of schools and the urgency for their reconstruction. Thus was born—from the mother of necessity—an acknowledgment of the need for more integrative leadership styles that hinge on the school's stakeholders participating as members of a school team. In this bottom-up orientation to leadership, the principal's role shifts dramatically from autocrat and chief to mobilizer of teams and facilitator of collaboration mechanisms among the school's wide range of stakeholders.

The complexity of schools as organizations today can ill afford an autocratic, top-down, one-directional orientation to leadership and communication. In their research on leadership and school culture, Sashkin and Walberg (1993) describe the need for change in the organizational communication networking that has historically existed in schools in this country:

There is no question that in the 1990s, U.S. schools face a changing and turbulent environment, and will have to cope with nonroutine problems on a daily basis. Modern organization theory stresses that if an organization is to be successful within this environment, it must have multiway communication networks and a high degree of flexibility in the conduct of its work. Communication structures in the organization must be established to meet the challenges of the environment and the purposes of the organization. Schools are clearly in a changing environment, and their current stated purpose is to educate all students to a high level of academic attainment. (pp. 127–128)

How does a principal facilitate internal communication? What structures are needed to facilitate not only two-way, but a truly dynamic flow of, communication in schools that connects people in ways that have heretofore been largely missing? And what types of communication structures are most likely to improve teaching and learning? As with any other dimension of a school's operation, the unique context of any school with its own set of strengths and weaknesses will need to be considered in deciding how best to facilitate multidirectional communication and collaboration in a school. It comes as no surprise that researchers frequently report effective instructional leadership does not exist outside or separate from effective organizational leadership. It is only one component of leadership in general, all areas of which are interconnected. Any leadership strategy that enhances the opportunity for interaction, involvement, and a sense of ownership shared by the many players in a school community is likely to impact positively the school's quality of instruction, and thus students' achievement.

Principal's Behaviors for Facilitating Collaboration

Collaboration suggests a higher level of teamwork than does *cooperation*, which is often interpreted as being more compliance-oriented than collaboration. Collaborative teamwork is characterized by members' willingness to enthusiastically endorse and support the achievement of the goals of the group and organization. To achieve this higher level of performance, effective instructional leaders must set the tone for such shared teamwork. They accomplish this by establishing an open-door policy and an open demeanor—one in which teachers, parents, students, staff, and community are made to feel welcome and essential as true partners in its operation. As partners, they are comfortable approaching the principal in the school or in his or her office without always having to have an appointment or feeling apologetic about the interruption. Elaine McEwan (2003) puts it this way: "Only salespersons need appointments with instructional leaders" (p. 71). The principal closes his or her door only for confidential conferences. Otherwise, the door should remain open, and the principal should be accessible and approachable.

In addition to being accessible while in the office, the principal who is frequently visible in the halls, on the campus, in the cafeteria (often having lunch with students and teachers), and in classrooms can be a powerful communication channel, both as a means for gathering input and for disseminating information and reinforcing the focus on the school's vision, goals, and the importance of teaching and learning. Where and how principals choose to spend their time sends a much louder message about what they stand for and where their priorities lie than what the principal may say or write.

School leaders' participation in social and political events outside the school also opens up lines of communication and offers an opportunity for getting acquainted with staff, parents, students, and members of the community outside of the school setting, as well as for being an advocate for the school and students' education. Deciding to what extent such participation is possible is important and will depend on your own set of personal circumstances. However, it is important for the principal to participate actively in the social and political life of the school and community. The principal's role as chief communicator for the school and vocal advocate for teaching and learning has become a major one as the pool of stakeholders in the affairs of schooling has expanded exponentially due in part to the accountability movement, with its greater exposure of schools to public scrutiny.

Learning to use effectively, and availing oneself appropriately of, the many in-house communication media—in-house televised broadcasts, intercom, Internet venues, memoranda, newsletters, faculty meetings, school assemblies, student councils—to connect with students and staff provides the principal with multiple ways to disseminate and receive information more accurately and to reinforce the school's mission, with its central purpose of teaching and learning. Multiple media are vital for communication in larger schools, where direct contact—by far the most desirable form—is more difficult across the entire school. The key is not to abuse by overuse or neglect any of the many channels of communication but rather to learn to match the communication purpose with the most appropriate medium for either sending or receiving information. Surveys, telephone calls, personal visits, letters, and e-mails are all appropriate additional ways to communicate, depending on the purpose and the situation. Being sensitive to the context and the purpose of the communication is essential to effective communication.

Facilitating Teacher Collaboration

An informal communication network—the proverbial grapevine—always operates in an organization with or without anyone's sanctions. However, it may be more of a hindrance than a help, depending on the professional status of the school culture, how the grapevine operates, and who the key communicators are within it. In any case, more reliable, professionally focused structures of collaboration should also be operative in schools to ensure the best forms of internal communication. The establishment of formal mechanisms for collaboration between teachers is vital to effective teaching and learning, and fundamental to participatory, integrative leadership. Historically, teachers have had very little time or encouragement to engage in professional dialogue about the difficult, complex task of teaching. Sashkin and Walberg (1993) state,

> From a historical perspective, the isolated nature of the teaching profession has carried forward [from the days of the one-room

schoolhouse] into contemporary schools. Teachers are now assigned their classroom with students typically at one age level, although they are more likely than not to group them by ability level within the classroom. Although cooperation between principals and teachers has been a rare event, so has cooperation among teachers. It has not been uncommon for us to enter a school building in April of any given school year and find that a teacher knows little or nothing about how another teacher at the same grade level conducts her classroom. Further, it is commonly reported experience that conversations in teachers' lounges rarely focus on instructional issues. (pp. 125–126)

What these researchers recommend is the establishment of communication structures that coordinate as well as regulate; maintain feelings of personal worth, interpersonal relationships, and organizational values; and focus on new ideas and new ways of doing things (Sashkin & Walberg, 1993, p. 126). They suggest the formation of teams of teachers who work to solve problems, are connected by liaisons, and are reformulated as new problems arise and goals change.

Recommendations for the creation of working teacher teams proliferate in the current professional literature. These groups are given a variety of labels—work-study groups, dialogue teams, professional focus teams, quality circles, leadership committees, problem-solving teams, planning groups—but the objective is often the same: to provide time and focus for professional dialogue to problem solve and improve the school and the quality of teaching and learning in the classrooms. Tanck (1994) suggests using many forms of active teacher collaboration, such as

1. Instruction councils as the locus of faculty leadership for ensuring competent professional practice and student performance
2. A site-based school improvement project that involves the entire faculty (e.g., an excellent model for school improvement is Onward to Excellence developed at the Northwest Regional Educational Laboratory)
3. Collegial development teams for teachers to share their expertise and provide mutual support for reaching professional goals in small groups of four to six
4. Peer coaching, wherein teachers observe each other and provide feedback on the efficacy of instruction

Participants in collegial development teams report a strong commitment to the process and agree that their efforts improve instruction and student achievement . . . While there is evidence that site-based management *per se* does not improve student achievement in schools, there is evidence that a collaborative focus on effective school practice does enhance student learning. (Tanck, 1994, pp. 94–95)

Mary Newman and Warren Simmons (2000), directors of the Leadership Development initiative of the Annenberg Institute for School Reform at Brown University, espouse the benefits of distributed leadership for student learning:

> One effective way to create a common culture that values continuous learning for everyone is to create professional learning communities— small groups of practitioners who work together to foster reflective practice, collegiality, and collaboration and who develop and focus on a coherent set of standards-driven goals connected to teaching and learning. For example, a team in a school or district community can develop or adopt a process for giving and receiving feedback through peer observation, examining student work, and shoring teachers' and principals' work. By "de-privatizing" practice and sharing their work with one another, members of a school/district community can come to common understandings about the purpose of schooling, the curriculum, and best practices. (p. 11)

Effective instructional leaders help to make professionally focused talk the superglue of the school and its culture, and an expectation among the faculty, staff, and students—part of the school's norms. The principal and other teacher leaders must be role models, responsible for reinforcing professional dialogue and setting in motion the creation of such opportunities for others, for providing the resources and time teachers need to engage in such discussions, for helping to keep the discussions centered on improving instruction, and for being active participants in the discussion groups.

A key process in a school that operates with participatory decision making is the ability for the many groups at work to be able to reach consensus. A necessary part of participatory style leadership is the ability to lead and teach others how to use a healthy group process for dealing with varied opinions and ideas in order for the group ultimately to make a decision that everyone is able to not only live with, but feel good about and support. While there are many formal and informal ways to go about catalyzing consensus, one reliable method is the Nominal Group Technique. This process has several advantages: it allows the person in charge to (1) control the meeting and discussion, (2) keep the group working toward the task at hand, (3) insure that everyone participates by presenting his/her ideas, and (4) set priorities and reach consensus on the goals, problems, solution, or program suggestions proposed by the group. The process has a strong research base supporting its usefulness in facilitating group decision making (Lunenburg & Ornstein, 2008).

"My campus used this process in determining the emotional issue of mandatory staff cuts due to district level budget constraints," says Dr. Nancy Adams, Associate Professor of Educational Leadership at Lamar University in Beaumont, Texas, and veteran principal who received the 2007 Galveston Independent School District's Principal of the Year award.

"I have seen it used at the district level in deciding which campus would be closed due to declining enrollment. It gives everyone a voice and plays out as a fair process to all parties involved when the stakes and emotions are running high. All principals need to have a strategy like this one in their back pocket. I have been impressed as I watched this technique used. It works!!" (Adams, Author's Feedback Form, October 2008)

At the elementary level, too often the only collaborative team structure is seen in the form of grade-level teams. At the high school level, the most systematic collaborative teamwork is found among members of a department, usually formed around subject areas. Middle school team structures for teacher collaboration often follow either the elementary or the high school structure, depending on their predominant orientation. Although such unilateral forms of collaboration may work well for grade-level or departmental coordination, they fall far short of providing other important kinds of cross-grade-level and whole-school interaction that tap teachers' problem-solving capacity and foster their spirit as a united, schoolwide team of professionals working toward larger goals than those within grade levels or departments.

True participatory leaders identify early the leadership talent among their faculty and capitalize on this readily accessed leadership resource. One way to operationalize shared leadership is through the formation of a schoolwide leadership team that ideally is representative of the various grade levels and disciplines. The members of such a team can be valuable partners in shared school leadership, and reliable communication conduits for helping to disseminate valid information and to gather input and feedback critical to good schoolwide decision making and continuous improvement efforts.

Another strategy for ensuring the best possible teaching and learning is establishing formal, team-based induction programs for new teachers and teachers new to the school. The collaborative, team-based approach to induction of new teachers, with the mentor being only one part of a larger team, helps to distribute the responsibility among the faculty, increases the sense of professionalism and ownership among the faculty for the wellbeing of the new teacher, and provides a stronger base of support for new faculty. Obviously, the sooner new teachers are made to feel a part of the school family by becoming familiar with the people and the resources, becoming oriented to the culture, and being given the support and guidance they need to deal with their first-year problems, and thus feeling adequate in the classroom, everyone benefits—the new teacher, other faculty, the principal, and the community—in addition, of course, to the students. Strong orientation systems for new staff can greatly enhance a principal's efforts to reshape and change the school's culture by ensuring that new staff get the positive support and assistance they need to be successful and feel competent.

Good induction programs help to expedite new teachers' effectiveness and confidence in the classroom, thereby enhancing the possibility that they will remain in the profession. The mass exodus of classroom teachers in this country due to retirement, combined with the increasing demands on teachers and the high rate of attrition of new teachers, makes it imperative that proper care be given to the incoming new generation of teachers. It is not only good business, and it is more than facilitating better instruction; it is the moral, decent thing to do. New teachers today, more than ever before, need the kind of support afforded entry-level persons in other professions—a period of mediated entry into the classroom, with strong support and nurturing, to ensure their competency before they are treated as fully fledged, veteran teachers.

A word of caution regarding collaborative structures: The interdependent connection between collaboration and school culture is especially critical to the success of various forms of principal-imposed structures for teacher collaboration. If the initiatives employed by the leader to increase the professionalism and collegiality among teachers are what Sergiovanni (1992) calls "contrived collegiality," the results are likely to backfire. Sergiovanni warns, "Contrived collegiality, by forcing people together, can take a toll on teachers' time and compromise their professional autonomy" (1992, p. 90). He speculates on the historical cause for much of the lack of professionalism among faculties and in school cultures:

> The problem seems to result partly from a culture of schooling whose management is captured by bureaucratic norms and whose teachers are captured by the norms of isolation and privatism. These norms seem impervious to change strategies and leadership practices that rely on bureaucratic, psychological, and technical-rational authority. For example, administrators who push for collegiality by altering structures and introducing such innovations as team teaching and peer coaching in a school, without addressing the norm structure, may be superimposing a form of collegiality on an unaccepting culture. (p. 89)

In other words, true integrative, participatory leadership recognized by the school and community is a prerequisite for professional attitudes and behaviors to emerge from teachers and for these to become a part of the school culture. Without a principal's sincerity of purpose to share leadership and empower others, no strategy or superimposed mechanism for increasing cooperation and collaboration among teachers will work to achieve significant, positive school improvement. Teachers themselves must ultimately assume professional behaviors that will necessarily include collaboration for improvement. The principal merely paves the way for such collaboration, first by genuinely having and exhibiting the expectation that teachers are professionals with much to contribute to the leadership of the school. With such an expectation borne out by behaviors, the principal can then—and *only* then—facilitate teachers' collegiality by increasing opportunities and professional purposes for them to engage in collaborative endeavors.

Facilitating Student Collaboration

Students must actively be included in the information loop if the school is to operate most effectively. The structures most appropriate for soliciting their input and involving them in meaningful ways in the operation of the school are contextually dependent. That is, the degree and kind of participation will depend on students' ages, sophistication, and experiences with purposeful collaboration among themselves as well as with the adults in their environment. Unfortunately, students' views about their educational experiences and the operation of their school are too often overlooked.

The most obvious, prolific communication conduit with students is in the day-to-day interaction with them in the halls, on the campus, in the cafeteria, on the playground, on the athletic field, and in the classrooms. The tone and type of messages sent and received during these myriad less-formal interactions between adults and students, and among the students themselves, are a vital means of communicating with students. The culture of the school is most impacted by the degree of respect, the expectations for achievement and behavior, and the individual attention shown throughout the school day among the school's myriad of interpersonal interactions. However, in addition to the input teachers and principals get and the messages they send (by word, deed, and body language) to students in their informal interactions with them, more deliberate, formal mechanisms can also be useful in opening and maintaining lines of communication with students. Their deliberate inclusion in the information web of the school community is essential for them to acquire a high degree of identification with the school, a strong sense of community and team spirit, and a feeling of ownership that comes only from involvement in an organization's operation.

One oldie-but-goodie means of communicating with students more formally is through the establishment of a student council or student advisory committee. Most students are quite capable of participating in such a capacity by the middle grades. To be a valuable communication channel, however, the council should participate in the school's operation in meaningful ways. When students are given opportunities to participate in purposeful projects and school problem solving, everyone benefits. Adults are frequently surprised and delighted by the quality and number of ideas students generate. And students gain experience with group problem solving, are better informed about the school's mission and purpose, feel more connected to the adults and each other as a part of a community, and feel valued and respected as contributing members of the organization of their school. These are powerful culture builders as well as communication conduits.

An easy way to facilitate communication with and among students (and others) is to have a suggestion box for students to deposit their ideas for school improvement. Awarding students for the "best idea of the week" or month will add interest and spark enthusiasm for participation in this strategy. Having a group of teachers and students judge the suggestions and choose the winners could add more interest and broaden participation in the activity. This idea will have positive results only if students' suggestions are given serious consideration and follow-up.

Student work-study teams can be formed on an ad hoc basis as the need arises; this is a process with which students could assist—improving the cleanliness of the building and grounds, improving student conduct, participating in community service activities, or planning for special events, such as Grandparents Day, are possible reasons to form a team. Students could also serve on the adult work-study teams as needs arise that are appropriate to their participation. Work-study teams may often involve the participation of teachers, students, administrators, and parents in cooperative endeavors.

Peer tutors and support groups can be an effective way to use the talent and skill of many students, get them involved in helping each other, and tap into the varied interests and needs of the student population. Such groups can involve teachers and community members as well as students, depending on the strengths and resources of the school community.

It is important to be certain that varied communication channels are operative and open for all students, not just a select group. Ideally, each student should have opportunities to be an active, contributing member of the school community. When only the academically gifted students or children from the top socioeconomic echelons are asked to participate in student leadership and are the primary students included in the organization's communication loop, the other students eventually get the message that not much is expected of them and that what they have to offer is not as valuable as the contributions of those students in the loop. It naturally follows that when students feel marginalized or less than good about their participation in school, they find subgroups with which to identify and from which to gain personal value and esteem.

CONNECTING WITH PARENTS AND THE COMMUNITY AS PARTNERS

"Nothing motivates a child more," Michael Fullan (1994) points out in his book about the principalship, "than when learning is valued by school, family, and community working in partnership" (p. 22). In making a case for the importance of establishing partnerships with parents in the education of children, Dolan (1994) offers these powerful ideas:

To educate children without a deep partnership of teacher and parent is hopeless, and going in we have conditioned everyone to minimal interaction, indifference, maybe even suspicion. This is the [steady state] in most of the country. And, it has to change . . . In a school, where mistrust between the community and the administration is the major issue, you might begin to deal with it by making sure that parents were present at every major event, every meeting, every challenge. Within the discomfort of that presence, the learning and the healing could begin. (p. 159)

Yet schools often report repeated failed initiatives and feeling helpless in trying to reach out to and involve parents in the education of their children. However, research has provided good insight into what will and won't work in this important obligation of schools. A word of caution: The work is not easy and is more than just "keeping parents/families informed" . . . this won't qualify as "involving or engaging" them as partners. For example, in their extensive research synthesis regarding parental and community involvement's impact on student achievement, titled *A New Wave of Evidence: The Impact of School, Family, and Community Connections on Student Achievement*, Ann Henderson and Karen Mapp (2002) identify the following proven ways that schools can assist families in developing their capacity to support their children's education:

1. Engage them at school so they understand what their children are learning.
2. Give them a voice in what happens to their children.
3. Provide information about how to help their children at home, what their children need to learn, and how to plan for college, postsecondary education, and a career.
4. Foster social connections among families and with teachers.
5. Build families' understanding of the education system and how to guide their children through it successfully.
6. Offer access to social services and community agencies.
7. Identify and build on strengths in the community and among families. (2002, p. 74)

This research synthesis is an excellent source for outstanding recommendations and innovative strategies to engage parents, families, and communities as real partners in education—strategies that have a solid track record of success in schools from all types of communities where there is a broad range of cultural, economic, and educational backgrounds. Despite these differences, there is an overriding interest that is common to all communities and shared with all educators: the desire to have their children learn and do well in school. That common desire is what brings the varied constituencies together and is the core incentive that paves the way for such partnerships to work.

Forming Partnerships

Families and the community collaborating with schools as partners is simply a must for schools to be effective in their central mission of caring for and educating children. An important point made by Henderson and Mapp (2002) concerns the kinds of partnerships that are most likely to be successful: "Parent and community involvement that is linked to student learning has a greater effect on achievement than more general forms of involvement. To be effective, the form of involvement should be focused on improving achievement and be designed to engage families and students in developing specific knowledge and skills" (p. 38).

The job of educating children is far too complex for educators to be successful if they are attempting to do it alone. Healthy partnerships are needed for students to succeed at school, but these partnerships require strong systems of two-way communication and collaboration between the school, parents and families, and the community. The school must be able to send messages in a reliable, efficient manner and likewise be able to seek—and genuinely seeking to receive—feedback and input from all stakeholders. The strategies discussed in this section are some of the more reliable tools principals can use in establishing open lines of communication and strong alliances with their parent and community partners, an essential role of today's instructional leadership.

School councils or advisory committees that include representative stakeholders are an important part of today's school operations. Rather than seeing such groups as necessary annoyances or window dressings, today's most progressive school leaders incorporate them as "part of a systemic shift in the relationship between the communities and schools that is both inevitable and that contains the seeds of a necessary realignment with the family and other social agencies" (Fullan, 1994, p. 22). Ideally, councils work on problems and help the school garner the resources needed to make change happen, rather than make major decisions. It is the principal's job, however, to explain the parameters and purposes for councils' functioning and to help them learn to work collaboratively as a group, brainstorm ideas to improve the school, and coalesce for the benefit of the children. Councils should not be viewed as panaceas or the sole means of involving parents and community members as partners of the school, but rather as one strategy for soliciting these stakeholders' participation in the school that has the potential to be beneficial to everyone.

An important new role for principals today is serving as a mediator—facilitating the participation of parents and community members and ensuring that such councils understand their advisory capacity and serve useful purposes. Councils should generally not get so heavily entangled in trying to make decisions that their energy and morale are drained off in petty power struggles. Fullan (1994) writes both of the potential benefits and the limitations of such councils, which should be clearly understood by the school leader if such groups are to benefit the school's operation:

> The role of the council is to help mobilize the forces and resources for change by developing the skills of parents, teachers, students, and principals as leaders in "group problem-solving," "dealing with conflict," and "making content expertise accessible" ... The establishment of a council involving a handful of parents could not possibly improve the learning for the hundreds of students in the school. What does make a difference is the multiple forms of particular involvement deliberately fostered, developed and supported. (pp. 22–24)

Facilitating Mutual Understanding

Surveys can be an effective way of gathering the information needed by today's principal when it comes to analyzing and understanding the community. The newspaper, the Internet, mail, personal interviews, and the telephone are all viable vehicles for surveying parents and community members. Each method has its advantages and disadvantages, which should be considered in choosing the method most appropriate for each school context. Surveys and questionnaires can be constructed to fit the needs of the school and used to glean attitudes and opinions related to issues about which parents and community have an interest or concern. Finding out how the community at large feels about issues that are usually of concern to them— discipline, drugs, violence, school grounds and facilities—are easily accessed via surveys. Parents' concerns are usually more closely linked to issues involving teaching and learning. Including parents and citizens in the development of the questions usually enhances both the quality and receptivity of the survey. Resources abound for assisting with the development of a survey. One such helpful resource is a book by Gallagher, Bagin, and Kindred (1996), titled *The School and Community*. Carefully developing the survey or questionnaire and piloting it for feedback and revision before using it on a wide scale, or selecting one already developed that serves your purposes, can prevent many mistakes and ensure that the survey best meets your needs.

Dissemination strategies to get the word out or to keep parents and community regularly informed include informative school Web sites; letters or newsletters from the principal, the teachers, or both; a school newspaper; a local newspaper column; and local radio and television spots. With today's technological advances, additional communication conduits linking schools to parents and community in two-way exchanges of information are limited only by the time and imagination of the school's leadership and include the Internet, e-mail correspondence, blogs, blasts, live conferences and chat rooms in addition to the more traditional conduits of homework hotlines, back-to-school open houses, regularly scheduled parent–teacher conferences, and PTO or PTA meetings. The point is not to seek one perfect channel of communication with the public but to have a system consisting of multiple conduits or channels to facilitate dynamic, multidirectional flows of communication and opportunities for community-based interaction and dialogue about the school and the students.

With stakeholders in today's schools representing many diverse interests and perspectives, such interaction with parents and community as partners in the education of children is vital to the school's effectiveness in fulfilling its central mission: teaching and learning. Stephen Covey (1992) saliently warns, however, of the shallowness of strategies that defy or ignore the importance of trust and sincerity emanating from the leadership in the organization:

> Until we cultivate principle-centered leadership inside our organizations, our efforts to improve communications will have little permanent value. The foundation lies with people and relationships. When we ignore the foundation, our improvement initiatives will fail or falter. Effective communication is built on the cement of trust. And trust is based on trustworthiness, not politics. (p. 118)

Nor will any of these recommended strategies work without principals accepting "seeking first to understand" and "serving the child's best interest" as their working mantras.

And so it is that, at the end of this chapter on communication's role in instructional leadership, we come full circle once again to dealing with the core of who our leaders are as people. Marlin Tanck (1994) writes,

> The nature of moral leadership is portrayed to the staff and the public by the way in which things typically are done and how resources usually are used. Provision of higher-level moral leadership, which stresses professional ethics and service to students, is strongly stated by allocating adequate time for professional collaboration and by making instruction councils the focus of school organization. (pp. 91–92)

What motivates a principal most in coming to work each day and whose interest does he or she most passionately serve? Only when the interests of children propel the strategies and actions of school leaders, and they assume with understanding and skill their new role as team builders and chief agents of coalescence of multiple resources on behalf of children, are their efforts more than sounding brass and tinkling cymbal, making much noise but signifying very little for improving schools, teaching, or learning.

Walking the Talk

An example from the field of a principal's strategies to engage stakeholders as partners the operation of the school

Parents, teachers, business and community leaders are actively engaged on our campus through an active site base team, celebrations of success, programs, and field trips. Our site base team, which is made up of parents, teachers, business and community representatives, meets each month to discuss what is happening on our campus. Paraprofessionals and teachers of all special programs have a representative on the committee. The grade level chairpersons are ad hoc members. Every member of the campus has a representative to provide input and share what is discussed. All reports on state assessments from TEA, the Academic Indicator System (AEIS) report, and the Campus Report Card from TEA are discussed at open meetings of the committee. The members of the committee determine the goals for the campus and the strategies to meet the goals. The business and community leaders provide a great deal of insight and perspective from their point of view. They keep us aware of the skills our students need to be successful in the business world and community. They offer opportunities for our children to take part in service learning and participate with our students in activities like painting a map of the United States on our front driveway. Our school piloted Junior Achievement in the second grade in our area.

Parents, teachers, business and community leaders work together to provide opportunities for each of our students to be successful, whether it means providing for their basic needs or having an opportunity to further their innate talents. Many of our students have never been out to zoos, museums, cultural activities, restaurants, or even to a supermarket. The students in our Preschool Education Program go on a field trip to our local H. E. B. Store every year where they learn about healthy nutrition and the business world. Through field trips, our children learn that there is a world of opportunities for them. Parents and teachers make field trips possible by working with business and community leaders to provide funds for chartered buses and other expenses. Parents who never participate in any other event anxiously take advantage of an opportunity to go on a field trip with their children to places they have never been.

We invite parents and business and community members to speak to our children on special occasions and to celebrate the many cultures represented on our campus. Since 2001 our students have made a human flag to honor first responders and veterans on Veterans Day each year. Fourth grade students host a Cultural Fair each spring during which they share research on the cultures represented in Texas. Their parents provide native dishes that represent the different cultures and spend the day sharing the food and learning about one another's culture. Business and community leaders are invited to this event to share the history and culture of our community. (Karen Sue Noble, Author's Feedback Form Response, September 2008)

Karen Sue Noble is the principal of Hillcrest Elementary School serving PreK–fourth grades in the Nederland Independent School District in Texas, a position she has held for sixteen years. The school's 525 student population (20 percent Asian, 20 percent black, 20 percent Hispanic, and 40 percent white) has a free and reduced lunch rate of 60 percent, with 20 percent of them English language learners and 11 percent of them special education students, and with sixteen different languages spoken among the student population. Yet this school was chosen in 2005–2006 as one of only two National Title I Schools for Texas, and the school frequently receives an Exemplary rating from the Texas Accountability System.

POINTERS FOR THE PRINCIPAL

- Seek first to understand.
  - ○ Assess your communication skills—your strengths and deficiencies.
  - ○ Practice empathic listening to genuinely understand how people feel and what they are trying to tell you.
  - ○ Improve your attitude toward people to improve your listening skills.
  - ○ Monitor the quality of communication throughout the school.
  - ○ Actively seek feedback and input from others.
  - ○ Listen more; tell less.

- Facilitate opportunities for collaboration within the school.
  - ○ Encourage a climate of trust and respect.
  - ○ Be genuinely approachable and highly visible.
  - ○ Establish multiple forms of teacher/family/student teams that collaborate regularly to improve teaching and learning.
  - ○ Institute a school-based team approach to induction of new teachers.
  - ○ Avoid trying to paste on collegiality without doing the hard work of changing the culture.

- Treat parents/families and community as true partners in educating children.
  - ○ Assertively reach out to all parents on behalf of students.
  - ○ Establish multiple two-way lines of communication with parents and community.
  - ○ Capitalize on the potential benefits of a leadership advisory council, consisting of family and community representatives.
  - ○ Use media and up-to-date technology to expedite and improve communication.

6

A Learning Organization's Whetstones

Best Leadership Practices for Facilitating Professional Growth and Development

The hallmark of the artisan is the ability to reflect on practice.

—Thomas Sergiovanni (1995, p. 34)

Effective instructional leaders are eager learners.

—Elaine McEwan (2003, p. 36)

A combination of meaningful collaborative involvement and self-directed performance and accountability is what makes a profession strong and keeps competent persons in it.

—Marlin L. Tanck (1994, p. 94)

A school system truly committed to empowering teachers by giving them access to decision making must be prepared to foster a new professional culture in the schools, a culture that accords high priority to matters of the mind.

—Gene I. Maeroff (1994, p. 55)

We cannot achieve quality learning for all, or nearly all, students until quality development is attained and sustained for all teachers.

—Michael Fullan (1994, p. 246)

Meaningful and lasting change occurs when we look inside ourselves for answers.

—Carl R. Rogers and H. Jerome Freiberg (1994, p. 119)

Too many schools are so paralyzed by what teacher evaluation used to be that they resist promising new alternatives.

—Edward F. Iwanicki (2001, p. 59)

Research repeatedly indicates that the majority of a typical principal's day is spent on disciplining students, communicating with the central office staff, talking to parents, and dealing with myriad administrivia (management and operational tasks). "I believe," writes Gordon Cawelti (1993), Executive Director Emeritus of the Association of Supervision and Curriculum Development, "the building principals who would be called instructional leaders would spend at least half or more of their time engaged in the following activities: (1) curriculum planning, (2) clinical supervision, (3) staff development, and (4) teacher evaluation" (p. ix). He further postulates that these tasks are often deliberately avoided "simply because principals are not comfortable with them."

Today's school leader does not have to be the dominant expert in all of these complex areas, but he or she must recognize these school processes as the whetstones of an improving organization. The principal must be chief mobilizer of the school's talent and resources to maximize these processes as tools for organizational development. Thus, the case is further made for a participatory, distributive style of leadership for today's schools. A principal's role as a member of a school-based leadership team is primarily one of mobilizing, encouraging, and facilitating working teams. The principal is not expected to do it all. Rather, as a leader of leaders, the principal is expected to be involved in the work of curriculum planning, supervision, staff development, and evaluation—but as a working team member, not always the person in charge.

Along with the teachers, instructional leaders give these processes a considerable amount of time; lend their expertise where they have some and when they find it appropriate to share; take care to maintain high visibility and working team-member participation; and facilitate two-way communication channels with the school's working teams as well as multi-way communication channels between and among the various working teams themselves. The processes that support the continuing development of the organization and its people are complex and best handled by administrators and teachers working together in a collaborative fashion to share their skills, knowledge, and experience. The job is too big for an administrator to manage well alone but, more importantly, the collaborative processes themselves—as discussed in Chapter 5—hold the greatest potential for transforming the school into a learning community focused on improving teaching and learning. According to Hawley and Valli (2000),

> The essential characteristic of effective professional development is that it involves continuous teacher and administrator learning in the context of collaborative problem-solving. Thus it occurs in planned, structured ways and in ways that are incidental and informal. When professional development is seen as a program or series of formal scheduled events or is otherwise disconnected from authentic problem solving, it is unlikely to have much influence on teacher or student learning. (p. 9)

Reflective practice, *supportive* supervision, *cooperative* team-based evaluation, and *work-study groups* are the most professional, authentic approaches to the organization's processes of practice, supervision, evaluation, and group work if improvement of teaching and learning is the central motive. Ostensibly, these processes are intended to be positive and facilitative of growth and development of educators. Somewhere along the way, however, they often take a bad turn in the organization of schools: The practices of teaching and administration are too often prescription oriented rather than professional and reflective; supervision and evaluation are too often "snoopervision," with administrators observing and making judgments about (rather than collaboratively working with) teachers' performances, which often amount to "dog and pony shows" for the prearranged observation of the supervisor/evaluator; and the work of the school is too often performed by appointed committees to accomplish various task assignments that frequently have little to do with shared study to improve the school's operation by centering the work on students, teaching, and learning. The sad, nagging reality is that practitioners in education rarely have the time or expectation to reflect routinely on their performance; to be involved in supervision and evaluation processes that are professionally conceived and collaboratively implemented with improving teaching and student achievement as the obvious, sustaining motive; or to participate in large and small group work that emerges from the whole school team and is clearly focused on problem solving to improve teaching and student achievement. This chapter's recommended processes are the ones most often linked with schools characterized as "learning communities"—organizations that are in a continual state of improving led by teams of exemplary "learning leaders." While worthwhile staff development can legitimately take many other forms (e.g., workshops, guest speakers, invited consultants, professional conferences) reflective practice, supportive supervision, cooperative team-based evaluation, and work-study groups are often overlooked as viable forms of staff development with strong potential to have sustainable impact on teaching and learning. So why not make the most of this readily accessible potential? Professionally conceived and implemented with the intent of improving instruction rather than checking up on employees, telling them what they're doing wrong, or attempting to force external control for accountability, these traditionally dreaded school processes can become positive, powerful tools for facilitating "professional" growth and learning among the adults in school communities.

A spirit of taking responsibility and professional accountability for one's own performance is indicative of a healthy school culture, a true learning community, where teachers and administrators set the pace as "learning leaders." In positive, developing schools, professional development in the form of reflective practice, supportive supervision, cooperative evaluation, and work-study groups are routine practices in the day-to-day operation of administration, faculty, and staff; they emerge from the collective thinking and participation of all faculty and staff about how these processes can best facilitate improved instruction for student achievement.

REFLECTIVE PRACTICE

Someone once estimated that teachers rank second only to air-traffic controllers in the number of decisions they must make during their typical workday. Teaching and school administration both involve physically, emotionally, and intellectually demanding work. Ironically, the busy-ness of most schools undermines their most central business—matters of the mind. Genevieve Brown and Beverly Irby (2001) posit,

> Although it is difficult to find the time to step back and analyze decisions and subsequent actions, it is critical that the principal do so . . . Reflection by the principal necessitates the engagement in thoughtful and careful reporting and analysis of past practices, events, and experiences, thus offering valuable insights into one's leadership progress. Reflection takes the principal from a basic level of acceptance of the way things are in the

process of schooling to a level of critical examination, self-assessment, and new visions. (pp. 24–25)

These authors report the following commonalities among reflective administrators, which they purport "serve as benchmarks for principals who are interested in engaging in reflection to inform their practice" (p. 25).

1. They view self-assessment and reflection as priorities for school improvement.
2. They recognize that external and internal challenges result in growth.
3. They intentionally engage in activities aimed at challenging current beliefs and practice expanding understandings.
4. They understand that change is inevitable.
5. They recognize that chaos often accompanies change.
6. They share understandings with colleagues. (pp. 25–26)

Brown and Irby's handbook on the development of a principal's portfolio includes many suggestions for helping an administrator—new or veteran—to learn to use reflection as a tool for self-improvement as well as for facilitating reflective practice among teachers and students in the school community.

To be sure, schools traditionally have not been conducive to much reflection, especially among the adults. How is it that students are supposed to learn higher order thinking and practice in-depth reflection in a school context in which adult behavior is primarily characterized by reactionary, spontaneous behaviors, such as "putting out fires" and "keeping the lid on?" In writing about this ambiguous phenomenon, Michael Fullan (1994) states, "Schools as learning organizations are basically nonintellectual in the sense that the way they are organized, structurally and normatively, is not amenable to experimentation, critical reflection, continuous learning, assessment, or rethinking" (p. 243). Yet teachers themselves, both as individuals and collectively as faculty, should routinely be practicing these reflection-intensive processes. Members of professions are characterized by their recognition of the need to stay current and to be accountable for continuous improvement and adaptability to change. Sarason (1993) admonishes preservice teachers regarding the importance of understanding and participating in change:

Teaching is not and should not be for those unwilling or unable to be active agents of educational-institutional change. From the standpoint of the larger society, there is too much at stake to allow teachers to be passive participants in the dynamics and processes of change. (p. 19)

Being active participants in the dynamics and processes of change, as individuals and as members both of a team and an organization also involved in continuous change, necessitates reflective practice. It is highly complex, often ambiguous work because change processes are not neatly packaged events. Change not only is continuous but also is characterized by flux, unpredictability, and messiness.

In grappling with the kind of science that would best help educators to function in the chaotic world of schools as loosely coupled organizations, Sergiovanni (1995) suggests a "craftlike science, within which professional practice is characterized by interacting reflection and action and episodes" (p. 32). "Indeed," he continues, "professional knowledge is created in use as principals and teachers think, reflect, decide, and do" (p. 32). Sergiovanni describes what he calls "scruffie thinking" as serving a principal best in dealing with "complex problems in turbulent environments under indeterminate conditions": "Scruffies believe that because the principal, not the theoretician or the researcher, is in command of the idiosyncratic nature of the situation, she or he must be in control of the available scientific knowledge" (pp. 33–35). So what exists in the world of professional know-how and administrative theory to enhance a principal's decision-making acuity and skill? Sergiovanni (1995) readily attests to the significance of the field's scientific research base, but only when the contextual realities of each situation are given full consideration simultaneously:

> Professionals rely heavily on informed intuitions as they create knowledge in use. Intuition is informed by theoretical knowledge on the one hand and by interacting with the context of practice on the other. When teachers use informed intuition, they are engaging in reflective practice. When principals use informed intuition, they too are engaging in reflective practice. Knowing is in the action itself, and reflective professionals become students of their practice. They research the context and experiment with different courses of action. (p. 32)

Mid-continent Research for Education and Learning (McRel) (2000) synthesized the most current literature pertaining to leadership and school improvement up to that point in a monograph that also offered suggestions to school leaders based on the review. Building a learning organization was one of the six enumerated guidelines offered in this publication. Advice to principals regarding this guideline for becoming a more effective leader of change to improve teaching and learning is summarized in Box 6.1. (The change process and the role of the principal as a major agent of change are examined further in Chapter 9.)

BOX 6.1

Building a Learning Organization

- Keep the organization dynamic and adaptable to change by creating, acquiring, and transferring knowledge and modifying behavior to reflect new knowledge and insights.
- Use honest inquiry to examine the appropriateness of past practices or a charted path. Begin inquiries by evoking previous experiences, assumptions, values, and beliefs about issues at hand. Study groups, reflection groups, focus groups and storytelling groups are relevant options.
- Use every person and every situation as a resource for learning: outside consultants, workshops, print materials, conferences, as well as the expertise and experience of the internal faculty and staff working regularly in both whole and small groups to reflect on whether their instructional practices are working.
- Create a safe environment in which people are open to exploring and dialoguing about ideas and alternatives, many of which can be unsettling. Use balance as the leader between stimulating change and maintaining sufficient focus and stability to keep people moving positively.

Of course, the extent to which these suggestions are helpful is largely dependent on the degree of trust that exists among members of the group and the larger school community. Which comes first here, the chicken (professional dialoguing and experimenting) or the egg (trust)? Without ever having the opportunity to deal with unsettling ideas and to examine belief systems together, school members are not likely to develop a culture of trust, which must exist for professional reflection and dialoguing to be its best.

The superglue chapter, Chapter 4, dealt in some detail with how leaders can help to create positive, learner-centered school culture. Although such a culture built on trust takes time and many day-to-day interactions (both formal and informal) between the members of the school community to develop, it can be facilitated by leaders giving teachers safe opportunities to get to know each other well enough for trust to develop and setting structures and expectations in place for dialogue about teaching and learning.

"Generally, people in schools do not talk about their work—teaching—with each other," note Glickman, Gordon, and Ross-Gordon (2007). Yet research often finds that professionals (administrators and teachers) in high-performing schools, unlike most schools, do indeed talk to each other and dialogue often to problem solve and share ideas to improve teaching.

The practices recommended for instructional leadership in this chapter and throughout the text are based on the assumption that excellent teaching and learning cannot happen apart from a trusting community of learners, in which reflective practice and continuous learning are routine behaviors for everyone and are modeled best by teachers and administrators in a collaborative, problem-solving, learning and learner-centered environment. Leiberman (1995) states,

> People learn best through active involvement and through thinking about and becoming articulate about what they have learned. Processes, practices, and policies built on this view of learning are at the heart of a more expanded view of teacher development that encourages teachers to involve themselves as learners—in much the same way they wish their students would. (p. 592)

Reflective practice—for principals and teachers—is essential to maximizing professional people's growth and development, and thus to school improvement. As such, it is a recurring theme in this toolbox for instructional leadership. The reader can readily detect the reflective nature of the recommendations in each of the chapters thus far in this book (i.e., the significance of examining personal style, skills, values, vision, and personal mission as individuals in Chapters 1 and 2; creating a collectively shared mission, vision, and goals as members of a school community in Chapter 3; developing and maintaining a school culture focused on improving teaching and learning in Chapter 4; and the importance of collaboration and multiway channels for teachers, parents, students, and administrators to interact, dialogue, and focus on school improvement in Chapter 5).

Supportive supervision and cooperative evaluation are recommended approaches to these two basic functions of a school principalship. Sergiovanni (1991) contends that supervision and evaluation are inevitably intertwined processes:

> When the focus of supervision is on teaching and learning, evaluation is an unavoidable aspect of the process . . . Attempts to mask evaluation aspects of supervision by avoiding the use of the term, by denying that evaluation occurs, or by declaring that evaluation is reserved only for the annual administrative review . . . are viewed suspiciously by teachers and for good reason—evaluation cannot be separated from supervision. (p. 282)

It is no coincidence that the particular leadership approach to each of these functions encouraged in this chapter is highly dependent on reflection and dialogue as instrumental to the successes of these recommended honing tools. The organizational whetstones (i.e., tools for renewing and improving schools as an ongoing process) are given substantial credence by their association with many of today's best thinkers and instructional leaders.

SUPPORTIVE SUPERVISION

As with any of the functions of leadership, principals should reflect on and answer basic questions about their beliefs and values regarding education in general and the supervisory function in particular to decide the appropriate action to take in fulfilling the role. The leader's educational platform (discussed in Chapter 2) serves as a starting point for determining how one should behave in any of the basic leadership functions. Having thoughtfully developed an educational platform regarding his or her values and beliefs as a leader in education, a school principal is then prepared to respond to the three additional questions in Box 6.2 specifically focused on clarifying one's supervisory role and subsequent behavior.

BOX 6.2

Clarifying Questions

1. What is the purpose or goal of supervision?
2. How can this goal best be achieved?
3. What can I do as principal to facilitate the achievement of this goal?

In defining the purpose of supervision, today's most effective administrators are clearly moving away from a paradigm of "snoopervision" toward a role as facilitator of teachers' and staff's growth and development (Beck, 1994; Blase & Blase, 1998; Daresh & Playko, 1995; Glatthorn, 1984; Oliva & Pawlas, 1997; Sullivan & Glanz, 2005). When the purpose of supervision is perceived as a catalytic process to help people improve their performance, it becomes quite different from when supervision is perceived to be an autocratic, top-down exercise in quality control. Findings from the Blases' study (1998) regarding instructional leadership are representative of the conclusions drawn by many contemporary researchers who favor a more nurturing, facilitative approach to supervision:

> In essence, our findings confirm that good supervisory practice should no longer emphasize control and competition among teachers: The prevalent negative associations that derive from "control supervision" simply must give way to various forms of collegiality among educators. Supervision should avoid restrictive and intimidating approaches to teachers, as well as approaches that provoke little more than teachers "jumping through hoops" and giving "dog and pony shows" based on reductionist algorithms presumed to define good teaching in their classrooms. Instead, supervision should work toward the development of professional dialogue among educators. (p. 159)

Once the purpose of supervision has been determined, the second question concerns how this purpose can best be realized. The literature is replete with excellent models of supervision to assist a principal with different types of goals related to supervision focused on nurturing and facilitating better teaching. Supervision of this kind is supportive in its basic purpose. Regardless of its term, effective instructional leadership for today's schools is geared toward instructional improvement. Following is an annotated sampling of the most common models/types of supervision found in the literature for school leadership to date.

1. *Developmental supervision.* Among the foremost thinkers and writers on educational supervision is Carl Glickman (1985). His supervisory model includes four approaches, which he labels (1) directive control, (2) directive informational, (3) collaborative, and (4) nondirective. This comprehensive model of supervision has a developmental dimension to it, progressing from being highly controlled by the supervisor (directive control) to being primarily teacher controlled (nondirective). The idea is for principals to be able to provide teachers with a wide range of developmentally appropriate supervision. However, the directive control approach has little support in much of the current literature about best practices for supervision in today's schools.

2. *Autosupervision.* This is the Blases' term for teachers assuming primary responsibility for their instructional practices and professional development through self-analysis, reflectivity, monitoring one's own progress toward goals, and implementing changes based on reflection. Allan Glatthorn (1984) labels it self-directed development.

3. *Clinical supervision.* According to Goldhammer, Anderson, and Krajewski (1993), this form of supervision—among the most widely accepted and attempted supervisory models in the field—is the aspect of supervision that draws on data from firsthand observation of actual teaching, or other professional events, and involves face-to-face and other associated interactions between the observer(s) and person(s) observed in the course of analyzing the observed professional behaviors and activities, and seeking to define or develop (or both) the next steps toward improved performance (p. 34).

4. *Collegial supervision.* This is a form of peer supervision that Allan Glatthorn (1984) calls cooperative professional development. Glatthorn defines this approach to supervision as a moderately formalized process in which two or more teachers agree to work together for their own professional growth, usually by observing each other's classroom, giving each other feedback about the observation, and discussing shared professional concerns (p. 39). Sergiovanni (1995) refines this form of professional development into more of a supervisory process by stipulating the necessity of the team or pair of teachers to establish the rules and issues before an

observation is made that will also extend to follow-up conversations or conferences.

5. *Differentiated supervision.* As the name implies, this eclectic approach to supervision draws on many of the existing models in an effort to best meet the varying needs of teachers by matching the type of supervision with the teacher's professional developmental stage and his or her style of teaching and learning.

6. *Proactive supervision.* Daresh and Playko (1995) use this term to differentiate the more desirable practices of supervision for today from those stemming from the scientific management views of yesteryear. They describe this approach as one that must stem from an understanding of one's own basic attitudes, values, and assumptions about supervision and education. This approach to supervision is in harmony with participative leadership approaches.

The concept of supportive supervision is consistent with integrative, participatory leadership styles used by today's most effective principals. Although supervisory responsibilities can be assumed by a number of different people in the organization—from central office supervisors to supervising teachers—the role of principal is inherently linked to supervision. It is, as Daresh and Playko (1995) maintain, a moot point to try to separate leadership from supervision: "We continue to hold firmly our view that more effective educational programs will result from more effective leadership practice; we also continue to believe that effective leadership and proactive supervision are synonymous terms" (p. xiii).

Most of the models of supervision can be used in a positive, supportive fashion if the intent of the process is to improve teaching. Because of its comprehensive nature, however, reliance on the differentiated model of supervision is recommended as one that most clearly illustrates and embraces the values of supportiveness and individuation—using whatever means a principal has to help a teacher improve. "Matching supervisory options to individual needs . . . has great potential for increasing the motivation and commitment of teachers at work," states Sergiovanni (1995, p. 234). Although exact matches are unrealistic, considerations about what will work best with a teacher and his or her uniqueness should maximize supervision efforts. The more a principal knows about a teacher's abilities, intellect, learning style, teaching style, motivation, and work goals, the better the chances of making a good supervisory match between the principal and the teacher.

This approach to supervision requires more than a nurturing spirit and thorough acquaintance with faculty as individuals, however. Differentiated, supportive supervision also requires a great deal of skill and flexibility by the principal, who must be open to facilitating a wide range of supervisory support to meet the highly variable needs of most faculties.

This point leads to consideration of the third question posed at the beginning of this section: What can I do as principal to facilitate the accomplishment of the goal? Once the purpose of supervision is defined as improving teaching and learning, and the preferred approach to achievement of this goal is determined to be a kind of supportive approach to supervision of teachers—both as a collective group and as individuals—then defining the principal's role in accomplishing this goal naturally follows and is essential in order to act on the first two steps.

Supportive supervision necessitates differentiation and sensitivity to the needs of the individual teacher, much like good teaching requires attention to the individual needs of students. Sergiovanni (1995) writes,

> The key to the contingency view and at the heart of reflective practice within the principalship is a very simple but deceptive axiom. Teachers have work goals that are important to them. Given the opportunity, they will work very hard at achieving these goals . . . Supervisory options and styles should respond to these differences among teachers, for such responsiveness makes it easier for work goals to be realized. (p. 243)

The principal's role in providing a support system in which teachers can grow and further develop the complex skills of teaching is one of coordinator and integrator of many people to provide the best supervision in such a tailored fashion. The differentiated, supportive approach to supervision defies top-down, single-handed administrative styles. The principal's role in this ambitious, complex form of supervision is one of team member, motivator, resource gatherer, identifier of available talent, and scheduler. In other words, the principal provides oversight of the process and assumes much of the detail of the logistics for ensuring opportunities for differentiated supervision to occur, while involving teachers in assuming a major part of the responsibility for their own growth and development, both as individuals and as a collective faculty.

A comprehensive, supportive, differentiated system of supervision in a school has a number of components operating simultaneously (i.e., ongoing processes, rather than unilateral events) to ensure continuous reflection, dialogue, analysis, and planning for improving teaching. Strategies that are illustrative of supportive supervision systems are described in Box 6.3. Sergiovanni (1995) contends,

> Neither teacher development nor supervision are things that we can do for teachers, but are things that they must do for themselves . . . The test of leadership is to be able to extend to teachers in invitation to accept responsibility for themselves, and to have them accept it. (p. 244)

However, this is not likely to happen unless principals and school leaders provide a well-designed system of support and assistance in a professional context of high expectations for performance among the entire community.

BOX 6.3

Strategies for Supportive Supervision

- *Cooperative clinical supervision.* Teacher and supervisor (or master teacher) work together to establish goals, plan observations, and perform follow-up conferences. Administrators and teachers should become skilled in observing, analyzing, and conferencing for improvement. These can be intimidating processes, but tackled head on by the whole faculty, they can become valuable tools for improving teaching and sharing expertise among the staff. This form of supervision is intensive, reflective, and requires in-depth dialoguing to be maximized. Short-circuiting the complexity of the elements of good clinical supervision can reduce it to a robotic process—something that is more of a liability than an asset.
- *Collegial coaching.* A master teacher teams with a novice or veteran teacher needing assistance with an identified pedagogical skill.
- *Collegial study groups.* Small groups of teachers (which may also include administrators) work toward the accomplishment of a shared professional development goal.
- *Individualized, mediated entry programs.* Long-term, team-based, tailored support systems are established for new teachers (e.g., several years of close mentoring, nurturing, and support may occur before the teacher is assigned a full load of students; team-based support is available; plenty of coaching and opportunities to work with master teachers and administrators are provided).
- *Self-directed development activities.* Teachers audio or videotape themselves (or work with a colleague) for self-analysis and follow that by reflections in a journal or log leading to plans for improvement. Teachers may dialogue with colleague(s) and draw on feedback from students and parents to incorporate their own improvement plans. Professional reading and reflecting, and attending professional conferences, also take place.

Blase and Blase (2004) conclude from their study of effective instructional leaders that those principals who are most successful plan carefully for teachers to have adequate feedback, information, and assistance for their professional growth and development. Turning a school into a community of learners should begin with the adults in the environment setting high expectations and assuming primary responsibility for their own and each other's performance as professional educators. Principal leaders cannot force this to happen, but they can set the stage by modeling such behavior, providing opportunities for teachers to grow as professionals, and setting high expectations for themselves and everyone else in the school community.

As obvious as it should be to the profession by now that a strong program of mediated entry should be routine for all those entering teaching (as is induction into other professions), we continue to treat our vulnerable, new members as though they were no different than veteran educators. In fact, it is not unusual to find some of the worst tasks and some of the most problematic students assigned to new teaching staff. We know this is not right! Yet, even when such heinous acts are not committed, seldom are the resources made available or a system put in place to give new teachers (and teachers new to a school) the support they need to transition successfully into the complex world of teaching or to acclimate into a new school. Is it any wonder education continues to have the highest attrition rate of all the professions—and that the attrition rate is on the incline? Teachers exit the profession most often in the first five years of their career, with the greatest percentage of those leaving being among the brightest and best. Yes, these are the teachers who have choices and can find more gratifying work in other professions where they are treated with respect and given the support and guidance they need to grow and develop on the job.

Glickman et al. (2007) write about teachers having "unstaged careers"—unlike physicians, lawyers, engineers, and scientists, who experience many years of transitioning into greater degrees of responsibility and competency in their work. These authors explain that

> [t]eaching, on the other hand, has been unstaged from entry to exit. Education majors take courses, spend time in schools, perform as student teachers, and then graduate from college into their own classrooms as teachers. After that, no matter how many years they continue to teach, they do not move into another stage. The 20-year veteran teacher has the same classroom space, number of students, and requirements as the first-year teacher. Furthermore, for each year of experience, a teacher realizes a salary increase identical to that received by all others of comparable experience. (p. 27)

The pervasive lack of a support system in education for the teaching profession's novices shows blatant disregard for new faculty members, veteran faculty members, and teaching itself. It is irresponsible and disrespectful—if not outright indecent—to make teaching assignments and teaching pay scales that do not differentiate among the various organizational tasks and the skill levels needed to accomplish the complexities of providing good instruction and ensuring that all students are learning. No wonder members of the public often have such demeaning perceptions of the teaching profession when it is so obvious that the education profession itself does not acknowledge or give credence by the way it operates to the complexity of its own work.

COOPERATIVE EVALUATION

Closely allied, and perhaps even inseparably intertwined, with supervision is the leadership function of evaluation. Just as with other functions, principals equip themselves to deal best with the evaluation by returning to their educational platform, reviewing their fundamental values and beliefs, and adding questions that pertain to the purpose of, process for, and their role in the evaluation function that were posed in the previous section on supervision. "Two leadership tasks invariably affecting the instructional climate are supervision and evaluation of teachers," writes Lynn Beck (1994) in her book on administration as a caring profession. She continues,

> An ethic of care would influence administrators' understanding of purposes, processes, and roles in these activities. In recent years supervision and evaluation have been viewed as activities for monitoring teachers' work, judging their effectiveness based on student outcomes, and meting out rewards for "success" and punishments for "failures." Administrators guided by caring would reject these purposes, viewing them as patronizing, discouraging of teachers' professionalism, and ineffective in achieving desired results. Instead, they would consider supervision and evaluation as activities intended to promote personal and professional development and well-being. Viewing these as endeavors to support teaching and learning, caring instructional leaders would be considerate and fundamentally non-critical. With teachers they would assume the roles of professional colleagues, co-learners, supportive counselors, and friends. Furthermore, they would seek to be understanding listeners, creative problem solvers, and, when necessary, mediators or advocates. Formulating this type of understanding would, in all likelihood, require that leaders engage in thoughtful reflection and dialogue. (pp. 93–94)

Historically, the principal's function as evaluator has undermined the role of supervisor. The contradiction that exists in performing these two tasks is that—at its best—supervision has been interpreted as a helping function, whereas evaluation traditionally has been viewed as one of judging and rating. "Most writers in supervision," explains Ellett (1987), "assume that instructional supervision is a 'support' or 'helping' activity designed as a service for teachers and that this role is incompatible with the school principal's responsibilities as a manager and evaluator of personnel" (p. 304).

An enlightened perspective of evaluation is that it should be "simply one important aspect of the effort to match individual human abilities with organizational goals, objectives, and priorities" (Daresh & Playko, 1995, p. 284).

However, this interpretation is an idealistic one that often goes unnoticed by the players, who all too often see the process as being primarily punitive and aimed at making retention and non-renewal decisions at its most negative level or, at its most benign, a "dog and pony" show to satisfy state and district evaluation requirements. Rarely do teachers or administrators interpret the evaluation process as being very helpful in improving teaching and learning. Unfortunately, the evaluation function of the principalship is most often viewed as a time-consuming requirement that creates more problems—perhaps even impeding teachers' sense of professionalism—rather than facilitating growth and development among staff and faculty.

Although varying purposes for evaluating personnel may exist, instructional leadership necessitates that performance evaluation focus on facilitating growth and development among teachers to improve student learning. Instructional leaders must find ways to make performance evaluation (for everyone, including administrators) a positive, helpful process. It is possible for a school's professional staff working cooperatively to take state- and district-mandated evaluation systems that are less than ideal and turn them into useful, nurturing processes for improving teaching and learning. A school's professional community can literally transform evaluations from traditionally oriented observations, checklists, and ratings that are one way—top-down or bottom-up—to cooperative endeavors in which teachers and administrators work as team members to help each other learn, grow, and improve their performance.

The mechanistic processes of evaluation often used in schools today bear little resemblance to reflective practice; indeed, too often they make a mockery of professionalism and the true complexity of teaching and learning. Annual or biannual observations made by the administrator hardly equip an instructional leader to assess with any degree of accuracy or analysis the quality of instruction afforded children during a nine-month period. Furthermore, the oversimplified evaluative formats have the potential for doing more damage than good in terms of both process and product. The feedback from such observations, checklists, and ratings renders little to no useful feedback from which teachers can improve their performance and can often be more demoralizing than uplifting and helpful—even when the ratings are all top level. Who can feel professional pride in work that is reduced to evaluation by a couple of observations using a checklist and rating scale? The widgets in the domain of educational productivity defy such simple construction.

Chad Ellett's (1987) estimation of the state of the art in evaluation of teacher performance in the late 1980s sums up the problems that persist today:

> Recent case-study analyses of "exemplary" teacher evaluation programs administered at the local district level show that the development and use of teacher evaluation systems for both formative and summative purposes is indeed surrounded by many complex issues. A recent study of teacher evaluation instruments, procedures, and policies used by the one hundred largest school districts showed that:

1. few have comprehensive (3 or more days) training programs for users;

2. most pay "lip service" to fulfilling instructional improvement purposes, but are deficient in the diagnostic structure and procedures necessary to accomplish this task;

3. few are content-valid relative to the research literature on teacher effectiveness; and

4. few have explicitly stated rules or procedures for combining formative and summative observation data. (pp. 305–306)

Despite the national movement in the 1980s for more accountability from schools that led to most states developing and implementing large-scale performance assessment programs requiring systematic collection of data about the quantity and quality of instruction through direct classroom observations of teaching, educational accountability remains an issue mired in confusion. These original state initiatives in performance evaluation cost millions of dollars and were extremely time-consuming. Yet they have failed to resolve the accountability dilemma or the evaluation conundrum. According to Razik and Swanson (1995),

> Teacher evaluation is not characterized by a single best or universal method. For example, both the theory and practice of teacher evaluation reflect disagreements as to whether instructor evaluations should detect incompetencies, prevent incompetence, or correct deficiencies, all of which suggest different methodologies and approaches . . . [T]eacher evaluation may be accomplished for a variety of reasons, none of which are or can be explicitly measured in isolation. In this sense, teacher evaluation, in fact all evaluation, remains a problem. (p. 238)

For the principal *as instructional leader*, however, a primary reason for performance evaluation should be clear: to improve teaching and learning. Iwanicki (2001) suggests including the three questions in Box 6.4 to focus evaluation where it should be most centered—on student learning.

BOX 6.4

Questions for Focusing on Improving Performance Evaluation of Teachers

1. Were the objectives of the lesson worthwhile and challenging?

2. Did the teacher treat the students with dignity and respect?

3. To what extent did all students achieve the objectives of the lesson?

(Iwanicki, 2001, p. 57)

With the purpose clearly established, determining ways to answer these questions and satisfy the purpose for evaluation is less confusing. Lynn Beck's (1994) suggestions for evaluating staff are particularly appropriate for caring leaders who believe that teaching and learning improve best in schools where faculty and staff themselves are nurtured and given the respect and resources to grow and develop as a team, a community of learners:

> Caring leaders might also promote some fundamental changes in supervisory and evaluative assumptions and methods . . . They might actively work to change the pervasive belief that effective teaching can be readily quantified and measured and push for multiple approaches to assess the successes of schools, teachers, and students. These leaders might also shift responsibility for supervision to teachers. This could be done through the development of mentoring programs; through the support of teachers' professional organizations; and through relinquishing control of issues such as hiring, "salary, tenure, and forms of promotion." Further, caring leaders might consider subjecting themselves to some form of supervision and evaluation by inviting teachers, students, parents, and other administrators to help them improve professional practice. (p. 95)

Cooperative evaluation can take many forms, but its essence—similar to and closely allied with supportive supervision—is facilitating reflection and honest inquiry into how to improve teaching in its most complex of interpretations. Rogers and Freiberg (1994) assert,

> Teachers are able to build an internal locus of assessment when the principal and school environment support self-learning . . . Learning from one's successes and mistakes can be the best teacher of all . . . Knowledge is power, but knowledge about self is the greatest power. (pp. 118–120)

The points in Box 6.5 are examples of concrete ways cooperative evaluation may manifest itself in a school community. Teaching is a complex process that defies oversimplification in the form of quick and slick observation checklists and limited data on which to base evaluation and feedback. Allan Ornstein (1993) notes,

> As for teacher evaluation instruments, keep in mind that the human side of teaching is difficult to measure. As a result, it seldom shows up in teacher evaluations. In our attempts to be scientific—to predict and control behavior and assess group patterns—it's too easy to lose sight of the affective side of teaching and the individual differences among teachers. It's too easy to attend to specific types of behavior and cognitive results. (p. 187)

BOX 6.5

Exemplary Forms of Cooperative Evaluation

- *Peer-assisted or team-based evaluation.* Teachers pair up with one or more partners to observe each other, give feedback, dialogue, explore new strategies, and work as a team to help each other improve performance. The focus of evaluation would then be reporting on what the team accomplished for students in light of its own plan of action for addressing the school's improvement goals.
- *Faculty-derived evaluation processes.* Faculty and administrators plan together for the evaluation processes to be used each year.
- *Training in evaluation methods.* Faculty and administration are thoroughly trained in observation and evaluation skills and processes.
- *Teacher-chosen evaluator.* Marginal teachers' choices are included (among faculty- and administrator-selected master teachers/administrators) in forming their evaluation/support team.
- *Master-teachers as evaluators.* Master teachers are highly involved in evaluation and supervision of peers. In this role, master teachers are given adequate release time from teaching to mentor, observe, conference, coach, and conduct demonstration teaching.
- *Self-assessment.* Ample opportunity is given for, and high value placed on, a teacher's own reflections and analysis of his or her performance via journals, formative and summative conferences, and frequent reflective dialogues with a master teacher, mentor, or administrator.
- *Student feedback.* Student feedback and perspectives are routinely sought through developmentally appropriate ways, such as surveys, interviews, and frequent informal discussions with students about quality of teaching, lessons, activities, projects, and assignments.
- *Parent feedback.* Parent feedback (from all parents) is routinely sought regarding their perceptions of their children's progress, homework, attitudes, and the communication links with the teacher and school.
- *Evaluation themes.* Observations, dialogue, and reflections about instruction focus on what Rubin (1975) identifies as critical teaching areas: a teacher's (1) sense of purpose, (2) perception of students, (3) knowledge of subject matter, and (4) mastery of technique.

COLLABORATIVE PROFESSIONAL DEVELOPMENT

It should be obvious to the reader by now that a highly versatile, recommended tool in this instructional leader's toolbox is the use of various forms of work-study groups to facilitate collaboration, reflective practice, and continuous growth and development of people in a school conceptualized as a true learning community. In a community-based approach to school leadership, the whole faculty becomes a collaborative team that identifies strategies, formulates goals, and breaks up the work of improving the quality of instruction into more manageable pieces. "As teachers work together in study groups," write Murphy and Lick (2005), "they alter their practices to provide new and innovative opportunities for their students to learn in challenging and productive new ways" (p. 3). Teams form around mutual interests and complementary skills to pursue various dimensions of school improvement and bring input to the whole group for sharing and facilitating the larger group's goals. This form of institutional problem solving is highly recommended by the current research on effective school leadership today (i.e., Murphy & Lick, 2005; Stiggins, 1997; Sullivan & Glanz, 2005). Two of the eight learner-centered professional development principles recommended by Hawley and Valli (2000) are that professional development for teachers and administrators should do the following:

1. Provide learning opportunities that relate to individual needs but are, for the most part, organized around collaborative problem solving

2. Be continuous and ongoing, involving follow-up and support for further learning, including support from sources external to the school that can provide necessary resources and outside perspectives (p. 8).

Work-study groups are characteristic of a professional environment in which workers as professionals assume more responsibility for the quality, conditions, and standards of their performance and learning, and this is embedded in the culture. Dennis Sparks (2001), a vocal advocate of professional development via increased interaction among the school's faculty, writes,

> Teachers' learning must be encouraged within the school by high expectations for performance and nurtured by a culture that supports experimentation and collaboration. Such schools provide teachers with regularly scheduled time for learning, planning, and problem solving with other faculty members. (p. 56)

If teachers are expected to grow professionally and improve their teaching, they must have frequent, insightful, specific feedback on their performance; opportunities to dialogue about and reflect on the nuances of teaching and learning; meaningful participation in work-study groups focused on improving students' learning; and varied forms of assistance in the classroom to develop and refine their professional skills. One-shot workshops, one-size-fits-all approaches to staff development, mandates for improvement, and autocratic supervisory and evaluative styles are all unlikely to improve instruction significantly, if at all. It is difficult, time-intensive, usually tedious work, but attempts to oversimplify and shortcut around the complexities of improving instruction simply have not worked.

The precise forms that supportive supervision, cooperative evaluation, and collaborative work-study groups need to take are, like so much else, dependent on the context of the school. Make no mistake: building a professional work culture is no small feat. As Hawley and Valli (2000) write,

> Substantially strengthening teachers' opportunities to improve their teaching will require nothing less than school restructuring, new professional cultures, the reallocation of resources and time, and changes in the role of school districts and popular conceptions of how students and teachers learn. (p. 9)

A site-based, collaborative, whole-team approach to examining how the functions of supervision and evaluation and the use of work-study groups can best facilitate reflective practice and professional growth in a particular school setting is a critical first step to developing a school's internal whetstones for honing professional skills and ensuring peak performance among teachers and administrators as growing, learning members of the school community. One thing is certain: If teachers and administrators are not learning and growing professionally, students are not likely to be learning much either.

Walking the Talk

An example from the field of how a principal encourages professional growth and development of the faculty in her school

One of the most beneficial things I have found to encourage professional growth and development for the teachers on my campus is to take them to every conference or convention I attend. We attend the Texas Elementary Principals Association (TEPSA) conferences every fall and summer at which they have an opportunity to hear first hand from members of the Texas Education Agency (TEA), Title I directors, English as a Second Language (ESL) directors, Special Education directors, teachers from other schools and inspiring speakers like Ron Clark and Erin Gruell. We have attended National Texas Elementary Principal (NAESP) conferences, State and National Title I Conferences, and American Supervisors and Curriculum Development (ASCD) conferences. On these occasions we have an opportunity to learn together, discuss what we learn, and how we will apply what we learn to ensure the success of every child on our campus. We not only learn new methodology but reaffirm the methods and strategies we are using. Teachers enjoy hearing new ways of teaching and learning first hand. They also enjoy visiting the exhibitors, asking questions about products, and choosing what they think will improve instruction themselves. I sometimes take or send representatives from each grade level to enhance vertical planning and sometimes take or send all members of one grade level to encourage the teachers at a particular grade level to work and plan together. Depending on the main

(Continued)

(Continued)

issues at the time, I also take or send special education teachers, ESL teachers, and Title I teachers. I encourage all of my teachers to share what they learn when they plan and work together to ensure that all students receive the highest quality instruction. Many of the professional growth and development activities we attend are two- or five-hour trips with an overnight stay. Participants have an opportunity to bond, brainstorm, and plan on these trips. We have an opportunity to have meals together which gives us an opportunity to discuss what we learn. We stay up at night discussing how we will use new information to improve instruction. Our student population has changed rapidly and we have had to learn and change the way we teach to meet their needs. Any time a teacher or group of teachers approach me with a professional growth opportunity they feel will enhance their teaching skills, I find the resources to send them. Being able to attend, workshops, conferences, and conventions makes teachers feel appreciated and rewarded for their hard work and dedication. They return from professional growth opportunities refreshed and excited to share what they have learned.

I also provide opportunities for my teachers to visit other schools and observe each other. We have presented what we have found to be successful for other teachers, principals, and central office staff at conferences which has increased the self-esteem of my teachers and their willingness to work together for continued success. We have presented at TEPSA, State and National Title I conferences, for other school districts, and recently at the School Improvement Conference for schools that had not met national No Child left Behind (NCLB) Annual Yearly Progress (AYP) requirements. Because of the success of my teachers and students, I was chosen to participate in the Texas Principals Excellence Program to mentor principals whose schools received Academically Unacceptable ratings from the Texas State Accountability System. Through my participation in this program, I am modeling the continued professional growth and development I encourage.

My teachers enjoy continuing to grow and stay on the cutting edge of what is happening in education. I enjoy seeing my teachers grow and enjoy the success of their students as much as I enjoy watching my students grow and learn. There is nothing more rewarding than seeing the difference it makes in a teacher or a child when they develop self-confidence and self-esteem from success! (Karen Sue Noble, Author's Feedback Request Form, September 2008)

Karen Sue Noble, principal of Hillcrest Elementary School in Nederland Independent School District, Texas, since 1992.

POINTERS FOR THE PRINCIPAL

- Model and encourage reflective practice.
    - Look for ways to integrate old knowledge with new.
    - Routinely question how well-entrenched, past practices are working.
    - Minimize risks for experimentation to improve teaching and learning.
    - Be an active learner yourself, open to new ideas and practices.

- Practice supportive supervision.
  - o Clarify the purpose of supervision, for improving teaching and learning.
  - o Approach supervision as the responsibility of all professionals.
  - o Acquaint yourself well with your faculty as people and professionals.
  - o Differentiate the supervision to meet the needs of the teacher.
  - o Provide a team-based support system and mentors for new teachers.
  - o Actively seek resources to support teachers' learning.
  - o Seek continual improvement, but be quick to praise and to celebrate progress.

- Practice cooperative evaluation.
  - o Clarify the purpose of evaluation, for improving teaching and learning.
  - o Approach evaluation as the responsibility of all professionals.
  - o Focus on the worthiness of lessons, the quality of the interaction between a teacher and students, and students' achievement.
  - o Resist evaluation that oversimplifies the complexity of teaching.
  - o Remember, success breeds success—and failure does likewise.

- Rely on work-study groups as the hub of professional development.
  - o Involve the whole faculty in collaboration to help students succeed.
  - o Facilitate routine meetings of groups for dialogue and problem solving.
  - o Be an active participant in the collaborative process.
  - o Facilitate increased professional dialogue about teaching and learning.

7

The Lens of Instructional Leadership

What really counts in public education is that students succeed and become thinking, knowledgeable, and productive citizens, regardless of which path in life they choose.

—Amy Ciliberto (2001, p. 1)

The benefits of learner-centered practice extend to students, teachers, administrators, parents, and all other participants in the educational system.

—Barbara McCombs and Jo Sue Whisler (1997, p. 62)

Principals in the exceptionally good schools choose to be instructional leaders first and administrative leaders second.

—Gilbert R. Austin and Stephen P. Holowenzak (1985, p. 72)

In schools that show impressive achievement gains, educational leaders maintain a clear and consistent focus on improving the core tasks of schooling—teaching and learning, and they accept no excuses for failing to improve student learning.

—Kenneth A. Leithwood and Carolyn Riehl (2005, p. 25)

No one dimension of school leadership is more important than a principal's skill and commitment to focusing the school's work on the learner. How, one might ask, can educators ever *not* do this? Isn't this what the organization of school is all about? Of course it is! However, the learners—the ones most directly impacted by the school's efforts—are also captive participants dependent on their significant adult others to ensure that schools function on their behalf. They usually have little voice in their education or the ability to assess and impact its quality. Unlike businesses, whose consumers' pocketbooks rather quickly reflect the quality and appeal of the businesses' products and whose accountability and survival are directly linked to customer satisfaction, the school's mission—the education of children—is less quantifiable, more long range, and dependent on many variables (some of which are beyond the control of the school). Because of these very different circumstances, educators' work can more easily become poorly focused and misdirected, often without their even being aware of it. The business of education is a complex endeavor, dealing with complex processes of pedagogy and learning. That is why a skillful, dedicated leader is needed to focus the work of the school on the learner, to monitor the progress of students, and to facilitate continuous improvement among students and staff as a learning community.

No one strategy, tool, or skill is the unilateral key to or sole recipe for improving students' achievement and learning. From Chapter 1 to now, and subsequently in this book, the focus is on the multiple ways a school principal as an instructional leader influences and facilitates the quality of teaching and learning. Setting in motion a community of learners through approaching leadership from a perspective of shared governance; being guided with a central compass of doing what is best for students; mutual sharing and examination of personal and group beliefs and visions about students, teaching, and learning; developing and often revisiting through reflection and dialogue a shared school vision, mission, goals, and objectives centered on meeting the needs of students; creating a strong school culture of high expectations for students' and staff's performance; facilitating multidirectional communication and feedback loops among all of the school's stakeholders so that teams and work-study groups can dialogue, experiment, and solve problems related to teaching and learning; and capitalizing on processes of reflective practice, supportive supervision, and cooperative evaluation to promote continual growth and development of faculty and staff are all tools for improving teaching and learning.

This chapter zeroes in even more on the importance of the learner in this complex scenario called school, and focuses on educators' acquiring skills to ensure that the organization is appropriately channeling its efforts on students' behalf. As McCombs and Whisler (1997) assert, "People are at the heart of any living system; attention to learners and learning in educational redesign puts the focus where there is the maximum probability of enhancing positive outcomes" (p. 185). The impetus of schoolwork, with all of its rich dynamics, is taking care of children and facilitating their development as healthy human beings. Understanding children and learning is essential to the work of educators. The rapidly changing demographics of this nation should propel educators to reassess their notions of learners and learning. Anne C. Lewis (2001) posits,

> If I were a teacher or a school administrator, I would reflect on the statistics describing what this nation is becoming and realize that we have an opportunity to try out a different lens through which to view students and their potential. (p. 647)

Along with the dramatic changes in the ethnic makeup of the U.S. population and school-age children, research that illuminates our understanding of learning has rapidly increased over the last decade, giving educators considerably more reliable information on which to base decisions about programs, curricula, and teaching. Educators must assume the responsibility of keeping abreast of what research has to offer about how learning happens best and how schools, classrooms, principals, and teachers can facilitate the healthy growth, well-being, and learning of all children in our care. Principals as true instructional leaders are exemplars in their relentless quest for information that can be used to improve teaching and learning and to personalize the educational experience for each boy and girl.

FOCUSING ON LEARNERS AND LEARNING

Understanding children and how they grow and learn is essential to teaching and being an effective principal. Although there are developmental factors to consider in completing the educational equation—factors that are basic to human beings and that sweep across time and culture—there are also important differences that are unique to each individual, group, or generation, which are critical to making wise pedagogical choices. Nothing takes the place of interacting with students to get to know them as real people—and for them to get to know you as a real person, too—with all of the wonderful, unique qualities that characterize being human. According to Cohen and Ball (2001),

> Although many people think of instruction as what teachers do, it consists of interactions involving teachers, students, and content . . . [Lessons are] not the result simply of what [teachers] know and do . . . but of how the teachers and students interpret and interact with one another and with the task. (p. 75)

Developing an understanding of and true empathy with students as individuals is a prerequisite to meeting their educational needs and to infusing your work with the passion and caring essential for outstanding leadership. An instructional leader, principal, and teacher must interact often and freely with students throughout the school day; take a genuine, personal interest in students; and come to know and genuinely appreciate each student as a one-of-a-kind person with a unique background and individual talents, weaknesses, and motivations to learn.

Without question, the lens through which the most effective instructional leaders filter their work as principals is a learner-centered lens characterized by two important features, without which such a lens can never develop optimally:

1. *Enjoying children and getting to know them as individuals.* Genuinely enjoying being around and getting to know students greatly enhances a principal's learner-centered acuity. Without this element, the lens will forever be foggy.

2. *Keeping abreast of research on learners and learning.* Keeping the learner-centered lens intact and sharply focused also requires that the school's leadership team stay abreast of what research has to offer about children and learning, then working together to understand, translate, and best apply this continually evolving information to their own school setting and their students. Principals cannot do this work alone, however; they should ensure they are a dynamic part of this important dimension of a school's improvement process.

Research on learning, motivation, and human development so fundamental to improving schools has dramatically increased over the past twenty years. If school reform efforts today are to be aptly centered on the learner and improving children's chances of academic achievement and personal well-being, they should stem from the current research base on learning. One such potentially powerful source of information is a set of "learner-centered psychological principles" that emerged from a 1993 initiative (an appointed Presidential Task Force) of the American Psychological Association and the Mid-Continent Regional Educational Laboratory. These principles, revised by APA in 1997, were originally developed specifically to serve as guidelines for school redesign and reform.

The fourteen learner-centered psychological principles organized around four distinct domains are included in Box 7.1. These principles of learning can be the litmus test in making the most of today's school reform and improvement efforts. Such initiatives should be compatible with the learning principles, and implementation of a strategy should be monitored for its success with criteria drawn from the research on learners and learning. The principles have implications for all aspects of a school's operation, from such obvious areas as instruction, curriculum, and assessment to areas that are (unfortunately) less often tied directly to students' interests such as budgeting and professional development. When viewed through a student-centered lens, the whole school's operation and all decisions are most appropriately channeled and are indisputably focused toward a school's ultimate mission of doing what is best for students. A principal's role as a true instructional leader is facilitating teaching, learning and a learning environment, teachers' education and continued growth and development, family and community involvement, and policy making that is supportive of schools as centers of learning for everyone in them. It is incumbent on educators—especially leaders—to understand these principles and to work with faculty, parents, and other administrators to translate these understandings into practices that lead to improved student learning and well-being—*all* students' learning and well-being. This is what really counts in accountable leadership.

BOX 7.1

Learner-Centered Psychological Principles

Cognitive and Metacognitive Factors

Principle 1—The nature of the learning process. The learning of complex subject matter is most effective when it is an intentional process of constructing meaning from information and experience.

Principle 2—Goals of the learning process. The successful learner, over time and with support and instructional guidance, can create meaningful, coherent representations of knowledge.

Principle 3—Construction of knowledge. The successful learner can link new information with existing knowledge in meaningful ways.

Principle 4—Strategic thinking. The successful learner can create and use a repertiore of thinking and reasoning strategies to achieve complex learning goals.

Principle 5—Thinking about thinking. Higher order strategies for selecting and monitoring mental operations facilitate creative and critical thinking.

Principle 6—Context of learning. Learning is influenced by environmental factors, including culture, technology, and instructional practices.

Motivational and Affective Factors

Principle 7—Motivational and emotional influences on learning. What and how much is learned is influenced by the learner's motivation. Motivation to learn, in turn, is influenced by the individual's emotional states, beliefs, interests and goals, and habits of thinking.

Principle 8—Intrinsic motivation to learn. The learner's creativity, higher order thinking, and natural curiosity all contribute to motivation to learn. Intrinsic motivation is stimulated by tasks of optimal novelty and difficulty, relevant to personal interests, and providing for personal choice and control.

(Continued)

(Continued)

Principle 9—Effects of motivation on effort. Acquisition of complex knowledge and skills requires extended learner effort and guided practice. Without learners' motivation to learn, the willingness to exert this effort is unlikely without coercion.

Developmental and Social Factors

Principle 10—Developmental influences on learning. As individuals develop, there are different opportunities and constraints for learning. Learning is most effective when differential development within and across physical, intellectual, emotional, and social domains is taken into account.

Principle 11—Social influences on learning. Learning is influenced by social interactions, interpersonal relations, and communication with others.

Individual Differences Factors

Principle 12—Individual differences in learning. Learners have different strategies, approaches, and capabilities for learning that are a function of prior experience and heredity.

Principle 13—Learning and diversity. Learning is most effective when differences in learners' linguistic, cultural, and social backgrounds are taken into account.

Principle 14—Standards and assessment. Setting appropriately high and challenging standards and assessing the learners as well as learning progress—including diagnostic, process, and outcome assessment—are integral parts of the learning process.

Source: From "Learner-Centered Psychological Principles: A Framework for School Reform and Redesign." Copyright © 1997 by the American Psychological Association. Reproduced with permission. No further reproduction or distribution is permitted without written permission from the American Psychological Association. The full document may be viewed at http://www.apa.org/ed/cpse/LCPP.pdf. The "Learner-Centered Psychological Principles" is a historical document that was derived from a 1990 APA presidential task force, and was revised in 1997.

CREATING A CLIMATE FOR LEARNING

The school or classroom most conducive to students' learning is characterized by having a moderately warm climate—that is, one physically, emotionally, and intellectually inviting for all children and adults. The physical environment itself is the first thing noticeable about a school's climate. Too often schools look like institutions—cold, impersonal, rather uninviting places to spend most of the workday week. Attention to the various dimensions of a school's climate is essential to nurture and optimize teaching and learning.

Condition of Building and Grounds

At a minimum, the building and grounds should be safe, clean, and well maintained. With some creative endeavor and participation by all involved in the school, most campuses and buildings can be made reasonably attractive. The objective is to make schools as inviting and conducive to teaching and learning as possible. Hallways and classrooms should be replete with student products, artwork, posters espousing the school's core values and mission, and various manifestations of the school's team spirit and focus on student success. Flexible and adequate space for varied teaching approaches, storage, conferences, team planning, and professional development should be provided. Students and staff should periodically be surveyed for input on ways to improve the facility and grounds.

Psychological Climate

The actual building and grounds should be safe, comfortable, functional, and attractive, of course; but, more importantly, the psychological climate should be highly conducive to students' learning as well. Adults' indifference to students' feelings and distinctive personalities can result in student hostility toward learning, the school, and its authority due to resentment and a loss of respect for the adults who show little respect to them.

At the other extreme (a too-warm climate), however, too much coddling or too much control over students can lead them to become overly dependent on the adults in their environment. Such treatment stunts students' developmental progress toward greater self-reliance for their learning and assumption of responsibility for their behaviors. Attending to the learning climate and attempting to keep it healthily balanced—neither too cold nor too hot—and facilitative of students' growth as self-sufficient, independent learners is challenging work that requires genuinely liking children, understanding how they learn best, and having great interest in them as individuals with varying cultures, abilities, preferences, and learning styles.

Learner and Learning-Centered Change Strategies

According to Rossi and Montgomery (1994) in their research sponsored by the U.S. Department of Education's Office of Educational Research and Improvement, "young people need to have adults who are 'crazy' about them. Unfortunately, in our most troubled schools teachers aren't crazy about students, and students aren't crazy about teachers—instead, they are driving each other crazy" (p. 1). This extensive review of the current state of the art in reforming schools to serve all students' needs in the best possible way offers the following specific proposals for creating a healthy learning environment, "a challenging, non-stigmatizing learning environment that meets student needs":

1. *Changes in curriculum*—for example, focus on real-world experiences to attract student interest; integration of academic and vocational skills so that students are well-prepared for both college and the job market.

2. *Changes in instruction*—for example, adults as mentors or advocates; provision of race and gender role models; cooperative learning; peer tutors and mentors; one-on-one tutoring; using computer programs to develop higher order thinking skills, rather than simply as basic skill drills.

3. *Changes in assessment*—for example, alternative or authentic assessments; assessment and recognition of incremental student progress.

4. *Changes in school organization*—for example, creation of smaller academic units within larger schools, or schools within schools; team teaching.

5. *Closer connections with work or college*—for example, university outreach to students at risk; school-to-work apprenticeship programs. (p. 4)

Pull-out programs, special education classes, ability grouping by whole classes, and grade retention are traditional forms of responding to the special needs of students. Such practices have not worked well and may, in fact, have further limited certain students' chances of academic success, their self-esteem, their overall optimism toward school, and ultimately their life choices. "Remedial help, before- and after-school programs, summer school, instructional aides to work with target children in the regular classroom, and no-cost peer tutoring are all more effective than retention," conclude Shepard and Smith (1990, p. 86) in their synthesis of research on grade retention.

Royal Van Horn's (2008) book, *Bridging the Chasm Between Research and Practice: A Guide to Major Educational Research*, includes a chapter devoted to educational research's findings related to grade retention and its impact on students and their academic achievement in schools. Van Horn introduces his chapter with the following comment:

These days, we hear so much about the importance of education and of "leaving no child behind." It is time to take a close look at traditional educational practices and to re-evaluate their effectiveness. The flunking of kids in school, or grade retention, as it is more professionally labeled, is almost universally believed to be beneficial to children. Scientific evidence, however, refutes this belief. (p. 9)

Van Horn's chapter on the topic includes a thorough review of the major studies on retention, which consistently and overwhelmingly conclude the futility of the strategy in helping students succeed academically. In its mildest interpretation, the research on retention finds it to be a woefully unsuccessful strategy; the real sting, however, comes with the prevailing interpretations of research—such as the following quote—that call the practice outright harmful:

> Thus, the results yielded from recent reviews and meta-analysis provide converging prima fascia evidence suggesting a strong case could be made for grade retention as "educational malpractice" given that research has failed to demonstrate the effectiveness of grade retention as an academic intervention. (Jimerson 2004, in Van Horn, 2008, p. 12)

Although no one strategy is likely to provide the solution to meeting the diverse needs of today's students, researchers and educators are now turning to programs and strategies that emphasize higher order thinking skills, mainstreaming, cooperative learning, and inclusion as strategies most likely to help all students learn. These strategies are recommended for students having academic problems as well as for the high achievers and rely less on low-level drill-and-practice exercises, tracking, and grade retention as primary methods for assisting students who are underachievers.

COMMUNICATING HIGH EXPECTATIONS FOR LEARNING

High expectations for students' and teachers' successes are an essential building block in creating a healthy school culture, one focused on teaching and learning. "You usually get what you expect from people" is a frequently used quote, and in dealing with children or adults it usually holds true. Expectations for high achievement among adults and children in a school are manifested in many ways other than what is said. In fact, actions speak louder than words every time. The following questions can assist leaders in knowing what to look for as they enhance their learner-centered lens to analyze their school's daily operation and understand the messages being communicated in many—often subtle—ways about the performance expectations of teachers and students:

- How well kept are the building and grounds? Is the school an attractive, pleasant place to be? Does it beam with pride?
- How friendly, caring, and respectful are people to each other?
- How common is active teaching and learning in classrooms, with students clearly engaged in learning and interacting—with the teacher and each other—in the learning process?
- For what are rewards and celebrations given most frequently and to whom?

- What safety nets are in place to keep kids from falling through the cracks? What routine interventions are taken to ensure a child's academic success and feelings of well-being?
- What support systems are formally functioning to support new and veteran teachers to ensure their success and continued growth?
- Is instructional time protected and treated as a scarce, precious commodity?
- How upbeat and optimistic about learning are the behaviors, conversations, and attitudes of adults and children in the school?
- How welcome and seriously involved are community members and families as partners in learning and the education of their children (in ways more meaningful and central to children's learning than volunteer efforts and fundraising)?
- How much of the adult conversation (in lounges, faculty meetings, etc.) is focused on improving teaching and learning and helping students succeed?
- How often and how well (using multiple sources) are students' welfare and academic progress monitored?
- How clearly are expectations for performance communicated to all students (in developmentally appropriate ways) and are all students evaluated fairly and according to procedures made clear to them?
- How well are all students given opportunities to excel and be recognized for their individual strengths and unique abilities and talents?
- Are students (in developmentally appropriate ways) expected and encouraged to participate increasingly in the management of their own learning and have input into their classroom's and school's operations?
- How thoroughly do the principal and faculty collect, analyze, and disaggregate varied data to understand how well all children are learning and how data are used to make decisions?
- Do teachers and administrators frequently arrive early, stay late, or work in study groups to help children—and each other—succeed?
- Do you, the principal, enjoy being in your position and coming to work?

The importance of high expectations to learning has been well documented in the literature (e.g., Cotton's 1995 research synthesis on effective schooling practices; Leithwood & Riehl, 2005). Kenneth Leithwood and Carolyn Riehl make these research-based claims about the importance of teacher expectations and student achievement and the principal's role in setting high expectations:

> One of the strongest in-school influences on student learning appears to be teachers' expectations that students and will succeed. Teacher expectations help to determine the academic press of a

school and its classrooms, the curriculum to which students are exposed, and the efforts teachers will make to help students achieve at high levels. Expectations of marginalized students, including low-income students and racial/cultural minority students, remain persistently low in many contexts. Successful leaders in schools serving diverse groups of students emphasize the necessity of all staff having high expectations and developing corresponding ambitious learning goals for students. (p. 25)

However, high expectations for student learning are not a dimension that can easily or artificially be injected into a school's dynamics. High expectations for performance—everyone's performance in the school community—begin with strong, participatory leadership and a faculty and staff willing to come together as a team driven by a passion for children's well-being and learning.

One of the most consistent pieces of research on effective schools is research related to the high positive correlation between student achievement and family involvement (Austin & Holowenzak, 1985; Cotton, 1995; Epstein, 1987; Henderson & Mapp, 2002). A school culture and environment that communicates high expectations for students' success is one in which high expectations are also evident for parents and families as partners with the school in the hard work of educating children. High expectations for parents' participation in the education of their children should be clearly evident in the school culture. This important element of parental involvement sends important messages to children and sets the stage for their success or failure. Canter and Canter (1991) write,

> An uninvolved parent, justifiably or not, gives a child the message that the child just isn't important enough to warrant close attention. An involved parent, on the other hand, can provide the boost to a student's self-esteem that will lead to greater success in school and a more fulfilling and accomplished adulthood. (p. 5)

Parents and family are, after all, the most important people in a child's life, with the most potential to influence and motivate the child. It is, then, no surprise that their involvement is often listed as a critical variable for schools improving their effectiveness. In her review of research related to parental involvement, Epstein (1987) writes,

> The evidence is clear that parental encouragement, activities, and interest at home and participation in schools and classrooms affect children's achievements, attitudes, and aspirations, even after student ability and family socioeconomic status are taken into account. (p. 120)

What is surprising, however, is that though educators often lament the lack of parental interest in their child's education, few make aggressive, concerted efforts to involve parents and families in meaningful ways in students' education or to make them true partners in the work of the school, most especially in matters that most impact their children's learning. Epstein (1987) attempts an explanation for this dichotomy:

> The lack of active administrative leadership and attention is due, in part, to the dearth of useful, organized information on parent involvement in schools. There are many types of parent involvement, and it is unclear how each type contributes to school effectiveness. There are many real problems associated with parent involvement, and solving them takes time and perseverance. Yet, it is the administrator's role to orchestrate activities that will help the staff study and understand parent involvement, and to select or design, evaluate, and revise programs for parent involvement. (p. 120)

One major role of today's leaders is to oversee and ensure that policies and practices in the school (from PreK–Grade 12) affirm parents' roles as partners with teachers in their children's education. In a major study on parental involvement supported by the National Institute of Education, U.S. Department of Education (Epstein, 1987), results showed that

> surprisingly, large numbers of parents are excluded from some of the most common, traditional communications from the school. In our survey more than one-third of the parents had no conference with the teacher during the year. Almost two-thirds never talked with a teacher by phone. Although most teachers (over 95%) reported that they communicate with the parents of their students, most parents are not involved in deep, detailed, or frequent communications with teachers about their child's program or progress. (p. 124)

Better parental involvement should be more than a rhetorical aspiration of principals and teachers. In their study of exceptional schools, Austin and Holowenzak (1985) concluded that, in high performing schools,

> parents play an important and integral part. They feel their opinions are valued and they are involved in important decisions that affect the lives of their children. Principals who have high expectations for parents, teachers, and children must demonstrate this by involving them in meaningful ways. (p. 74)

Schools should take the initiative to pave the way through policy and good practice to develop better forms of parental participation in children's education. There are myriad ways an administrator can use his or her role to influence and guide better working relationships and communication between the home and school.

The recommendations resulting from the research of Joyce Epstein (1987) and a publication by Lee and Marlene Canter (1991) titled *Parents on Your Side* are helpful resources for assisting schools and leaders who are serious about initiating stronger links with parents and thereby improving considerably the probability of their students' success. The more recent research of Anne Henderson and Karen Mapp (2002), conducted under the auspices of the National Center for Family and Community, yields insightful analyses and thorough, up-to-date recommendations based on their synthetic review of studies conducted from 1993 to 2002 on the impact of family involvement on student achievement. These researchers conclude, among many things, "When we combine these recent studies with earlier research, we see strong steadily growing evidence that families can improve their children's academic performance in school" (2002, p. 73). The Canters (1991) further assert,

> The vast majority of parents of your students really do want to be involved. They do care about their children and want to provide needed support. In many cases, however, they just don't know what to do—or if they should do it at all. To put it into perspective, only 25% of parents report receiving systematic requests or directions from teachers on how they can help their children academically. However, when requested to give additional assistance, over 85% of parents immediately responded and were willing to spend at least 15 minutes per day working with their children. In short, when parents are contacted by skilled, trained teachers who communicate effectively, they will respond. (pp. 6–7)

Parent involvement may take many forms and must be tailored to the particular school and community setting, but in any school it should be far more than chauffeuring field trips and fundraising. Henderson and Mapp's (2002) research findings reiterate and affirm the earlier speculations by Joyce Epstein about the importance of *how* a family is involved with the school being critical to how much it will positively impact their child's learning: "the ways parents are involved at school should be linked to improving learning, developing students' skills in specific subjects, and steering students toward more challenging classes" (p. 73).

Administrators and teachers have the responsibility and the prime opportunity to take the initiative in forming stronger partnerships with families, partnerships that encourage their greater participation in their children's learning—the involvement that will pay back the biggest return for students. Leithwood and Riehl (2005) contend that two types of school initiatives have been shown to have the potential for strengthening parents' and families' resources and abilities to work productively with their children's schools: parent education programs and integrative social services. Furthermore, in both initiatives, the research indicates that school leaders play significant roles in championing and coordinating them. A child's education is, after all, a shared responsibility between the home and school; it follows that it should also be a shared endeavor.

High expectations are a result of a school-based team—a learning community—having committed itself to a shared mission, vision, and a set of group-defined goals for the organization and the team in meeting the needs of students. The processes for developing and maintaining these organizational blueprints help facilitate partnerships, team spirit, and energy that set in motion high expectations for success and keep them renewed and mirrored throughout the school, in the home, and—most important to the mission of schools—in the classroom, the center of teaching and learning.

LOOKING FOR INDICATORS OF EFFECTIVE TEACHING AND LEARNING

In their quest for instructional leadership as a major role, today's principals should not mistakenly diminish the importance of the teachers' role in instructional leadership in the school. In their recent article on school effectiveness, Thomas and Bainbridge (2001)—former school superintendents—assert unequivocally that the teacher is the primary instructional force in schools:

> Instructional effectiveness is the responsibility of teachers. The principal may be a leader, but accountability for effective instruction belongs to teachers. Principals may understand instruction and support it, but they do not teach the curriculum . . . Teachers are the heart and soul of any school system. They are the models we remember as adults. We must give teachers the instructional authority and the freedom to make individual decisions for each boy and girl in their classrooms. (p. 55)

What is effective instruction? Most performance evaluation checklists fall far short of nailing down good teaching. Is teaching an art or a science? Can it be defined or is it too much art, too little science? These conundrums remain with us, but they are less puzzling than they used to be. Learning research in the last couple of decades has produced some exceptionally helpful information to improve instruction. It has not, however, produced a unilaterally most preferred approach to teaching. Without question, teaching styles—as well as the definition of good teaching—vary widely. This should not, however, prevent educators from tapping into the increasing well of research on pedagogy and learning—studying it, discussing it, and drawing from good data on student performance to make decisions regarding instruction. That is what work-study groups should be doing; that is what the school leadership should be doing; that is what instructional leadership is all about.

The Complexity of Effective Teaching

Teaching is infinitely complex and challenging; this is both the thrill and the ill of the profession. There is no one right way to teach, just as there is no one right way to learn. Instruction based on what is known about how children learn best can vary widely in its individual interpretation and manifestation: "Not all learner-centered teachers believe or think in exactly the same way or engage in the same practices . . . [L]earner-centered teaching is as much a way of being, a disposition, as it is doing one thing or another" (McCombs & Whisler, 1997, p. 100).

According to Hoyle, English, and Steffy (1994), important indicators of teaching effectiveness are the teacher's maximization of time to increase learning, their matching of materials to the students' abilities, and the high expectations they exhibit for themselves and their students. These performances, though observable, are not overly prescriptive and are so closely tied to students' learning that it is impossible to see many of them without simultaneously looking at students and their performance. Hoyle et al. (p. 147) state that an effective teacher

- Motivates students to achieve
- Uses academic learning time effectively
- Demonstrates proficiency in subject areas
- Demonstrates command of the language
- Promotes student academic growth
- Establishes clear learning objectives
- Bases learning strategies on objectives
- Bases testing on objectives

Although there certainly are many other behaviors that contribute to a teacher's performance, Hoyle and colleagues (1994) contend that these are core essential elements, without which no other behavior holds much value.

Allan C. Ornstein (1993) cautions that research on teacher styles and teacher competencies—the two major categories of teaching research—both fail to deal adequately with the human element in teaching. In the profession's quest to quantify and analyze teaching in terms of a specified set of preferred behaviors, important human dimensions are overlooked or dismissed:

[Such research] fails to take into account the emotional, qualitative, and interpretive descriptions of classrooms and the joys of teaching. It takes little note of social and psychological factors in teaching, and it recommends few of these factors as effective . . . This research stresses narrow student outcomes based on knowledge-based achievement. But the researchers pay little attention to the thought processes involved in learning—especially the ability to think critically, solve problems, approach ideas creatively, and carry out other forms of high level cognition . . . Learning experiences that deal with character, spiritual outlook, and philosophy are absent. The personal and human dimension of teaching is usually ignored—a sad commentary for a helping profession. (p. 26)

Personalization of Students' Educational Experiences

There are many different ways to approach differentiating instruction and tailoring children's school experience to meet their individual needs while capitalizing on the students' strengths. Teachers relate to children in their own individual, sometimes very different but often equally effective, ways. It is not important that teachers behave the same way. What is important for all teachers, however, is to reach out—in their own special ways—and respond to children as individuals who need to know that they too are special, cared for, and appreciated for their differences by the adults in their world.

Such personalization of students' education is consistent with the learning principles outlined in the beginning of this chapter and can be recognized in classrooms by features such as the following:

- Students frequently have choices in how they pursue their learning (e.g., choosing their own projects, choosing whether to work individually or with a team, choosing how they would like to demonstrate competency).
- Students work at different paces, frequently doing different things.
- Students are actively engaged in learning, both individually and in groups.
- Students show excitement about learning new things.
- Multiple methods are used in assessing student achievement; assessments vary among students.
- Curriculum content is integrated, based on meaningful themes and units and students' interests, and often results in student projects.
- Students are encouraged to reflect often on their own progress (e.g., use of student portfolios; student-led, parent–teacher–student conferences regarding students' progress; self-assessment opportunities; journals and logs).
- Students have multiple channels for frequent feedback regarding their growth and progress.
- Students participate in classroom decisions.
- Students assume increasing responsibility for their conduct and learning.
- Students are encouraged to think for themselves.

- Interaction between students and the students and teacher is mutually respectful and kind.
- All students receive an equitable share of the teacher's attention.
- Students move about freely but are purposefully focused on learning.

"In the final analysis," conclude Keefe and Jenkins (2002), "personalized instruction reflects deep concerns for learners and the willingness to search for ways to adjust the teaching/learning environment to meet the learning needs of individual students" (p. 440). In the February 2002 issue of *Phi Delta Kappan*, a special section is devoted to personalized instruction. These two contributing authors, John Jenkins and James Keefe, describe how two schools (Thomas Haney Secondary Centre in Maple Ridge, British Columbia and Francis W. Parker Charter Essential School in Devens, Massachusetts) personalize instruction using their own unique approaches. Keefe and Jenkins (2002) point out that, though each school's approach is different, there are some commonalities underlying the differences, including the following: (1) a dual teacher role of coach and advisor; (2) the diagnosis of relevant student learning characteristics; (3) a collegial school culture; (4) an interactive learning environment; (5) flexible scheduling and pacing; and (6) authentic assessment (p. 450).

These personalizing features also characterize learner-centered classrooms and instruction, and are consistent with the principles of learning derived from research. They do not suggest a single way of achieving them, however. Ornstein (1993) espouses,

> The most effective teachers endow their students with a "can-do" attitude, with good feelings about themselves that are indirectly and eventually related to cognitive achievement . . . We're wrong to insist that all teachers must use certain methods and procedures. Instead, we must permit teachers to teach according to their own personalities, teaching philosophies, and goals . . . Although research on teacher competencies offers insight into good teaching, it can lead us to become too rigid in our view of effective teaching. (p. 27)

That is precisely why it is more important to center our attention on the learner and the research on learning, rather than on the teacher, the content, and the research on teaching. We know much more about learning than we do about teaching. After all, teaching has no meaning apart from learning; teaching is the means to an end: students' learning. Acting on what is good for learners and learning allows—even requires—various teaching styles and techniques that are suited to the strengths and talents of the individual teachers. Teachers working together routinely to share their ideas and to create a more challenging and rigorous instructional program that focuses on their particular group of students is the most credible strategy for improving the organization of schools for the purpose of providing students with a quality, personalized education. Educators—teachers and principals—operating throughout the day with an informed, learner-centered lens are better equipped to recognize when the learner-centered principles are being enacted and when they are being violated, and subsequently take more immediate and appropriate action to facilitate students' learning. Collaborating in study groups and as teams of professional educators, administrators and teachers are better able to attend to the complex, multifaceted needs of students and ensure that each child is given the attention and expertise to enable him or her to succeed. A well-developed learner-centered lens can enable educators—individually and collectively—to focus more clearly and directly on what matters most throughout the school's many functions: what is best for students, their well-being, and their education.

Walking the Talk

An example of how one principal tries to ensure the academic success of each child in her school

Because we have a very diverse student population with many special needs, I use Title I, Title III, Special Education, and Student Success Initiative funds to provide extra teachers and extra help personnel to provide small group instruction for every child in my school every day. Extra help teachers are as paid long term substitutes. Because pull out programs too often lower expectations for the students being pulled out, I have all of the special services people work with the students in one classroom at the same time to provide small group instruction. During small group instruction, every child receives the same curriculum and instruction. The classroom teacher plans the lesson and the instructional methods. The English as a Second Language (ESL) and special education teachers may have students who are English Language Learners (ELL), students who receive special education services, dyslexic students, ADD students, ADHD students, 504 students, and students who receive no special services. The classroom teacher and the Title I teacher may have the same mixture in their groups. This grouping allows ELL, special education students, and regular education students to learn from and with one another. This type of small group instruction assures the needs of all students are met, provides an opportunity for working in diverse groups, and minimizes the number of students who need special services. Students identified as Gifted and Talented also have small group instruction to ensure their special needs are challenged. The teacher plans instruction for all students and determines which students will be in each group. The groups are changed according to the instructional objective and the needs of the students. The special needs teachers attend the same professional growth opportunities the classroom teachers attend and spend time observing the methods and strategies the classroom teachers use for instruction. Depending on the teacher or the instructional method all teachers may go in the room or the special teachers make take a group to their room. All teachers have computers, camera documents, and projectors in their rooms and many have SmartBoards, because technology and visuals are important to student success in our interconnected and interdependent world.

All students are assigned to a regular education teacher. One special education teacher provides accelerated instruction for students who are two or more years behind. She has three paraprofessionals to help her provide the support the students need to achieve academic success. The students only go to her for the differentiated instruction they need. They remain in the regular classroom unless they need targeted assistance help to prevent them from reaching a frustration level that leads to a lack of self confidence. We have high expectations for every student. We tell them they are the smartest kids in Texas and they believe it and prove it every year when they take the Texas Assessment of Knowledge and Skills! (Karen Sue Noble, Author's Feedback Request Form, September 2008)

Karen Sue Noble is principal of Hillcrest Elementary School in Nederland Independent School District in Texas.

POINTERS FOR THE PRINCIPAL

- Focus your work on learners and learning.
  - o Enjoy, interact with, and really get to know your students and their families.
  - o Keep abreast of research on learning.
  - o Sharpen your learning/learner-centered lens through practice.

- Create a climate that nurtures learning.
  - o Encourage students' evolving independence as learners.
  - o Attend to the physical, emotional, and intellectual dimensions of the learning environment.
  - o Frequently seek and use student input to improve the school.
  - o Provide support for underachievers without stigmatizing them.

- Set high expectations for learning among students and adults.
  - o Expect, first and foremost, the best from yourself.
  - o Assess the school's performance through a learner-centered lens.
  - o Involve parents in authentic participation in their child's learning.
  - o Make sure your actions reflect learning as your top priority in the school.

- Be a familiar, supportive presence in classrooms.
  - o Improve your observation skills to assess more accurately the quality of teaching and learning in classrooms.
  - o Facilitate routine collaboration to improve students' success.
  - o Don't confuse teaching style and instructional effectiveness.
  - o Work with teachers as genuine partners in instructional leadership.

8

Tape Measures, Plumb Lines, and Common Sense

What Counts in Accountability

Our emphasis on accountability fails to take into consideration the single clear fact of life: children are different.

—Rex Knowles and Trudy Knowles (2001, p. 390)

Innovation was once the genius of this society, but when students all over the country are saying they have no time to discuss ideas or to learn to think critically, one worries about the big mistakes we are making.

—Anne C. Lewis (2008, p. 2)

What is needed is a results-oriented management system that focuses internal attention on producing quality schoolwork for children.

—Phillip C. Schlechty (1990, p. 142)

Student accountability should be based on multiple, formative assessments.

—"Students and Accountability," *ASCD's Education Update* (2001, p. 6)

There has to be a commitment on the part of leaders to develop a collective vision that goes beyond raising scores on state tests.

—Wendy McCloskey and Nancy McMunn (2000, p. 120)

The decisions so quickly available from intuition must sometimes be checked for accuracy by formal analysis, while those produced by careful analysis must generally be confirmed intuitively for face validity.

—Henry Mintzberg (1994, p. 1994)

No toolbox to assist principals today would be complete without tools for dealing with contemporary accountability issues: high-stakes testing and standards. Accountability and standards are the dominant national themes regarding education today, as they have been for over a decade. Closely allied with both the accountability and standards movement is the third, "dark horse" member of the group: high-stakes testing. Nine years ago, McCloskey and McMunn (2000) of the SouthEastern Regional Vision for Education (SERVE), commented, "High-stakes state tests with important consequences for educators and students have become the accountability tool of choice in many states as policy makers struggle to find ways to increase student achievement levels" (p. 115). While high-stakes testing has been around for many years now, with states struggling to find ways to use it appropriately and accountably, the passing of the now infamous and currently stalled federal No Child Left Behind (NCLB) Act of 2002 has left schools in a frenzied state, desperate to avoid the punitive consequences of not having every child make adequate yearly progress (determined by students' performance on tests) as defined and prescribed in the bill. Public recognition of the law's negative effects has resulted in a growing consensus in favor of a major overhaul of NCLB (Education Commission of the States, NCLB Reauthorization Database, 2007).

There is no single definition of accountability, no perfected set of standards, and most certainly no standardized test capable of coming even close to accurately accounting for student performance. The NCLB experience has made that excruciatingly clear. Accountability encompasses a broad spectrum of issues—accountability from whom, for what, and how are all separate and important dimensions of the issue. Across this nation, individual state-constructed systems chug away at their attempts to make public schools more accountable. And even with federally legislated mandates, each state handles the implementation and compliance strategies differently. "Increasingly," notes Robert L. Linn (2001), co-director of the National Center for Research on Evaluation, Standards, and Student Testing, "states are using their accountability systems as much for measuring school status as for student achievement . . . But the methods by which states rank schools or measure improvement vary greatly" (p. 1).

Although the public cries out for more accountability from educators, schools are faced with shrinking pools of resources to deal with mounting complexities in meeting students' needs: Teacher and principal shortages are now a nationwide phenomenon; tax dollars to support schools and education must be stretched to meet increased public needs; and meeting the needs of today's pluralistic student population to ensure students receive a good education requires more sophisticated and specialized skill as well as financial and human resources than in the past. It is no secret to today's educators that they are expected, and more often now legislated via mandates, to do more without the resources that are often promised by legislators, but are rarely delivered—as has been the case with the NCLB Act. This is not to say, however, that NCLB implementation has been cheap. The costs associated with the testing requirements of the act alone are steep. "The annual cost of high-stakes testing," report Baine and Stanley (2004, p. 8), "rivals the gross national product of some small countries, somewhere between $20 and $50 billion, or about 5.5 to 14 percent of every dollar spent for public schools" (in Van Horn, 2008, p. 100). And what about the time devoted to testing in our schools? Researcher Royal Van Horn offers this perspective:

> Very little has been written about the amount of time that is taken away from instruction that is then devoted to local, state, and federal testing. Here is an example from Duval County, Florida, the fifteenth-largest school district in the nation. Responding to the federal mandate that every student make AYP (Adequate Yearly Progress), the district has decided to test elementary school students three times a year . . . Unfortunately, one cannot give young children—for example, first graders—a group-administered, paper-and-pencil test. Instead, one must test each student individually. Using the test that the district has chosen takes about 20 minutes per child to administer. Testing three students a day takes the teacher about two weeks. Given that this testing is to be done three times a year, the total reading time devoted to testing and not to instruction is six weeks per school year. There are 36 weeks in a school year, so this testing takes one-sixth of a year. That is a lot of time taken away from instruction. (2008, p. 92)

One has to wonder about the accountability of this expenditure of time and energy. *Whose interest* is being served most by it in the final analysis? Accountability to the public for what is happening to students as a result of their school experience is essential and long overdue. However, the tail should not be wagging the dog: accounting to the public for what's happening in schools should be peripheral to schools' central mission: teaching and learning. The *way* schools and educators go about being more accountable and *why* they should be doing more of it should be redirected from high-stakes testing to better, authentic "assessing" of students' work in the classroom for the primary purpose of finding out more about how best to teach them—the most urgent and accountable reason for doing it in the first place. With better assessment of students' learning day in and day out, educators can make better decisions about how to improve instruction to meet students' needs. The job is much more complex and continuous, and requires more skill than high-stakes testing. It is also, however, the most direct route to improving student achievement, and certainly a better use of time and money. When teachers know more about what students need and are given the support and assistance required to deliver it, students will certainly learn more—the surest, *sanest* way to improve student achievement.

This chapter offers three types of enablers to assist today's school leaders in fulfilling their duty as accountable instructional leaders who have the skill and understanding to resist being sucked into the undertow of today's confusing forces for certain forms of accounting by the schools that are neither authentic representations of school's merit nor productive uses of schools' and states' scarce resources, time, and money. The tools should help, but dealing with mandated accountability is undoubtedly the most demoralizing and stressful of all the responsibilities of today's school leader. The tools offered in this chapter to assist principals and teacher leaders with these tough accountability issues cluster into three themes of recommended actions: (1) being positive, proactive, vocal advocates for schools assuming appropriate accountability for their role in students' learning; (2) understanding the mired accountability movement and knowing how to make appropriate uses of it to help schools improve; and (3) ensuring the competent assessment of students' classroom performance to significantly diminish the focus on annual, standardized testing as the primary proof of students' achievement and the school's accountability.

ASSUMING THE ACCOUNTABILITY REINS

Maintaining optimism and hope while dealing with dichotomous forces in the accountability fray requires great skill, dedication, and moral tenacity from educators. The most effective principals do more than ride the tide and hope to stay afloat; they provide leadership to a school community in dealing with these issues in proactive, positive ways that do not demoralize faculty, undermine the community's confidence, skirt the issues, or put the school on the defensive. "The principals of tomorrow's schools must be instructional leaders who possess the requisite skills, capacities, and commitment to lead the accountability parade, not follow it" (Tirozzi, 2001, p. 438). Being proactive by taking the initiative to account for what is happening in the school and how well children are learning is an important posture for today's principal to assume. Schlechty (1990) saliently deduces, "The results by which school systems must be led are the results that are consistent with the purpose of school, as that purpose is articulated in the school's vision statement and belief structure" (p. 141). A school with a well thought-out vision and mission that are alive and reflected in the school's operation should not be shaken by the turbulent winds of the accountability confusion sweeping the nation. Shared beliefs, values, mission, and goals all form the bedrock upon which a learning organization builds itself, and to which it returns frequently for reexamination, renewal, and guidance in dealing with the many issues on the educational landscape. Remaining steadfast and true to one's moral purpose in doing what's best for students, however, is easier said than done, with the unparalleled pressure of current federal involvement in attempting to force schools to be accountable for students' achievement—primarily via standardized test scores.

Unfortunately, we have not done so well as a professional community in taking the initiative to clarify and assume our rightful share of the responsibility for students' achievement. Despite platitudes and rhetoric about believing all children being can learn, we have stopped short of taking the lead in garnering the resources and support that many children must have to succeed in school. Schools cannot do it alone, nor should they be expected to. But they are in the ideal position to advocate for all children, and to coordinate and orchestrate bringing the various potential resources together to ensure children have what they need to succeed, in school and in life. Historically, educators' commitment to being accountable for children's learning seems to fade dramatically from paper to practice—from rhetorical mission statements and philosophical documents to behaviors in classrooms and throughout schools. Children don't respond to mission statements that remain dormant and unlived, a mission that is only a limp paper document. John Merrow (2001), executive producer of *The Merrow Report*, puts it this way:

> They [the public] have come by their mistrust honestly. [T]he obvious truth [is] . . . that educators have not held themselves accountable. The system has, for the most part, skated along with the attitude, "We taught the material, so don't blame us if they didn't learn it." This has been the unspoken modus operandi, which, if you think about it, is perfectly consistent with high sounding public platitudes like "All children can learn." ('They can, but it's up to them, and if they don't, it's their fault, not ours!' is the unspoken second half of the aphorism.) (p. 654)

This attitude has largely been responsible for landing educators in the position today of having to be on the defensive and of having to respond to outsiders—the public, business leaders, and politicians—who are attempting to force schools to prove accountability, which is unfortunately now defined by those outside the school. Merrow (2001) laments this dilemma, claiming, "Unfortunate decisions are being made as pressure for 'accountability' overwhelms common sense" (p. 654). As it has turned out, Merrow's comments in 2001 were sadly all too prophetic. One year later, the far-reaching federal legislation of the Bush administration, NCLB, was enacted for the purpose of holding schools accountable for students' academic progress and eliminating achieve-ment gaps correlated to economic status, race, ethnicity, and limited English proficiency. The act mandated, among a host of other things, specified levels and subject area testing of students annually, along with the requirement that states set "adequate yearly progress" goals and that they use the tests to deter-mine whether schools make adequate yearly progress toward 100 percent pro-ficiency for *all students* by the year 2013–2014. The high-stakes part of the law ties students' scores in a school and district to consequences . . . the old carrot and stick incentive to facilitate school improvement. So, how has this worked for us? The National Center for Fair and Open Testing (FairTest) issued its sta-tus report of NCLB's six-year track record in January 2008:

> After six years, there is overwhelming evidence that the deeply flawed, No Child Left Behind law is doing more harm than good in our nation's public schools. NCLB's test-and-punish approach to school reform relies on limited, one-size-fits all tools that reduce education to little more than test prep. It produces unfair decisions and requires unproven, often irrational "solutions" to complex problems. NCLB is clearly under-funded, but fully funding a bad law is not a solution.

FairTest's summation of NCLB's lack of effectiveness is reflective of the public's current overwhelmingly negative sentiments toward this law. The fate of NCLB—awaiting reauthorization by Congress since fall of 2007—is now in the hands of a new president and administration as of the time of writing (November 2008). One thing is certain, the recommendations for improving NCLB for reauthorization are extensive and come from wide-spread, powerful sources (for a comprehensive detailing of the recom-mendations proposed and who is proposing what, see the Web site of the Education Commission of the States, www.ecs.org/nclbreauthorization).

Educational leaders have the responsibility to take the lead in advo-cating for what needs to happen to this law . . . to make it better or get rid of it. Anne C. Lewis (2008), well-known *Kappan* contributor, national edu-cation policy writer, and vocal critic of NCLB, finds the act to have been costly and to have done more harm than good in beefing up America's schools and improving student achievement:

> The corruption of learning in this country can be stopped if policy makers halt the irrational accountability requirements. States that have already developed their own thoughtful measurements that encourage deep learning ought to be allowed to continue their work. For most other states, exploring growth models would be a good start. More realistic targets ought to be devised, using the available research. Policy makers need to work along with researchers and the public in fashioning testing and accountability systems that reflect agreed-upon values about what students should know and be able to do and that encourage excellent teaching. (p. 2)

Lewis (2008) sums up the prevailing opinions of the majority of educators when she writes, "The biggest mistake about the current testing mess is thinking that the biggest mistakes going on are the mistakes in scoring by the testing giants. This is truly a minor problem compared to the really big one: continuing to cling to the status model of adequate yearly progress (AYP) under the No Child Left Behind Act" (p. 1).

Given the mobility of students today, coupled with the fierce competition for dwindling public resources, having more common standards nationwide and being more accountable for students' education seems only prudent. Having standards in education—all kinds of them—and being accountable are fundamentally sound processes for any enterprise. The problem is agreeing on what constitutes reasonable and fair standards, who should be accountable for what in a child's educational experience, and how schools can best account for their role in a child's education . . . not nearly as simple as being accountable for a manufactured product.

Viewing schools as mere factories and children as widget-like products leads to flawed thinking about appropriate measures of school accountability. Schlechty (1990) writes,

> A results-oriented management system will have little chance of success so long as students are viewed as products. Such a view allows for too much scapegoating, and it is based on assumptions that are not believable to teachers and administrators . . . Schools will never improve if educators allow others to put them into the test-score, keeping-children-in-school, reducing-vandalism-rates, and reducing-suspensions business. (pp. 139–140)

Accountability

No one best system of accountability for students' performance seems to exist, but Linn (2001) makes suggestions for states to follow that will help to put the focus for accountability where it should be—on students, teaching, and learning, not on test scores. His article on standards-based accountability systems across this nation includes the following sound recommendations for maximizing the likelihood of an accountability system's contributing to improved student learning while minimizing negative consequences:

1. Place more emphasis on school improvement than on current performance.

2. Report the margin of error for any school result.

3. As required by the Standards for Educational and Psychological Testing, evaluate the validity of the uses and interpretations of assessment results.

4. Validate trends with results from other indicators such as the National Assessment of Educational Progress and other state tests. (p. 4)

The important points made by Linn are that school accountability should be based on multiple criteria and should include school improvement processes substantiated by a smorgasbord of data, only one piece of which would be standardized test results. Such an approach to accountability would then itself be most accountable.

Systemic processes for ensuring that schools are appropriately focused on teaching and learning are well supported and documented in the extant research on organizational effectiveness. Accountability measures should be focused on those things we know are important about schools, children, and learning. Assessing a school for the quality of its system's fundamental processes can be one very legitimate means of holding educators accountable in the short term, while the processes in place have the time needed to make changes that will ultimately impact student achievement in the long run. "Real change and real accountability depend on a whole-school reform agenda with a systemic plan that ensures continued interaction among faculty members at all levels and across disciplines" (Tirozzi, 2001, p. 438). Such process standards would not attempt to dictate how a school functions but, rather, would describe the kinds of systemic functions characteristic of a healthy organization centered properly on the well-being of its charges and central mission—teaching and learning.

Characteristics of an accountable, well-run school would include the existence of fundamentally sound processes that may take a variety of site-specific forms, such as the following:

- Multidirectional channels of communication and interaction exist among all stakeholders for input as well as feedback and information sharing.

- A reflective, inquiry-driven school culture brings to life the school's shared vision and mission, with high expectations for everyone's performance.

- Clearly written and well-communicated instructional vision, mission, goals, and objectives are tailored by the stakeholders at the school level for that school's particular student population.

- School renewal processes and curriculum development are viewed as continuous, are focused on students' learning, and are a readily discernable part of the school's daily operation.

- Faculty, community members, students, and administrators collaborate in work-study teams (i.e., interdepartmental, subject area, cross-grade-level, grade-level, ad hoc problem-solving) that have frequent, routine time for reflection and dialogue.

- Student assessment is multifaceted, with tasks treated as learning experiences more than as tools for grading and sorting students, used to provide specific input and direction to teachers for further instruction, responded to with detailed feedback to students for improvement, and heavily oriented toward authentic performances to demonstrate learning and skill. Collective approaches to evaluation are included as a valued form

of assessing students' work. Teachers work together o
as developing evaluation rubrics; use of portfolios
giving more helpful, concrete feedback to students
students to make assessment most meaningful fo↕
key learning opportunity—and for the teachers th↕
performances to analyze their own teaching skill and s↕

• Many opportunities exist for staff to work with admin↕
each other to give and receive feedback on their instruction and ↕
mance as members of a school community of learners. Teachers are treate↕
as professionals who are capable of improving, and eager to improve, their
effectiveness and be those most in charge of their own improvement, with
ample support from the school and district and frequent feedback from
colleagues, administrators, students, and parents.

• Learning and improvement are the primary agenda for the entire
school community. Although children's growth and development come first,
the school as a learning organization systematically and routinely expects,
supports, and encourages the continued learning and development of everyone in the school; professional development with mentoring and support for
new teachers is ongoing via the work-study groups and various collaborative
endeavors taking place throughout the school's weekly operation.
Opportunities for faculty to observe each other, visit selected sites off campus, attend conferences and participate in arranged workshops are also available as additional means of growth and development—all of which are
appropriate forms of professional growth when matched well to the purpose
and when clearly focused on the improvement of teaching and learning.

• Evaluation and supervision processes focus on facilitating teacher
growth and development and are cooperative endeavors that are clearly
linked to students' achievement.

• All stakeholders are involved in meaningful ways in the operation of
the school and have ownership of the school's vision, mission, goals, and
strategies through their shared development with others in the school
community.

• Children are encouraged to take an active part in their learning and
assessment. They are involved in their own learning and assessment in
ways appropriate to their level and age, and may even take the lead in conferences to discuss their progress with their parents and teachers.

The following lists include rudimentary dos and don'ts for administrators to consider, which in some instances require leaders to do some
strategizing, get better informed about testing, and generally be proactive
in dealing accountably with standardized testing and its data. Few shortcuts exist on the road to school improvement and excellent leadership, but
following these few pieces of advice should prove well worth the time and
effort required of school leaders and faculty who see the importance of
asserting their influence in the accountability movement.

- Dig deeply! Take the time and find the resources to understand and teach to faculty (who should share with parents) all about the standardized tests that students must take and what the test data mean (and do not mean) and what they actually reveal about student achievement.
- Keep reports to the media and board straightforward and simple, using charts or graphs to illustrate for better understanding when possible.
- Be so well informed about standardized testing that you can (and do) speak with professional prowess about its limitations as a high-stakes device for promotion, graduation, or schools' and educators' accountability.
- Always be honest about strengths and weaknesses indicated by the test results.
- Whenever possible, use annual test results longitudinally to track achievement of students over time; be aware, however, of problems created by revised forms of a test and other changes in the tests used when trying to compare a certain year's set of data with another.
- Use disaggregated test data to see how well particular groups of children are achieving (e.g., by race, gender, socioeconomic status) and strategize as a community to enhance the achievement of underperforming groups.
- Analyze test data to see how students in the school are performing on specific skills and use this data as one source of input for renewing and revising curriculum, planning instruction, and planning for staff development.
- Plan broadly for student assessment with faculty, parents, and students so that everyone understands that the standardized test is only one source of data used to account for students' achievement and should be taken seriously, but not inappropriately emphasized.

Don't:

- Be afraid to ask questions and speak up when you don't understand how the test functions and what the test data mean. Otherwise, improper uses of data are likely to be made. It is imperative for the principal and faculty to understand what standardized testing is and what it is not, what its data can tell us, and how they can be abused.
- Be afraid to speak up for what you believe in and to share with parents and the community the limitations of standardized testing as a high-stakes assessment tool.

- Overemphasize standardized testing by either overstressing its importance over other indicators of student success or trying to defend the school because of poor test results.
- Take valuable time out of the school day to have practice sessions on taking the test.
- Put unnecessary stress on teachers to teach to the test. If curriculum work is ongoing among the faculty, test data and standards will be properly used to emphasize certain content objectives and will be reflected in daily classroom instruction.
- Marginalize the importance of test data. If they are important to the public, they had better be important to the school. Put the test in perspective and remember to use it to focus on how to improve student achievement.
- Set yourself up to be on the defensive about test data. Make it routine to present to the board and media student achievement data from all sources, together with the school's plan to make the most use of the data to improve teaching and learning. This way, standardized test scores are more legitimately used as part of a larger picture of student performance indicators and are less likely to throw the school or system a curve ball with warped or skewed data.

MAKING GOOD SENSE AND BEST USE OF STANDARDS

In the frenzied, diffused flurry to force improvement on the schools, too often policy makers and legislators (and sometimes educators) overlook the complexity of the task. "Voting for standards," Merrow (2001) insightfully notes, "is a lot easier than actually creating them" (p. 655).

There is a profusion of standards today. It seems only prudent for educators—especially those who would be leaders—to be able to clarify just what we mean when we take a stand for or against them. There are student performance standards, content standards, teacher certification standards, principal licensure standards, program standards, evaluation standards, state standards, national standards, and a growing number of professional organizations' own versions of standards (e.g., NCTM, NCSS, ISLLC, NCATE, AASA, NASSP, NAESP). Just keeping up with the latest set of standards in the education profession is difficult to do. Many standards are quite useful as guides for improving everything from leadership preparation programs and professional assessment and growth to implementation of curricular innovations, to name just a few. The most controversial of the standards, however, are those tied to K–12 schools' accountability: content and performance standards.

Content standards define the curriculum—what should be taught to students—while performance standards answer how the standards will be assessed—what students must do to demonstrate mastery of the content. A third type of standard that is mentioned less often but which is noteworthy is the type sometimes referred to as *opportunity to learn* standards. These standards stipulate what students must have had available to them in school for them to be held accountable for meeting the standards for promotion or graduation (Nave, Meich, & Mosteller, 2000, p. 129).

None of these standards is simple or easy to develop, but all three types are important to include, and—if done well—they have the potential to facilitate badly needed reform in schools where too many students are simply not receiving a quality education sufficient for their success as contributing members of this society. Having good standards in the first place is one issue; another is using them in ways that truly benefit schools and students. "Rather than trying so hard to bring up test scores by concentrating solely on tests themselves," writes John Franklin (2001, p. 8), "educators and administrators could bring those scores up by incorporating the standards into their curricula and using them to prepare their students instead." In other words, standards should be used primarily for guiding school improvement and accreditation processes, rather than for mandating specified curriculum content and requiring accountability based on students' performance on a standardized test. If the standards are not well written or dealt with in a competent, professional manner, they—like anything else—are more a liability than an asset in school improvement initiatives. The reform focus is too often oversimplified and operates on what seems to be the assumption that mandates, and in many cases rewards and punishments, will be sufficient incentives to improve instruction and raise student achievement. This approach is particularly heinous to the education profession because it does not acknowledge the possibility that if teachers and administrators had the skills, knowledge, and resources to improve, they would probably have already done so. McCloskey and McMunn (2000) make an important, related point:

> In our work with schools, we have observed that translating state standards into clear instructional goals (and classroom assessments) is often an overwhelming and difficult task for educators . . . Studies of high-performing schools make it clear that improving school quality is at heart a people process—teachers collaboratively implementing a challenging curriculum and getting support to reflect on how they can make instruction and assessment powerful and engaging . . . Finding the time to give teachers for this kind of improvement of practice is a key problem that leaders at all levels need to address. (pp. 118–119)

Yet the public outcry is for short-term, fast results and school improvement accounted for by almost exclusive reliance on standardized test results. In their recent article on the problems with the accountability movement, Rex Knowles and Trudy Knowles (2001) observe,

Even the most naïve statistician knows that half of all people who take a norm-referenced test will be below average. That's what average means. Statistical accountability makes some children "leftovers." . . . And teaching merely to get test results not only deprives students of the opportunity to think, question, reason, or disagree, it also informs 50% of the group that they are below average and tells 10% that they are just no good at all! (p. 391)

Due in part to the poor quality of most current content standards, the related performance standards and tests for accountability lack the depth and breadth of what education at its best should be. Merrow (2001) suggests that "the move to create standards is out of synch with what is actually happening in schools right now. Today, we're testing with a vengeance, well before the system has had time to get ready" (p. 654).

As a unilateral device, testing for accountability does little or nothing to improve schools, and may indeed make them even worse—especially for some children. The Knowles (2001) vehemently express their malcontent with the accountability movement today: "In our emphasis on accountability, we operate as though individual differences don't exist. That's just plain stupid. But we also operate as though differences shouldn't exist, and that's just plain cruel" (p. 392). The most insidious dangers of the standards movement are too rigidly interpreting and applying them to all children, expecting results too fast, and trying to account for them with annually administered, standardized test scores alone. Such practices rob students and teachers of opportunities for the most complex, dynamic aspects of teaching and learning—unbridled play with imagination and creativity and time to laugh, to get to know each other as individuals, and to find joy in learning.

Allan Jones (2001), a principal in Illinois, makes a convincing case against today's standards movement:

We must begin to remove the obstacles that prevent teachers and administrators from doing their jobs well. These obstacles range from state mandates that generate mountains of paperwork to a lack of basic resources—access to a telephone, a computer, a room in which to talk alone with a colleague. Creating learning experiences that are meaningful and engaging requires an enormous amount of thought and energy. (p. 464)

Anne Lewis (2008) voices similar concerns about what's happening to the quality of instruction, specifically in the wake of NCLB: "Recent improvements in professional development have tried to help teachers achieve a broader understanding of content, often through analyzing student work and tying formative assessments to standards. The AYP craze, however, is undermining all of these efforts" (p. 2).

No superimposed set of standards, pen and paper, or standardized tests for accountability can short-circuit the reflective processes that are essential for good teaching and learning to take place. As Bohn and Sleeter (2000) assert, "The more detailed and specific a set of standards is, the less room it affords teachers . . . to bring their own thinking or children's own experiences to the task of teaching and learning" (p. 158). This concern for what the Knowles (2001) term a "foolish emphasis on sameness" in the accountability and standards movement is shared by a growing number of educators:

> If the word [accountability] meant that teachers are to be account-able for the respect they show to children, we would rejoice. If it meant that teachers are to be accountable for helping students to find joy in learning and to become lifelong contributors to their soci-ety, we would rejoice. If it meant that teachers are to be accountable for ensuring that all children are successful and that those teachers will be required to find the means to guide students and to assess students in multiple ways, we would rejoice . . . If teachers are to be held accountable, will those students who are below average in reading be pushed, mauled, and remediated? Shouldn't we instead tinker with the regular education regimen and get on with the process of educating the child? But that's not what we do. We take children with eyes that won't focus, fingers that won't cooperate, association areas that won't associate, neurons that don't fire appro-priately, connections that aren't connected, brains that won't attend and we say, "Sorry, but you must read anyway." (p. 391)

There are many staunch and vocal adversaries among the educational community when it comes to the standards approach to reform; however, upon closer scrutiny of their objections, their argument seems most often to be with high-stakes testing rather than with standards-based school reform efforts. Should the baby (well-written standards that embrace the notion of pluralism rather than one-size-fits-all instruction) be thrown out with the dirty bathwater (high-stakes, standardized testing that straitjack-ets teaching and learning) to move past this nationwide dilemma? Opinions vary widely about this issue too.

Defenders of the standards movement point out that judging student performance against a standard is indeed a better practice than the alterna-tives: comparing students' work with other students' performance or the practice of teachers simply shooting from the hip in grading and scoring. "Those who wish for the abandonment of standards," contends Douglas Reeves (2001), director of the Center for Performance Assessment in Denver, Colorado, "should ask themselves whether the days of the bell curve is really the alternative they prefer" (p. 6). Without question, identifying and working toward standards is a process commonly associated with out-standing performers, in all walks of life and in most types of organization.

The primary problem—albeit not the only one—with the accountability and standards movement is undoubtedly how it is being interpreted and managed by forcing the companion use of high-stakes testing of students as the sole means of assessing mastery of the standards. "The standards movement's preoccupation with measurement is one of its most troubling aspects," observe Bohn and Sleeter (2000, p. 157). They go on to state:

> Standardizing "output" measurements tends to lead people toward standardizing "inputs" and framing human variation as a problem to be contained. In the case of schools, the "input" that the movement toward standardization leads educators to standardize is the curriculum; the rich human variations of children and of pluralism then become problems to be minimized. (p. 157)

Having standards should not be misinterpreted to mean standardizing the educational experience for all students. Quite the contrary should be true; one primary purpose for having standards should be to enhance the personalization of education for students to facilitate their academic success. Any such movement to reform schools to better serve children should have from the outset an approach that is consistent with what we know is likely to help them. Using the learner-centered lens formed by the psychological principles of teaching and learning (refer to Chapter 6 in this volume) make excellent criteria through which all proposed policies and practices should be scrutinized.

Common sense, if nothing more, should inform us of the utter insanity and counterproductivity of many of the shortsighted strategies for improving students' test scores that are often used in schools today. McCloskey and McMunn (2000) explain,

> Interestingly, strategies designed primarily to familiarize students with the test may not translate into real learning gains . . . The fact that some schools are implementing short-term test-preparation strategies as their primary response to high-stakes tests suggests that perhaps school capacity for taking on long-term instructional reform is not where it needs to be if high-stakes testing is going to translate into meaningful and thoughtful strategies for improved learning at the classroom level. (p. 119)

"Where high-stakes tests are being imposed by states, it has thrown many teachers and students into a state of anxiety," observes John Merrow (2001, p. 657). And educators are not alone in their anxiety about these standards and tests. Weekly reports of parents and students protesting these high-stakes tests have sprung up all over the nation (e.g., well-attended, formal protests against state-mandated tests occurred in May 2001 in New York and Boston, and this was before the enactment of NCLB). In understanding the standards movement, a distinction must be made between it and the movement toward high-stakes testing. In writing about what he calls the twin movements, Scott Thompson (2001) makes important distinctions between what he terms the authentic (standards-based reform) and the evil (high-stakes, test-based reform) twins. Table 8.1 summarizes important differences that exist between the two reform movements, which should be

Table 8.1   Differences Between Standards-Based Reform and High-Stakes Testing

Authentic Standards-Based Reform Movement	High-Stakes Testing Movement
Fundamentally concerned with equity and high expectations for all students and staff	Focused on testing to sort and track, reward and punish
Most interested in evidence of improvement	Most concerned about current student performance, test scores
Complex and based on multiple forms of monitoring and assessing students' academic progress	Overly simplistic in equating student achievement to performance on a single test; abusive, inappropriate use of standardized tests
Focused on improving quality of curriculum and instruction for all students, in all schools	Focused on quickly derived, quantifiable, annual test scores that are easily reported and understood by politicians and the public
Focused on facilitating all students' success	Focused on measuring, ranking, and sorting schools and students
Involves teachers, parents, and others as active participants in developing and refining standards	Tests written by "experts" used as single indicators of students' degree of success, thus making them the standards
Describes what children should be learning	Defines the scores that students and schools must make to pass
Requires heavy investment in professional development of teachers and administrators to facilitate improved teaching and learning	Emphasizes drill and kill in classrooms to help children score well on tests
Requires provision of intensive help for students, rather than merely penalizing some of them for their at-risk potential	Focuses on test taking to the neglect of learning, particularly in the spring just before testing
Requires schools to operate as collaborative communities of learners, focused on problem solving, reflection, and dialogue as primary means for continuous growth and development of everyone in the school	Often requires teaching and learning to take second place to practice sessions in preparation for the annual test
Emphasizes complex learning, which is not easily tested	Encourages a focus on isolated skills and low-level, easily tested objectives

understood more clearly—especially by educational leaders (Ciliberto, 2001; Reeves, 2001; Stiggins, 1997).

Janie Ray Smith (2001) attempts to make sense of the confusion around standards-based education and high-stakes testing and concludes that, when handled well, standards can be used to improve teaching and learning. Like Thompson, Ciliberto, Stiggins, and others who find hope in the standards-based reform movement, however, Smith contends that only when "schools are committed to standards-based instruction through a systemic, long term process" will standards be usefully employed and make a positive impact on teaching and learning (p. 4). When based on quick fixes and the test, the standards movement will quickly fail, concede Smith and most other standards advocates. Among the greatest good coming from the standards movement to date in school districts that have tackled standards-based reform from a systemic, all-encompassing perspective, suggests Smith (2001), are better analysis and use of data to make instructional decisions, better forms of reliable and varied performance assessments, and large strides in reaching all children more equitably, especially special populations. These results are indeed promising, but practices that led to these good results in a number of districts cited by Smith are more the exception than the rule.

Just what is the business of school? Determining what schools are and are not responsible for in a child's education, what they can and cannot reasonably do, is essential for making schools truly accountable. Schlechty (1990) asserts that the primary business of school is to "produce school-work that will engage the young to the point that they try it, stick with it, and succeed at it" (p. 141). This primary business takes place in classrooms, where the most pertinent indicators of a school's accountability and authentic evidences of student achievement exist.

FOCUSING ON CLASSROOMS FOR ACCOUNTABILITY AND STUDENTS' ACHIEVEMENT

What strategies are there besides high-stakes, standardized tests for assessing standards and holding students and educators accountable? What role should school leaders play—what can principals and teacher leaders do right here and now—to minimize the potential damage to schools and students in this nationally debated scenario? What's a good instructional leader to do to make the best of the testing situation today without giving in to bad practices and contributing to the problem? "The problems with NCLB," assert Glickman, Gordon, and Ross-Gordon (2007), "place supervisors and teachers across the nation in one of the great moral dilemmas of our time. They cannot simply declare NCLB immoral and refuse to help students prepare for the state's high-stakes test" (p. 458).

Besides the moral obligation educators have to work to make poor legislation work *for* rather than to the detriment of students, Glickman et al. (2007)

propose both short- and long-term strategies to deal with the dilemma in what they believe is a morally responsible fashion by not sacrificing the principles of good teaching at the altar of the unholy high-stakes tests. Among the short-term strategies they propose are to limit test-taking practices; differentiate instruction; use formative assessment extensively; and embed state standards and test objectives into a comprehensive curriculum that includes more holistic and meaningful learning opportunities. Their long-term strategy recommendations include the following: develop at national and state levels more realistic school improvement goals; shift from reliance on high-stakes testing to multiple measures including local assessment systems; measure academic progress of same students over time; provide adequate realistic resources for improving teaching and learning conditions (pp. 458–461).

To assess how well a school is doing in a truly accountable fashion, Eisner (2001), like Schlechty, Kohn (2001), and other seasoned, credible educators, suggests we look carefully in classrooms and examine closely the kinds of activities children are involved in, then ask questions such as the following:

- What is the educational significance of the content students encounter?
- How well are students able to pose meaningful questions rather than solve problems?
- What connections are students helped to make between what they study in school and the world outside?
- What opportunities do students have to formulate their own purposes and to design ways to achieve them?
- What opportunities do children have to work cooperatively on problems they deem important?
- To what extent are students able to work in depth in domains that relate to their unique abilities and aptitudes?
- Do students participate in assessment of their own work?
- Are teachers given the time to observe and work with one another?
- Are parents helped to understand what their child has accomplished in class? (pp. 370–372)

These are quality-oriented and legitimate—albeit less quantifiable—criteria for judging a school's accountability. Such questions are about looking at what's happening with students and teachers in the school as authentic, insightful indicators of how well a school is ensuring that children are learning, rather than narrowly focusing on an end-product in the form of standardized test scores.

School leaders can be a viable force in taking the initiative to focus on more credible classroom-based evidences of students' achievement, which cover many dimensions of human development not assessed well on such tests, thereby preventing the abuse of standardized, machine-scored tests as the sole or even the primary measure of children's—and thus schools'—accomplishments. Being appropriately accountable for students' learning requires schools to monitor their performance and analyze well-selected data; it does not translate into annual test results on which students' presumed achievement, and thus educators' accountability, must primarily rest. Reeves (2001) addresses this issue specifically:

> The participants in the increasingly vituperative debate on standards and assessments are missing the point. They throw their rhetorical missiles at one another, unencumbered by the evidence and focused on a particularly vexing conundrum: the relationship of standards to a single high-stakes test. Advocates demand accountability and opponents demand fairness, but neither side appears to be willing to shift the focus of the debate from an annual test event in the gymnasium to the primary location for effective assessment: the classroom. (p. 5)

John Franklin (2001) suggests, "Good assessment should be thought of as a photo album rather than a snapshot." He continues, "We should use different pictures and different lenses to get at different aspects of learning over time" (p. 8). The performance of students over time in the classroom—not a few hours spent once a year taking a test—is the obvious place to focus on credible and varied ways of determining (e.g., multiple-choice tests, portfolios of student work that contain concrete examples of children's progress over time, multiple forms of students' actual performances) what children are and are not learning. As Reeves (2001) sagely suggests, "The key to effective assessment is balance" (p. 8). Locally developed, more reliable, varied assessments of students' performance for multiple purposes help administrators and teachers become better informed about student achievement. "District designed performance assessments and thoughtfully designed classroom assessments can enable educators to have multiple measurements to determine achievement toward standards, to guide instruction, and to assess individual student needs" (Smith, 2001, p. 5).

An important dimension of classroom assessment is the significance of student–teacher interaction that is essential for finding out most specifically and reliably how well individual students are learning. Through regular and prompt feedback from teachers and each other, students have the greatest opportunity to grow, learn, and improve their performance. After all, the aim is improving learning, not measuring it. "A primary leadership responsibility of any principal is to provide opportunities for their teachers to learn to embed effective classroom assessment in the teaching and learning process" (Stiggins, 2001, p. 19). Teachers must have opportunities to learn and improve their assessment practices as an integral part of improving instruction. Principals and district administrators should facilitate ongoing professional development opportunities designed specifically to include student assessment practices.

In a *Phi Delta Kappan* article, Black and Wiliam (1998) report strong research evidence for the link between what happens in classrooms (particularly with assessment) and student achievement. These authors raise important questions for policy makers in their quest to raise standards and make schools more accountable:

> In terms of systems engineering, present policies in the U.S. and in many other countries seem to treat the classroom as a black box . . . But what is happening inside the box? How can anyone be sure that a particular set of new inputs will produce better outputs if we don't at least study what happens inside? And why is it that most of the reform initiatives . . . are not aimed at giving direct help and support to the work of teachers in the classroom? (p. 140)

Black and Wiliam (1998) offer their concrete, research-based responses to improving formative assessment in classrooms:

1. Feedback to any pupil should be about the particular qualities of his or her work, with advice on what he or she can do to improve, and should avoid comparisons with other pupils.

2. If formative assessment is to be productive, pupils should be trained in self-assessment so that they can understand the main purposes of their learning and thereby grasp what they need to do to achieve.

3. Opportunities for pupils to express their understanding should be designed into any piece of teaching, for this will initiate the interaction through which formative assessment aids learning.

4. The dialogue between pupils and a teacher should be thoughtful, reflective, focused to evoke and explore understanding, and conducted so that all pupils have an opportunity to think and to express their ideas.

5. Feedback on tests, seatwork, and homework should give each pupil guidance on how to improve, and each pupil must be given help and an opportunity to work on the improvement. (pp. 142–146)

These authors conclude their suggestions by acknowledging the critical role played by a teacher's beliefs about learning and each child's potential to learn in the child's chances of academic success. Indeed, a teacher's positive expectations for students' learning must be intact for other teaching strategies to be effective.

It is one thing to be responsibly accountable and to have ideals, goals, and some benchmarks in the form of standards to facilitate educators in their pursuit of quality assurances that students are getting a good, equitable slice of the nation's education pie. It is quite another to treat the standards as empirically derived or sanctioned by Divinity. Today's standards are not passed down from Moses or written in stone. Nor is it written in anyone's book of right living that educators should be held any more accountable for students' achievement than their families, communities, peers, legislators, and society in general. Paul Houston (2001), executive director of American Association of School Administrators (1994–2008), contends,

> It takes a village to raise achievement . . . [I]f we are to truly be a nation where the children of poverty are able to run alongside the children of privilege, then a total strategy and a commitment by all is needed. The village must be galvanized to action. (p. 46)

Commissioner of New York State Education Department Richard Mills (2001) reminds us of the importance of staying focused on children and not letting the distractions throw us off course or demoralize us. He too suggests educators prepare not to have all the answers but rather to ask the hard questions that lead the whole community to more serious thought about issues. He encourages educators to insist and persist by emphasizing the right things and by repeatedly retelling the tale because the public, board members, and state legislatures are forever changing and have short memories. "We shouldn't play along with those want us to stand there with all the answers," he warns. "How can we close the gaps in student achievement right here in our community? Now that's a question for parents, educators, students, everyone" (p. 40).

Finally, in dealing accountably with standards and tests, like any other practice, it is absolutely necessary to remember that at the heart of this education enterprise is the well-being of children . . . as individuals, first and foremost, not as collective groups of students whose test scores yield data for making comparisons, rating schools', teachers', and principals' performances, and giving politicians campaign fodder. Any practice that clouds or pulls us too much from that central mission is badly flawed. "Supervision and Instructional Leadership," remind Glickman, Gordon, and Ross-Gordon, advocates of leadership that is grounded in moral principles, "is foremost about the ideas of goodness, purpose, and hope for all of our students" (2007, p. 462).

Leadership for instructional excellence wears the "lens" of student-centeredness, attempting to interpret all practice in light of what is best for students in dealing with the tough issues that challenge educators today, not the least of which is today's accountability movement, with its emphasis on standards and high-stakes testing.

Walking the Talk

A recent principal shares an approach she used in her school to manage and deal responsibly with the state-mandated curriculum and annual standardized testing of students

Every student deserves to learn the prescribed curriculum and meet the required standards for their grade level. Your campus rating can sometimes hinge on the performance of one subgroup or even one student in a subgroup, as well. You want to

(Continued)

(Continued)

make sure that your plans are inclusive and precise in offering help to every student as needed. It is important to have a plan for students who are not achieving at the pace expected in the classroom. Benchmark scores should be disaggregated by subgroup each time you test. Deficits on each tested objective must be targeted. At my school, we used a tracking chart devised by district curriculum specialists that aligned the objectives taught and tested. Students, with the help of their teachers, filled in the squares on the tracking chart for the objectives they mastered on benchmarks. Those students who did not master all objectives filled in their squares as each objective was *retaught*, tested, and mastered. Using this tracking system, both students and teachers were able to track their progress individually and were consistently mindful of the areas not yet mastered. This system required students to set goals for their own learning and share the responsibility for monitoring their progress, a strategy noted in Robert Marzano's *What Works in Schools*. The special tutors, funded through Title funds in our case, worked in small groups with those students in the areas of defined weakness to fill in the gaps.

The pace of the curriculum in the classrroom continued, as well. The use of tutorials, whether in school or after school, is one way to address the needs of those students who are in need of intensive help. It is important to secure the most qualified tutors. We found great retired teachers, and those with small children who wanted to work part time. Whether your tutors are full time or part time, they need to be a real part of the team, attending all training that impacts student performance. They must plan regularly with regular classroom teachers, and function with them in a team effort to close the skill gaps of the students they share. The principal is instrumental in setting the guidelines that make this happen. After the first administration of the test, the students who did not pass were grouped by need and the regular classroom teacher pulled those students for small group tutorials while the tutor took over the regular class instruction. The philosophy behind this plan was that as the teacher of record, they *owned* the scores of these students, and they deserved the opportunity to work with them within the school day, individually and in small groups apart from the regular classroom setting. This worked well in our case as one way to provide for students who needed the most "intensive care". Your campus rating can sometimes depend on the performance of one student, and *every* student deserves to pass the test and be promoted to the next grade level. (Dr. Nancy Adams, Author's Feedback Request Form, Fall 2008)

Dr. Nancy Adams was the principal of Parker Elementary School in Galveston Independent School District, Texas, from 1995–2000.

POINTERS FOR THE PRINCIPAL

- Don't dodge accountability.
  - Actively assume responsibility for the school's role in student learning.
  - Facilitate conversations about accountability among all stakeholders.

- o Lead stakeholders to define who is responsible and for what in a child's education.
- o Know the national, state, and local perspectives and legislation on schools and accountability.
- o Embrace standards that support pluralism among teachers and learners.
- o Resist high-stakes, standardized testing as the major means of assessing students' performance and thus a school's accountability.
- o Assertively monitor, document, and report through multiple means how well students are learning.

- Know what educators and students are actually doing in the school.
  - o Be vigilant about the quality of activities and interactions in the school.
  - o Be keenly aware of activities in which students and teachers are routinely engaged.
  - o Participate regularly in dialogues about the quality of school life.
  - o Assist teachers, parents, and students in assuming appropriate, active roles.
  - o Lead the school in the practice of asking in-depth questions, especially about what's happening in classrooms.

- Make assessment more authentic and representative of students' achievement.
  - o Facilitate a multifaceted approach to assessing student performance.
  - o Understand and use standardized tests scores appropriately—as only one of multiple indicators of student performance.
  - o Encourage and support teachers' efforts to improve classroom assessment.
  - o Keep parents informed and involved in monitoring the progress of students.
  - o Report regularly to the board and community on varied indicators of student progress, both positive and negative data.
  - o Based on students' performance, adapt the school's goals for improvement.

9

The Instructional Leader's Power Tools

Cutting-Edge Leadership Strategies

Districts need to start fixing their sights on the schools they want to build, rather than maintaining the schools they have.

— Mary Neuman and Judith Pelchat (2001, p. 736)

Failure to discipline shared decisions by results means that the decisions will be disciplined by reference to the interests of factions, groups, and parties, rather than the interests of children.

— Phillip C. Schlechty (1990, p. 62)

Data for making informed decisions and reporting objectives are essential to the operation and leadership of the profession.

— Marlin L. Tanck (1994, p. 92)

Innovations that have been succeeding have been doing so because they combine good ideas with good implementation decision and support systems.

— Michael G. Fullan (1982, p. 113)

A systems approach to effective behavioral and instructional support requires the use of data or evidence to support decision-making.

—U.S. Office of Special Education Programs (2000, pp. 5–6)

Research, experimentation, and data gathering are built into the daily routine of learning organizations.

—Taher A. Razik and Austin D. Swanson (2001, p. 454)

The only constant is change itself. We've all heard it. We all know it at some level, but most of us operate primarily from a change-resistant mentality. The literature is replete with issues of change and its impact on us as individuals, families, groups, and society at large. For some time now, our society has made much ado about the increasingly fast rate of change in our world and its impact on everything from rushed children, stress levels, and heart attacks to the way organizations must now operate and be led to remain relevant and at the cutting edge. Processes such as long-range and strategic planning, forecasting, and even visionary leadership have been very much about the need for organizations to deal with phenomenal changes taking place at record-breaking speeds. Before a textbook reaches the classroom, much of its content is obsolete. Curricula at all levels, including preparation programs for teachers and administrators, must peddle faster to approach relevancy in what was already deemed an outmoded, stuck-in-the-mud endeavor. Before a piece of technology is installed and operable, a newer, improved model is on the market. It is no wonder that the traditional model of principal as one who simply "puts out fires" or keeps from "rocking the boat" is no longer adequate for today's schools. How does today's principal protect the organization from the potential havoc change can wreak? Or can change actually be a principal's friend? Are there ways to capitalize on change phenomena to facilitate teaching and learning and school improvement processes?

This chapter offers principals a critical set of up-to-date yet well-documented and essential power tools for dealing with change, so they can provide leadership at its cutting-edge best. These tools include (1) having a perspective on change that is proactive and positive, (2) understanding the processes fundamental to dealing with data, and using it and research more competently in making decisions and driving reform initiatives focused on improving teaching and learning, and (3) maximizing technology as a power tool for managing data and facilitating school improvement.

THE LEADER AS ARCHITECT OF CHANGE

Effective principals today do more than manage organizations. To be their best—and in many cases now even to survive—they must be leaders who get their impetus and power from empowering others, tapping talent throughout the school community, and mobilizing teams and structures for distributed leadership from among the entire spectrum of stakehold-ers. A primary distinction between management and leadership is that management suggests maintenance of the status quo. Leadership, on the other hand, is about effecting change.

Douglas Reeves defines leaders as "architects of individual and organi-zational improvement" (2006, p. 27). Organizations that thrive and are healthy are frequently referred to as *learning organizations,* characterized by continual growth and renewal among all school community members with the goal of improvement. Today's school leader must be an effective agent of change, with skills to facilitate the processes essential for the organiza-tion and its people to continue to improve. But, more than this, to be most effective today's principal must view change as an opportunity to redirect and fine-tune the organization in its mission to care for and educate chil-dren. An attitude that embraces change's positive potentials, skills that cap-italize on and steer change for school improvement, and understanding the complexities of how change occurs in people and organizations can equip a principal to move beyond being able to cope with change to being empowered as a change-shaper, an architectural leader. The architectural leader assembles and orchestrates the entire team of diverse talents that make up a school's operation (from bus drivers, cafeteria workers, and cus-todians to administrative assistants, teachers, and teacher assistants) to get the work done and accomplish the school's purposes (Reeves, 2006). No small feat and definitely not for the faint of heart.

Attitude Adjustment: Embracing Change

The literature is replete with opinions on what it takes to be a great leader (Covey, 1991; Fullan, 1995; Goldberg, 2001; Reeves, 2006). Although the ingre-dients for outstanding leadership offered by authors often vary, most include references to the capacity of great leaders to deal with change and make change work for them and the organization, rather than merely coping with change as though it were an adversarial, event-oriented phenomenon. Such an attitude is critical to making the most of change and leading a school, rather than tentatively addressing, enduring, or coping with change. This is an important distinction that outstanding leaders understand, and one on which they base a positive view of change as a tool for facilitating continual school improvement. An organization always involved in improving itself is less likely to feel the trauma of change events, often superimposed on it because it has entropied—stopped growing on its own as healthy organiza-tions do. Without processes in place for an organization to perpetually exam-ine itself and make adjustments and adaptations to improve its operation and outcomes, the more likely is the organization to find itself faced with having to make significant changes—an inevitable situation after years of stagnation and lack of internal renewal.

If an organization is not improving, then it most likely is getting worse. There is no static state of existence for human beings, organisms, or organiza-tions. Try as we humans may, we cannot stop change. The best we can do is to understand that change is, after all, what keeps life interesting by giving us repeated opportunities to grow and giving us renewed hope and optimism for a better tomorrow. The key for principals, teachers, parents, and community members is to funnel this reality of life-as-change into an ever-improving state of being for the entire learning community, the organization of school. Being far-sighted, proactive, reflective, and adapting to needed change routinely, rather than always having to respond or react to it, helps a school shape its destiny by channeling its energy into attaining its goals and mission.

"Change begins with a new way of thinking—it starts in the hearts and minds of individuals and results in seeing learning and learners differently . . . Like learning, change is a lifelong and continuous process." (Presidential Task Force on Psychology in Education & American Psychological Association, 1993, p. 56)

Key Skills of a Change Agent

Effective leaders do not facilitate change and improve schools alone. A major role for the principal is to involve the school's stakeholders in meaningful, learner-centered school improvement processes in ways that are appropriate and best suited to the various talents of the individual members. Indeed, a pivotal function for today's principal is involving everyone in continuous school improvement initiatives. Work-study groups and well-designed communication conduits provide the fundamental structures for schools to be learning organizations and for change to be embedded in the culture of their everyday operations. Principals and school leaders set these conduits and systems of communication in motion, thereby empowering others to be a part of continuous improvement in accomplishing the school's central role of educating young people.

Which employees should be included in this loop of continuous improvement? Every employee in the school should be a part of this meaningful work. Classified and professional personnel alike are critical to the success of the school operation and should be included in relevant functions that will help all those involved feel valued, perform their work better, and know that their work is important to the successful operation of the school in fulfilling its mission.

Today's principal as change-agent facilitates a change-friendly, improvement-oriented culture of risk taking and innovation to advance learning and success for everyone. According to Schwahn and Spady (1998),

Cultural leaders know that real change happens from the inside out, with the paradigm perspectives, beliefs, values, and goals of the individual . . . [W]ith a new perspective and a safe place to explore change, individuals can participate in a process with confidence that it will "work" for them. (p. 77)

Supervision and evaluation practices that are conceived as primarily supportive and cooperative endeavors (as described in Chapter 6) help to ensure such confidence and nurture the risk-taking spirit so integral to growth and improvement among faculty and staff.

Understanding change as a process, not an event, is essential for principals as well as teachers and other stakeholders involved in today's inclusive-oriented, participatory style of school leadership espoused in this text and widely accepted in organizational thinking universally. Change, viewed more authentically as a process, can be broken down into stages or phases. Understanding these stages helps those involved in such processes to understand change's complexities, thereby minimizing the frustrations that often accompany unrealistic expectations about making change happen. Predicting, for example, that during the implementation of a new strategy or program some stakeholders will be frustrated at first by their awkwardness with the innovation can enable educators to prepare for better support systems and backup plans to assist with such anticipated problems. Such proaction reduces anxiety and lowers frustration levels, which in turn paves the way for success and greater acceptance of future innovation and change.

Understanding the Complexity of Change

This text does not attempt to deal comprehensively with the complex concept of change. There are many excellent books on change and the multiple dimensions of it. For example, there is good change and there is bad change. Change is not inherently a good thing, as often it is implied to be. Change is only good if it leads to improvement, and most preferably improvement that can be sustained over time. There are short-term change strategies and long-term change strategies, usually happening simultaneously. Then there's the perspective of change from a "systems" view that looks at schools as being embedded within the multiple larger administrative, political, and social contexts which must be understood and dealt with in making change that inevitably impacts the way individuals in the school practice (students, teachers, principals, etc.). Changing practice (i.e., changing the way people do things) is the toughest, albeit the most important and key, role of leadership. Suffice to say in this chapter that there is much to learn if one wants to really understand the dynamics of change.

To be sure, instructional leaders will need to have not only an extensive knowledge and understanding of the complexity of change and its predictable stages, but just as important, the determination and skill to manage change as a process that must be tended and steered to keep it focused on ultimately improving what is happening in the classroom.

Throughout the extensive literature on change, its process is often described as a set of critical stages through which those involved in the innovation must pass. Although the labels and terms for the phases differ, basically the following are included in most models of change as process:

Awareness or readiness—the importance of all individuals involved in the change initiative to understand the need to change

Preparation—exploring and learning more about how the change initiative and how it will apply both to the school community collectively and to each individual specifically

Implementation—practicing new behaviors and skills and adapting to change

Refinement—routinizing a practice, assessing it, and improving on it

Of course, schools do not neatly deal with one change at a time. Change is happening at many different levels all around us. Various of these four change stages are operative at any one time in our personal lives, at work, in the community, and in society at large. Even though this change process is easily discerned in all phases of our lives and has been dealt with intellectually and well covered in the professional literature for some time now, few folks give it the credence that it deserves when dealing with change or innovation, particularly in school reform and improvement. I see school district after school district attempting to make rather dramatic change but giving short shrift to change as a process by attempting to treat it as an event—a workshop, most often, with little to no support or follow-up in the implementation stages in the classroom, where it counts most. Understanding that change is, indeed, a process that typically will occur in predictable stages can enable administrators to plan ahead for adequately providing the resources to support continuous school improvement.

If the purpose of change in a district or school is as it should be—to improve teaching and learning—then there must be a stronger recognition of the complexity of improving classroom practices and how this can best be facilitated. "You can make all the changes you want at the state level, but nothing is going to happen unless change takes place at the classroom and school levels," maintain members of the Southern Regional Education Board in their publication on school accountability caution (1998, p. 13). And changing what takes place in the classroom is not easy. Susan Fuhrman (2003) addresses the difficulty of making changes and improving schools:

Improvement is slow, unending, not particularly glamorous, hard work. It involves deep investment in teacher quality and knowledge, through recruiting, compensating, and developing teachers. It involves thoughtful, well-funded professional development that is intensive, extensive (over a period of time), focused on the curriculum that teachers are teaching, and followed up by coaching and other on-site support. (p. 10)

A major whetstone of school improvement is well-conceived staff development. "Indeed," asserts Schlechty (1990), "human resource development becomes the linchpin upon which all improvement efforts are based" (p. 139). Effective leaders understand this, and work fearlessly and tenaciously to ensure that adequate support and resources are provided to teachers, who are usually the ones who must deal with the lion's share of making things happen in the classroom. Embracing change as ongoing school improvement, skillfully nurturing a change-friendly culture that includes all employees and stakeholders, and understanding the complexities of change well enough to facilitate improvement that is lasting and sustainable are an instructional leader's best tools for ensuring the organization is a true "learning community."

PUTTING DATA TO WORK

It is increasingly evident in the research and literature that the schools making dramatic strides in improving educational achievement and equity make constructive use of data (Reeves, 2006, p. 89). Instructional leaders must depend on systematic, varied data and up-to-date research to guide their decisions and strategies for continual improvement and accountability for what's happening in their schools and how well students are achieving. "Without good information, an organization is blind to its past achievements and failures and to its future potential" (Razik & Swanson, 2001, p. 453). Information on both process and product is absolutely essential to direct change and maximize improvement efforts focused on teaching and learning. For example, although it is important, it simply isn't enough to know that third-grade students are not performing well in mathematics. In addition to the need to know more specifically which mathematical processes and functions are in question, it is imperative to know which students are performing well and which are not, as well as what's happening with mathematics instruction in classrooms (instructional approaches, curriculum, materials, schedule) to make sound decisions for change. The Southern Regional Education Board (1998) concludes,

> Most teachers have little experience in using data to determine where improvements are needed. Assistance . . . should ensure that teachers know what is expected, how to use performance data to identify problem areas, and how to develop and carry out a successful plan of action. Without this focus the school is unlikely to continue progressing toward high standards. (p. 25)

Data-enhanced (suggested recently as preferred to the term "data-driven") decisions and research-based strategies must be more than the stuff about which articles are written if school leadership is ever to be instructionally focused. Understanding what data are important, the multiple sources of relevant data, alternative methods of accessing and analyzing data, as well as using the results in making decisions are all important aspects of maximizing data to improve teaching and learning. "School leaders," assert Hoyle, English, and Steffy (1994), "must be skilled at interpreting and conducting research, evaluating programs, and planning for the future. Each skill is dependent on the other and must be mastered" (p. 246). Nor does data analysis have to be complex. Theodore B. Creighton, author of *Schools and Data: The Educator's Guide for Using Data to Improve Decision Making* (2001b), explains,

> Statistics is not advanced mathematics. The majority of statistical analyses useful to administrators can be completed with a basic understanding of mathematics and is more conceptual than requiring complex calculations . . . Data analysis in schools involves the collection of data and the use of available data to improve teaching and learning . . . Rather than complex statistical formulas and tests, it is generally simple counts, averages, percentages and rates that we are interested in. (pp. 7–8)

Existing findings based on research studies and what other schools and districts have learned about programs and strategies are also important sources of data for making informed, cogent decisions for improving teaching and learning. To ignore what others are doing and what is in the research literature on teaching and learning is not only inefficient and much like trying to reinvent the wheel, it is irresponsible and unprofessional.

Skillful collection, storage, analysis, and use of data, and routinely examining up-to-date research, are power tools for change because data and research provide information that enables educators to make the most of their time, resources, and improvement initiatives by streamlining strategies to meet the specific needs of their students. In short, a comprehensive system of information management is needed for a school to deal most competently with and maximally use the wealth of data pertinent and available to today's school leadership. Skillfully dealing with data should result in the formation of an information management system, which includes a more regulated, formalized approach to accessing and collecting data; analyzing data; and being able to use and report data more easily and accurately via the development of multiple databases and a user-friendly, school data synopsis—a school profile.

Accessing and Collecting Data

What data are important to collect and include in school decision making and improvement? Data are needed to establish what's in place, what's working, what our goals are, and how we improve student achievement (U.S. Office of Special Education Programs, 2000, p. 6). Bernhardt's (1998, p. 15) four classifications of the data important for schools to collect to make sound decisions for student achievement provide a useful framework for thinking about data, its sources, and its types. Bernhardt's data classifications include demographic data, perceptual data, data on student learning, and data related to school programs and processes. Thinking of data in these clusters helps to put large quantities of data into a more manageable system that has a wide spectrum of relevant information from which to draw, and on which to base decisions.

Demographic data include information on students, such as name, gender, ethnicity, special needs, age, grade, attendance, socioeconomic characteristics, educational history, and relevant family and contact information. Demographic data related to the faculty and community are also important to have. Much of this information is objective, frequently numerically categorized, and already available somewhere in most school districts. Using the data more effectively requires first putting them into an easily accessed data bank in the school.

Student learning data include standardized, norm-referenced and criterion-referenced test data, teacher observations, and an array of more informal classroom assessments. If accountability for students' achievement is ever to depend on more than standardized test scores, educators must collect, use, and actively promote a broader range of data as better, more authentic representations of student performance. More important, instructional decisions cannot be most responsive to students' needs without such data being collected continuously and used throughout the school's daily operation and decision-making processes.

Perceptual data are important because of their impact on learning. The values, beliefs, and attitudes of learners, teachers, parents, and community members are strong influences on the school's culture, the learning environment, and ultimately student performance. This set of data is more subjective and more difficult to quantify. Yet it must not be excluded from a school's database for reflecting and making good decisions about students and learning. Much of it must be collected via questionnaires, surveys, interviews, and understandings gleaned from carefully attending to the behaviors and language of, and feedback from, students, parents, and community members. "What data shows our commitment or if our classes are exciting, creative places?" asks George Goens (2001, p. 32), a former superintendent of schools in Wisconsin. Lest one thinks that such qualitative, soft data are less than helpful, he or she needs only to review the research-based, documented principles of learning from Chapter 7 of this book. The importance of perceptions and attitudes to teaching and learning are readily visible throughout these documented principles, this text's recommended lens for making students and learning the focus of the school's total operation.

Finally, the last of Bernhardt's (1998) classifications of data important for schools to collect, analyze, and use in decision making is data related to school processes and programs. Schools have primary control of these constructs when designing to facilitate student achievement. Schools' decision-making processes regarding programs (e.g., curriculum content, materials, projects) and processes (e.g., student–teacher interaction, instruction, collaboration, communication) should be based on thorough analyses of—and continually adapted to—students' achievement and well-being. The effectiveness of these processes and programs should, of course, be reflected ultimately in students' performance. It is important, however, to document more than students' test scores and to know what is going on in schools and how decisions are made that relate to students' interest as the rationale and guiding compass. In this way, adjustments can be made and processes and programs more routinely examined and accounted for in light of what is happening to students.

Also important in collecting data about programs and processes is accounting for the resources required to implement and maintain them (e.g., personnel, materials, space, time, equipment, professional development). Data about faculty, their special skills and training, and their credentials represent important information to have readily available. It is critical as well to analyze programs and processes in terms of cost factors. Too often, educators fail to deal as responsibly as they should with the public's tax dollar, and as a result taxpayers are usually suspicious of and reluctant to respond to the school's request for increased funding. Data that help to analyze cost factors related to programs and processes initiated by the school are essential to making decisions that can be justified on the bases of both effectiveness and efficiency issues.

The case was made in Chapter 8 of this book for accountability criteria to include processes and programs that are most often within the purview of the school as an important component for school-based accountability. Also acknowledged in the last chapter was that accountability for students' achievement does not rest solely with the school; it belongs to the "village." What is happening in the school in the way of processes and programs to facilitate the school's role in students' learning, however, is highly relevant accountability criteria over which a school and district have infinitely more control, and for which they should rightfully be held accountable. "Accountability is more than a list of scores," Reeves (2006) sagely reminds readers. "Rather, accountability includes the actions of adults, not merely the scores of students" (p. 83).

When presented with the question of how he knew whether his district's schools were successfully educating children, Superintendent Gary Burton (2001) of Wayland Public Schools in Massachusetts thought of more than test scores, scholarships and the number of students accepted into universities for substantiating data. His indicators of how well the district was educating its young included the ability of the system to recruit and retain outstanding teachers, the good salaries that the community pays its educators as indicators of their commitment to children's education, the near-perfect student attendance rate, the absence of vandalism on campuses, the few children labeled by the district as troubled, and the high level of parent involvement with the schools from kindergarten through the twelfth grade. But most impressive was how he dug even deeper and turned to what he calls true benchmarks of the degree of success of educating children—benchmarks which he admitted were not very measurable: unsolicited letters of praise to the local paper about teachers or students; evidence of community service performed by students; the number of citizens who choose to vote in elections; and, most revealing, how students ten years beyond graduation have fared with college, jobs, relationships, and with demonstrating a community spirit of giving to and helping others (p. 42).

Truly, the success of the village itself must be the ultimate test of how well America is educating its young—a task that belongs to all of us and for which we should look broadly to access data and monitor our progress. The school's role is to do its best to find measures of its success within its scope of capability and responsibility as only one player—albeit a major one—in the village's education of its young. These measures will most often be more short term than is most desirable or authentic in the larger scheme of things. As Burton (2001) has concluded, the real proof is in how children fare in the long run as adults and members of the larger society. Meantime, schools and leaders can at least insist on asking more reflective, deeper questions and forcing the public to look beyond superficial data as measures of a school's accountability in its role in educating children. If student performance is authentically interpreted to include a broad spectrum of indicators chosen by the school's stakeholder community as important and indicative of students' achievement, then schools can be more accountable for how programs and processes within the school are impacting students' learning. It would behoove educators and school stakeholders to systematically collect data related to these admittedly complex, but infinitely more legitimate, indicators of students' achievement. Reeves (2006) calls this kind of broad-based accountability "holistic accountability," which he contends is one of five key characteristics of high-achieving schools (p. 83).

Analyzing Data

Data collected from the four broad categories identified by Bernhardt (1998), and from sources within and outside the school contexts, can then be used to make better, data-based decisions, rather than knee-jerk responses based on limited or skewed pieces of information or nonapplicable or inappropriate perspectives.

Varied forms of more in-depth analysis of frequently collected qualitative and quantitative data can be most useful in determining how to improve teaching and learning. "It seems to me," conclude Neuman and Pelchat (2001), "that if we really want to improve the results, then we have to start thinking about how we're teaching, what we're doing in the classroom" (p. 736.) Such analysis can provide insight into, for example, who is learning what, to what degree, using which program, in which classrooms, and at what costs. Philip Streifer (2001), a former school district superintendent, writes about what he calls a drill-down process useful in taking data apart, much like peeling off layers of an onion. Streifer makes an important point about the danger of taking a too-shallow approach to data and prematurely jumping to conclusions before thorough analysis of it has taken place. He finds three types of data analysis most useful in answering questions that large sets of aggregated data alone will not yield: (1) disaggregation of data across one or more factors, (2) longitudinal analyses over time, and (3) exploring, which he describes as using logic to analyze problems for which there is no clear, predetermined direction to follow. These are practical, responsible tools for digging deeper into data to make better decisions.

Streifer (2001) offers a number of very practical suggestions for schools and districts to consider in developing wholesome processes that support a data-driven environment. The following are adaptations of his recommendations that seem practical and timely for schools and districts to make the most of data available to them:

- Develop data work teams with people who have the expertise to deal with critical areas, such as curriculum, testing, database manipulation, and basic research.
- Give teams adequate time and perhaps even compensation for their work.
- Focus on patterns and trends in the data over time. Armed with diagnostic information gained through drill-down analyses, teams should rely on their judgment and expertise in planning program changes.
- Once the team believes it has identified the root cause of a problem, check the research to avoid reinventing the wheel.
- Build a culture that supports the review and use of data for decision making by including it regularly in the school improvement process, not just when a major problem emerges or the board or local news media asks for a report. (p. 18)

A culture that supports the wise use of good data for making decisions, particularly related to teaching and learning, generally operates from a perspective that includes the following approaches to and attitudes about data:

1. Disaggregate group test results and large sets of district and school data to find out how particular groups are faring (e.g., by class, gender, race, socioeconomic level, program, instructional method).

2. Focus on tracking the progress of children over time more than on comparing one group's scores with another group by looking at how students at each grade level compare to students from past years. Raymond Yeagley (2001), superintendent of the Rochester School Department in New Hampshire, recommends using a unique indentification number to follow a student from kindergarten through the twelfth grade.

3. Look for patterns of student and teacher performance over time to indicate possible strengths and weaknesses in teaching, programs, and organization.

4. Decide which data are worth collecting and analyzing. Think of data as more than test scores and numerical information. Emphasizing the potential of data to improve the organization, Razik and Swanson (2001) comment,

Data are to be used to isolate problem areas, to design corrective action, and to identify staff training needs. Data do not have to be of the standard statistical variety, however; the most useful kinds of data are frequently those generated by the employees themselves. (p. 454)

5. Use qualitative data in the form of surveys, opinion polls, interviews, feedback of all sorts from all stakeholders, and informal observations to gain insightful information. The use of varied data, soft and hard, formal and informal, formative and summative, is most likely to yield the best, most reliable information.

6. Do not overlook the importance of tracking and analyzing data on administrators, faculty, and staff, as well as students, as an important part of data analysis (e.g., attendance; portfolio development; student achievement; health and fitness; parental feedback; participation in professional growth opportunities, such as school and community activities, leadership, and work-study groups).

7. Encourage and support initiatives to assist faculty in becoming skilled and competent in classroom assessment of students' achievement, so they can rely more confidently and competently on these data in making decisions related to teaching and learning and in dealing with parents and community about accountability for children's achievement.

Finally, in thinking about collecting and analyzing various forms of data, it is important not to get lost in a sea of numbers and end-of-year reports, and drift from the purpose. Goens (2001) reminds us:

> Schools are sanctuaries for children where they can learn, make mistakes and find out about themselves and the world. When we focus so hard on numbers—test scores, attendance, data—we lose sight of the kids. We're in danger of making major issues minor and minor issues major. (p. 32)

We must look beyond easily accessed hard numbers to data that may not be as readily collected or numerically reportable. Because of the complexity of dealing with such quality-oriented data, it becomes more important for a school to dig deep when using data, to work as a team of stakeholders focused on teaching and learning who seek ways of answering more complex and more authentic questions. The stakeholders should determine for themselves the most important and truest indicators of the quality of their children's educational experiences, based on their shared beliefs, school vision, and mission, and not get sidetracked by statistical jargon and overly simplistic approaches to measuing student achievement.

Developing a School Profile and a Data Wall

It is one thing to collect data well, another to analyze it appropriately, and still another to interpret and maximize its use. In writing about how to capitalize on the data available to schools and districts, Superintendent Raymond Yeagley (2001) contends, "A greater challenge than collecting data is creating a process to transform the data into easily accessible, useful information that staff members will employ for school improvement" (p. 12). One way of handling the various data that Yeagley and a growing number of savvy administrators are using is to develop a data-based picture or profile of the school, which in itself becomes a more user-friendly format for accessing data, making decisions, and reporting school results. In making a case for collecting good data and developing a school profile, Marlin Tanck (1994) contends,

> Data for making informed decisions and reporting objectives are essential to the operation and leadership of the profession. A school data profile can describe the context in which learning occurs, some of the processes that influence learning, and the resulting attitudes, achievement, and performance of students. Such information provides a tool for setting goals, a context for individual classroom planning, and a basis for objective reporting to the public. It is vital to professional competence and accountability. (p. 92)

In the plentiful literature on school improvement processes, a first step often recommended is for stakeholders to develop an accurate and succinct profile of the students and community served by the school. A profile can be created in a number of ways, and many good resources exist to assist a school in using data that oftentimes are already available to develop the profile. Geannie Wells (2001), director of the Center for Accountability Solutions under the auspices of the American Association of School Administrators, writes,

> Through our experience we have found that each district's unique needs will determine which tool is best for them. There is no one-size-fits-all solution. New tools are being developed as we write, and districts should explore other available tools before making a decision. (p. 8)

Web sites of professional organizations such as the American Association of School Administrators (www.aasa.org), the Association of Supervision and Curriculum Development (www.ascd.org), and the National Staff Development Council (www.nsdc.org) are easily accessed, veritable treasure troves of current information on all types of resources available to school districts. These Web sites frequently include recommendations and reviews of multiple software packages for dealing with data, some of which are offered online free of charge (e.g., Quality School

Portfolio, developed by the National Center for Research on Evaluation, Standards, and Student Testing).

Data not already available to the school or district should be collected to form a comprehensive school profile, consisting of at least four major sections:

1. School and community demographics

2. Student performance indicators

3. School resources, programs, processes

4. Perceptual data about the quality of the school from all stakeholders

As expected, these areas parallel the data sources identified by Bernhardt (1998) and described in greater detail earlier in this chapter. Tanck (1994) recommends adding a fifth section containing diagnostic information that supports analysis and planning for a specific school improvement effort (p. 93).

Finally, a sixth component is recommended in creating a powerful, comprehensive school profile—a description of the school culture. Such a section tells the school's story by including those elements that make up the character of the school—the beliefs, values, norms of the school's stakeholders, its traditions, and any significant historical data that may have contributed to shaping the school's culture. The National Study of School Evaluation (NSSE), in its comprehensive work to assist schools with the implementation of improvement processes (Fitzpatrick, 1998), has this to say about the importance and purpose of a school profile:

> The value of a reliable information base cannot be overemphasized. Collection and careful analysis of pertinent information [are] critical in determining the effectiveness of the existing programs and services in your school. Moreover, the types of data collected for the profile can assist schools in planning and sustaining their school improvement initiatives in behalf of student learning . . . In short, the school's profile should provide a purposeful collection of the critical domains of information that tell the story of the school. All or any part of the information contained in the school's profile could be used to create reports for different audiences and may be disseminated in conventional ways, such as printed reports, or alternative ways, such as the school's Internet Web site. (pp. 1–1, 1–2)

Thus, although the profile is created from the collection and analysis of data from the six domains, it then becomes a data source itself for more accessible information that is easy to interpret and to keep updated for making decisions about teaching and learning and for sharing about the school and students with others. The collaborative, developmental process for creating a school profile is valuable as an end itself; however, the profile as a product is indeed a powerful tool for reporting to various audiences, for further directing the school's goals and objectives, and in planning most appropriately for instruction.

A good idea for making data more visible and user friendly is what Douglas Reeves (2006) calls the "Data Wall," a portable display using the cardboard three-panel displays frequently used for student science fairs with test data on the left panel, teaching strategies related to the tested subjects on the middle panel, and references and conclusions on the right panel. Advantages of this strategy for using data are that the displays

- Are simple to construct and do not create additional work
- Provide a valuable technique to jump-start better use of data, and
- Will ensure that the analysis of student data is not isolated to a single seminar or staff development program on data, but rather, becomes a continuous part of faculty and administrative decision making throughout the school year (pp. 196–199)

Reeves' book contains a thorough description of this strategy that is simple to implement but has great potential for improving the visibility and use of available data that too often remain dormant on a hard-drive or in a filing cabinet.

Research-Based, Data-Enhanced Decision Making

Too many bandwagons and panaceas to cure education's ills have diffused and distracted efforts toward more serious, painstaking reform needed by many of our country's schools in the past twenty years. The this-too-shall-pass mentality that often hinders legitimate school improvement efforts is primarily the result of educators' falling prey to claims of quick fixes for problems that, in reality, require substantial work and for which there are few, if any, shortcuts. If experience is not a sufficient lesson, then even a modicum of understanding about the dimensions of change should prevent principals and teachers from being so duped by greedy charlatans who flock to feed off the reform frenzy with their dubious wares—the latest fad or fantasy. Research about change is replete with validation of what it takes to impact the classroom and substantially improve teaching and learning. School practices that have proved most effective are based on sound principles and validated by strong research:

> The adoption of effective practices that are based on trustworthy research can be enormously difficult for schools because the temptation is to adopt fads that overemphasize ease and social or emotional appeal. These fads lack empirical evidence of their effectiveness and are based on invalid theoretical tenets . . . An essential feature of the implementation of research-based practices is that data on student performance must be collected frequently

and reliably to monitor the fidelity of the implementation . . . and the effectiveness of the practice. (U.S. Office of Special Education Programs, 2000, p. 5)

Systematically collecting and analyzing data related to programs and student achievement are a critically important dimension of what the literature calls practitioner-oriented, action-based research. Once a program or intervention based on reliable, research-validated practices in the field is adopted, then it becomes the school's responsibility to monitor that program during its implementation for the following purposes

- To provide a support system to assist faculty and staff with the new practice
- To ensure that what is identified as essential features of the new program are indeed being implemented as prescribed by the program
- To follow closely the progress of children
- To make reasonable adaptations that meet the unique needs of students and teachers involved, yet do not violate the program's essential features or sound educational practices

Throughout this text, the importance of participatory decision making has been emphasized. The degree of success of a new program's implementation is highly correlated to the degree of teacher participation in the decision-making process that leads to its adoption. The research on educational change is clear about the importance of stakeholders being involved from the start in innovation that hinges on their acceptance and implementation skill. "Educational change depends on what teachers do and think— it's as simple and as complex as that," writes Michael Fullan (1982, p. 107).

As teachers and administrators, parents, and community members work together to improve teaching and learning, it is important for them to look for sound, research-validated practices and programs to adopt. It is also important, once an innovation is implemented, to conduct a school's own action research by closely monitoring and supporting individuals as they become more skilled and acclimated to new practices and programs, by collecting data that can be used to make responsible, additional decisions about the adaptation and use of the new program and by analyzing the data related to student success (what is working, what is not, and with whom), as well as related costs over time for responsible, objective evaluation of the degree of the program's overall worth and effectiveness. Assistant Principal Eileen Greenspun (2001) contends,

Unless we do serious research and look carefully at results we are doomed to mediocrity. Let's do things like account for halo effects, do cost-benefit analyses, and try to stop selling the next best thing without looking carefully at it. (p. 644)

These research-oriented practices are absolutely essential to educators' accountability, and well within the capability and scope of their responsibility.

TAPPING INTO THE POWER OF TECHNOLOGY

"Because educational institutions are an integral part of the information industry, the remarkable advances in information and communication technologies hold enormous potential for revolutionizing schooling," claim Razik and Swanson (2001), who further state, "To date, however, that potential is largely unrealized" (p. 456). It is no secret that most schools lag behind most organizations in capitalizing on the multiple benefits of the wide array of technology available—computers, instructional television, recorders and cameras, interactive media, virtual classrooms, distance learning, and more. Today's technology has the potential for improving schools; it is multifaceted and has the power to totally transform schools as we know them. The following are uses of today's technology that improve schools most dramatically:

Data management—This might include anything from collection and storage, analysis and interpretation, to reporting varied data on students, staff, budgets, facilities, and materials.

Communicating, networking, connecting, marketing—Technology for communication can include communication among all stakeholders within and outside of the school and with other communities of learners both near and far away (e.g., other schools, parents, museums, libraries, community resources).

Professional development—Administrators, faculty, and staff can share ideas via the Internet and e-mail, participate in distance learning, and form study groups made up of local, state, national, and even global members.

Instruction—Technology can be used not just as an add-on to traditional forms of instruction but as a useful delivery tool to provide alternatives that improve access to and quality of instruction for all students by matching the needs of the child and the learning objective to the most powerful instructional medium. E-learning and virtual schools now make it possible to greatly enhance the personalization of instruction to meet students' divergent needs.

Curriculum management—Technology can be used to manage goals, objectives, units, timelines, teaching resources, and testing. Curriculum development processes of renewal, enrichment, and updating done with today's technology can be significantly more responsive to the needs of students and to changes necessary for the curriculum to be most relevant and current. Curriculum work facilitated by the power of technology can become most authentic by being approached as a fluid and continuously evolving process rather than as a product-oriented activity that is static and episodic.

Access to up-to-date research and information for staff, parents, and students—Technology provides ready access to a world of current information from professional organizations, government, schools and districts, technical and business experts, not to mention immediate access to many individuals, researchers, and original sources. Textbooks as the primary information source in classrooms are slowly, but surely, being replaced by digital media which is faster, more broad based, and in the long run more cost efficient as well.

Public schools must integrate the use of the power of technology similar to business and industry, which employ new technologies to increase productivity, not as an add-on to the curriculum or a high-tech frill in management processes. Using technology to replace certain management and instructional functions of the school in a more effective and cost-efficient manner is essential for educators. The U.S. Department of Education's Office of Educational Technology has developed "Action Steps" for schools and districts to take to upgrade their use of technology; these include specific recommendations for each of the following proposed actions:

1. Strengthen Leadership
2. Consider Innovative Budgeting
3. Improve Teacher Training
4. Support E-Learning and Virtual Schools
5. Encourage Broadband Access
6. Move Toward Digital Content
7. Integrate Data Systems

The report concludes with the statement, "Integrated, interoperable data systems are the key to better allocation of resources, greater management efficiency, and online and technology-based assessments of student performance that empower educators to transform teaching and personalize instruction" (U.S. Department of Education, 2004, p. 3).

Finally, with regard to technology's potential, it is important to understand that although equipment considerations consume the lion's share of time, attention, energy, and technology budgets in schools and districts, without well-selected, high-quality software, staff development, and sufficient planning by those who will use the equipment, the equipment's potential will surely go untapped. Even worse, having expensive technology that people do not know how to use or for which there is little or poor software is demoralizing and frustrating to staff and can actually detract from the quality of a school. As with anything new or innovative, education and training in how to use computers and related technology most effectively must be provided and must be ongoing. Such training is expensive, but in the long run it saves time and money by maximizing the potential of the equipment investments. In their article on technologies in schools, Schwab and Foa (2001) reported on what was then the current state of the art:

> The computer revolution in education continues to gather force. Judging from the media, one would assume that almost every student was learning on the Internet. But what's reported are the innovative examples, the pioneering teachers, and the "wow" potential. The reality is that there are still thousands of schools that have only aging computers in the library or a few newer machines clustered in a difficult-to-access computer lab. And even if there are computers in the classroom, there are still many more thousands of teachers who, while they know how to do word processing or even to search the Internet, don't have the slightest clue how to truly integrate technology into their teaching. The problem for educators nationwide is to scale up effective training to reach tens of thousands of teachers quickly. (p. 620)

Tapping the potential of today's technology is no longer an option or a luxury in providing accountable leadership. It is an essential, twenty-first-century power tool that has significant versatility in the hands of a skilled principal and staff in facilitating the school and community's efforts to improve the quality of teaching and learning for each child. Without it, the rhetoric about reaching all children is not likely to move past platitudes, mission statements, and campaign slogans. With technology properly used, schools and communities now have the opportunity to be truly responsive to each child's educational needs. Interestingly, the skilled use of technology holds the most promise for reaching all children and personalizing their school experiences in today's schools. Such is the irony: Technology, which is typically perceived as being cold and impersonal, has the potential to transform schools from formal institutions into warm, inviting, interactive learning communities.

In stark contrast to Schwab and Foa's (2001) rendition of the state of the technology art in most schools today, Razik and Swanson (2001) offer an exciting view of what they call emerging information-age schools that have tapped into the power of technology and have transformed themselves. These new-age schools are ones in which instruction is highly variable and responsive to the needs of the individual learner; the role of the teacher is reconceptualized into one of diagnostician, prescriber, motivator, facilitator, evaluator, and adviser; the focus is shifted almost entirely from teaching to learning that is highly prescriptive for each child and is continuous; traditional teaching is but one of many methods; school is viewed as a place of learning but not the center of learning, which is shifted to the student; and learning no longer is defined by time, place, or age but is continuous and supported throughout all segments of society. Razik and Swanson add,

> In an increasingly literate and sophisticated society, ways are being found to meet the unique needs of individual students at current or reduced costs. No longer need these two goals be mutually exclusive. They are being obtained concurrently in a few new schools designed specifically for the information age. These schools (1) place the learner in a role of active participant; (2) restructure the ratio of human and capital inputs in the schooling process, and (3) take advantage of existing information and communication technologies. To make them cost effective, these schools are designed systemically, making the use of instructional technology an integral part of the teaching-learning process. Innovations in pedagogy, curriculum, assessment, and school organization are developed simultaneously with innovations in instructional technology. (p. 458)

The power to make this transformation into today's information era is here, knocking at the schoolhouse door, and cramping outmoded approaches to education. Most lacking in our schools and communities are the vision, will, and determination to make the changes that are clearly within our grasp, empowered by the technology available to educators today.

Walking the Talk

An example of one state's commitment to integrate technology in its schools and its recognition of schools as being part of a system that must be considered when attempting to change any practice . . . of students, teachers, or administrators.

Supporting Change in Student Practice

The transition from a traditional teaching model to the effective utilization of one to one laptop access for all learners in Maine's schools recognizes that changing student practice is a core responsibility. *To this end, we must* realize that any school is a complex system, and that student practice cannot be changed independently of other system participants. This makes it clear that in order to change student practice, teacher practices must change, and in order for teacher practices to change, administrative practices must change, and community practices drive those *administrative practices*. MLTI supports Maine schools in recognizing and acting on an understanding of the complex nature of systems to work continuously to affect meaningful change. (www.Mainelearns .org/ovc/story_files/laptop_transition)

POINTERS FOR THE PRINCIPAL

- Capitalize on change to improve teaching and learning.
  - o Be proactive and try to shape change rather than simply adapting to it.
  - o Involve all stakeholders in school improvement initiatives.
  - o Encourage well-calculated risks to improve teaching and learning.
  - o Prepare stakeholders for the implementation dip (negative impact on student achievement) that frequently occurs in the first year of a new program.
  - o Treat change as a complex process, not an event.
  - o Plan ahead for the predictable stages people go through in changing.
  - o Focus primarily on how change will impact students and learning.

- Put data to work.
  - o Think broadly and gain access to a wide array of pertinent data.
  - o Collect qualitative and perceptual data in addition to numerical.
  - o Analyze data using disaggregation and longitudinal profiling.
  - o Develop a data-based school profile that can be easily accessed.
  - o Train and involve teachers and community in using data to make better decisions.

- Tap into the power of technology.
  - o Use technology to help you put data to work and to dig deeply into it.
  - o Maintain user-friendly databases on students, faculty, and community.
  - o Integrate technology into the school management systems, classrooms, and curriculum.
  - o Transform and personalize instruction with technology; infuse the curriculum with technology.
  - o Think of technology as an architectural and instructional tool, not as a frill or simply another piece to be added to the patchwork curriculum.
  - o Make technological training an ongoing must for everyone.
  - o Consider hiring a school-based technology specialist!

10

The Ultimate Leadership Tool

Personal Fitness

The busy principal asks, "How can I afford to take the time for personal fitness?" The wise principal knows, "I can't afford not to!"

We all understand too well the metaphor of the plumber with leaky pipes. Education's thrust is taking care of people. Yet too often educators neglect themselves and their own families in trying to fulfill their professional role as nurturers and care providers. This text's ultimate power can be realized only through the integrated use of the recommended strategies as tools in the strong hands, mind, and heart of a dedicated, caring, ever-developing, personally and professionally fit school leader. None of the tools in this text—not even maximized technology and good use of data—is powerful enough to compensate for a principal who does not feel well, lacks optimism, or is otherwise distracted by the problems often created by personal neglect.

The tools offered in this text for facilitating better instructional leadership are useful only when considered in tandem with each other and with the skills of a school leader who is personally fit and equipped with physical, mental, and spiritual stamina. A well-balanced, wholesome lifestyle is essential for the strong work ethic, physical fitness, nurturing spirit, wellspring of optimism, and an eagerness to continue to grow and learn that are required for a principal to lead a school to excellence.

Volumes have been written on how to live a good life. Obviously, because it is easier said (and written about) than done, there are far more how-to books on the subject than there are live role models for us to emulate. Despite the difficulty, leading a balanced life and maintaining one's fitness while in a position as demanding as a school principalship are imperative to providing lasting, excellent leadership. The magnitude of the principal's workload and the significance of the work are simply too great to expect less than healthy people to assume them with any degree of competence.

INVESTING IN PERSONAL FITNESS

Personal investments are essential to fitness and the ability to deal optimally with life and work, but this does not always mean spending excessive amounts of time and money on fitness programs, equipment, therapists, and expensive vacations. The most worthwhile personal investments we can make are our daily efforts to develop a healthy lifestyle, which translates into living a well-balanced life. Balance is achieved only if we attend to all aspects of our humanness, which include the following:

- Our physical well-being, which entails the need for proper diet, exercise, and rest
- Our spiritual well-being, which entails the need for reflection and introspection about the meaning of life, this world, and our place in it
- Our social well-being, which entails the need for companionship, love, and wholesome interaction with others
- Our intellectual well-being, which entails the need for learning and mental growth throughout our lives
- Our emotional well-being, which entails the need for us to understand the uniqueness of our psychological makeup and how it influences our interaction with others

What indicators are critical and fundamental to personal well-being? If you've not taken the time or had the will recently to indulge in just one more *Oprah Winfrey Show* or read Dr. Phil's or Dr. Laura's take on personal improvement, perhaps the following questions will help you take stock and reflect on what's involved in taking good care of yourself:

Physical Fitness

- How many calories do you consume on average in a typical day?
- How nutrition conscious are you? For example, approximately what percentage of your diet is made up of fresh fruits and vegetables?

- How has your weight changed in the past five, ten, or fifteen years?
- How have you adapted your diet and exercise to meet your changing needs during the past five, ten, or fifteen years?
- How often do you engage in some form of moderately rigorous, physical exertion that lasts more than ten minutes?
- How are your agility and reflexes? How do you keep them sharp?
- When's the last time you tried touching your toes? Doing jumping jacks? Walking at a brisk pace for at least a mile?
- Do you regularly get enough sleep? Do you usually awaken refreshed?
- Do you have at least one physical checkup annually?
- What's your average blood pressure?
- Do you pay sufficient attention to your personal grooming?

Emotional and Social Fitness

- How easily do you get frustrated, upset, or angry?
- Are you able to cope with life's ups and downs and maintain an even keel most of the time?
- Are you optimistic about solving problems and the goodness of humankind?
- When is the last time you took at least a week's vacation with your family?
- When is the last time you had a whole weekend devoted solely to family, hobbies, and relaxation?
- How hooked are you on TV, cell phones, video games, PDAs?
- What do you do to unwind that completely removes you from your work?
- How regularly do you indulge in your own personal interests and those of your family?
- How many really good friends do you have? How often do you socialize with them?
- Do you have a network of mutually supportive others in your life?
- How satisfied are you with your relationships with loved ones (spouse, children, friends, neighbors, relatives)?
- How good do you feel about yourself and your appearance?

Intellectual Fitness

- What's the most recent book you've read?
- What new something have you learned to do in the past year?
- Do you actively seek ways to increase your mental abilities (memory, alertness, perception, openness)?
- How well can you concentrate and focus your attention on in-depth, complex tasks?
- How easily distracted are you?

- Do you seek (or avoid) challenges to continue learning and growing?
- Do you usually see change as a threat or as an opportunity for growth and development?
- Are you afraid of problems or do you accept them as a way of life and learn to hone your problem-solving skills as a major key to living well?

Spiritual Fitness

- How do you replenish your inner sources of strength and resilience?
- On what do you rely for regular spiritual renewal?
- How often do you reflect on the things in life that mean most to you?
- Do your use of time and your behaviors reflect your values?
- How well can you articulate your philosophy of life?
- Can people recognize your philosophy by how you live?
- What are your life priorities? Are they evident in the way you live?
- Do you spend your time and energy on the things that you cherish most?
- What are your strongest sources of personal motivation?
- How satisfied are you with the way you feel and how you live your life?

COMMON PITFALLS OF THE PRINCIPALSHIP

Do not be discouraged or misled. The position of school principal can be one of the most rewarding professions on earth; however, it can also wreak havoc on one's personal life. Heed the following problems that frequently plague principals and take the necessary precautions to avoid their striking home.

Too Much Work and Little of Anything Else

Shortchanging any of the dimensions of our humanness eventually takes its toll on our lives and our work. When one dimension of our lives becomes too dominant, it eventually leads to some form of atrophy in one way or another, and because the various facets of our lives are all connected, other parts will eventually suffer from the effects of the weakened link.

There is no such thing as separating one's personal and professional lives. To excel at work over time, a person must strategize to do what Steven Covey (2004) calls "sharpening the saw," maintaining balance in one's life with regular, sufficient investments in all areas of humanness to sustain and renew oneself.

Ignoring One's Own Mortality

Pay attention to your ever-changing needs. We are always changing. If we are healthy beings, the changes involve learning, adapting, and getting better at being our best. However, too often we form habits of behavior that are resistant to change, despite our need to make continuing adjustments and adaptations. No area seems more illustrative of our lifelong metamorphosis than our bodies. Diet and exercise are important at any age, but the specifics of how best to provide nutrition and exercise are continually changing. Most of us know what we are reluctant to heed: At age forty-five, we should not expect to be able to eat the way we did at twenty-five unless we increase our physical activity to compensate for the decline in metabolic rate. However, not only are most people less active, but also many people actually eat more than they did when they were younger. So the pounds pile on, the energy goes down, and the exercise is further diminished by the excess weight and lethargy—a surefire formula for obesity and a host of related physical problems.

Most principals are at the time in their lives when they need to pay closer attention to eating leaner foods, exercising more deliberately, and including a variety of physical activities in their leisure time. Because our individual needs vary, it is important to bone up on the nutrition and diet literature and experiment to find out what works best for you to maintain healthy weight, strength, and good muscle tone. It is vital to pay attention to your changing needs, invest time and effort to learn about what works for you and your body, and then do your best to eat right and exercise regularly to look and feel your best—and lead most ably.

Marginalizing Spiritual Needs

Most of us have our own preferred ways of being spiritually replenished. For some, the church and an active religious life help to meet that need. But there are many other forms of spiritual renewal. For many of us, communing with nature can be pure therapy for a troubled mind and cluttered brain. There is no greater source of spiritual regeneration for me than a stroll under crystal blue skies, the feel and smell of lush green grass, gentle breezes rustling the leaves of trees on a summer afternoon, or a walk under the stars on a clear, moonlit night. Taking time to enjoy a peaceful, quiet time outside is balm to a soul and can help us return more easily to our spiritual roots and core values that anchor us in difficult times.

Listening to music, nurturing a friendship, reading a good book, or indulging in a recreation or hobby are other ways of replenishing one's spiritual self. These enjoyable experiences are too often viewed as luxuries, rather than as the essential fuel for the soul that they are. The time we invest in our spirituality is well spent, makes us stronger people, and—of course—impacts the quality of our performance at work. Our need for spiritual investing should not be trivialized or neglected any more than our need for adequate food and exercise, and each of us must find those forms of spiritual regeneration that work best for us.

Confusing Positional Authority With Personal Power

The position of the principalship brings with it a degree of authority that has little to do with who you are or what you stand for. Such a position of leadership also brings with it the assurance that sometime, somehow, you are going to make someone unhappy, just by responsibly doing your job. On the flipside, your authority will assure you of a certain degree of prestige that can also have little to do with you as an individual. No one is indispensable—not even you or I. Resist taking yourself too seriously and forgetting that the esteem you have is, at least in part, related to the position, not to you.

Although you certainly want (and need) the approval of your constituencies overall, you will never make an outstanding principal if you are overly concerned about being popular. Effective principals develop their personal power by acting with integrity and doing their best to stay focused on the welfare of students, day in and day out. Do your best while you are in the position to make the most of the authority it grants you to develop your personal power through consistently acting with honesty, fairness, and purpose to make a positive difference in the lives of students. This steadfastness builds trust and respect—which are much preferred and more effective and lasting than popularity.

Neglecting Significant Others

A job and career are important, but being a principal should not be the top priority in your life. Principals (good ones) are some of the busiest people I know. The demands of the principalship can consume you, unless you make a commitment to yourself and your family to put your family first. Everyone needs love and nurturing. We need to nurture our loved ones and be nurtured in return. Most intelligent people know this, but many conscientious principals get so caught up in their work that they forget it is not what will sustain them over the long haul. Time must be made for family and friends for the relationships to thrive. Everything that gives to us in life must in turn be given to. The no-free-lunch principle operates across the board.

Divorce and estrangement tear at the threads of all family members' fabric of well-being and usually lead to a multitude of peripheral problems. Sadly, a divorce often has a far more lasting impact than the marriage. It is impossible for most folks ever to rid themselves completely of the ravages of a divorce. The problems that generally ensue (e.g., emotional stress, confused children, financial losses) take their toll on the rest of family members' lives. Unfortunately, principals are particularly susceptible to marital problems and divorce, and statistics are particularly grim for female school administrators, who are even more likely to be divorced or single than their male counterparts.

Acquiring a Lone Ranger Mentality

Despite how much credit or blame you give yourself, other people to whom you are connected are vital players in your successes and failures. Principals often try to carry the weight of the world on their shoulders. Regardless of how independent and solitary the phrase "the buck stops here" sounds, no man, woman, husband, wife, or principal is an island. Graciously accepting our inevitable human interdependency and deliberately nurturing a personal network of supportive others will enhance our ability to involve people in our lives in wholesome ways that not only affirm our respect for them and acknowledge their importance to us but also improve the quality of our personal effectiveness. Lone-ranger thinking can lead to inflated notions of importance, wherein a person is inclined to take all the credit for successes, assume all the blame for failures, or both. Either perspective minimizes the importance of others' contributions and is badly flawed, grossly exaggerated, and ultimately self-destructive.

Becoming an "Administriviator"

"Make time," advises Wayne Dyer (2007), "to do something you've never done before—it could be walking barefoot in the rain, taking a yoga class, speaking before a group at a Toastmaster's Club . . . or anything else you've always wanted to do. Recognize that you've created restrictions for yourself that keep you from new and expanding experiences, and find the time now to close your personal rule book and plunge in where you've never before wandered" (p. 277).

It is hoped that you are among the majority of us who purport our motivation for choosing education to be our love of helping others—especially children—to succeed. Revisit that internal value often, lest you forget it under a pile of stuff to do on your desk, in your hard-drive, or at the meeting downtown. Remember the joy that comes from mingling with students, getting acquainted with them as individuals, and building relationships with parents, teachers, and community that maximize support for students' success. These are the most important politics of the position, which should not be denied or neglected and without which many principals find themselves depleted of their original enthusiasm as an educator, a significant contributor to being an effective leader. Stay in touch with what energizes and excites you about your profession—and life in general.

Best of luck to each of you, school leaders, as you make the most of your personal strengths, professional prowess, and the opportunities of your day in the sun (positions of leadership) to contribute your best to society through your work for our children.

IN CONCLUSION

Taken together, this compendium text of skills, suggestions, and strategies becomes a collection of integrated, interrelated, powerful tools for leaders to transform schools into learning communities in which they can most effectively channel the work of the organization toward accomplishing education's primary mission: students' achievement and success. These should be the threads that bind a healthy, learning village—the village's mutual concerns for children's well-being—which, when woven together, create a strong alliance, a safety net, a security blanket for students that will ultimately transform the at-risk populations into increasing numbers of students who are most likely to succeed—at school, at home, in the community, and beyond. What else is more important in this world?

Recommended Toolbox Resources

CHAPTERS 1 AND 2

Compass and Nuts and Bolts of Leadership

Web Sites

http://www.ccsso/ISLLC2008Research: a comprehensive online database provided by the Council of Chief State School Officers, with empirical research reports, policy analyses, leadership texts, and other credible resources which support the six 2008 ISLLC standards

http://www.naesp.org: Web site of the National Association of Elementary School Principals

http://www.nassp.org: Web site of the National Association of Secondary School Principals

http://www.truenorthleadership.com: contains a variety of well-known organizational and leadership assessment instruments (e.g., Inventory of Leadership Style; Myers-Briggs Type Indicator; Emotional Competence Inventory created by Daniel Goleman and Richard Boyatzis; Emotional Quotient Inventory)

Workbooks

Bennis, W. G., & Goldsmith, J. (2003). *Learning to lead: A workbook on becoming a leader.* Reading, MA: Perseus.

Brubaker, D., & Coble, L. (2005). *The hidden leader: Leadership lessons on the potential within.* Thousand Oaks, CA: Corwin.

Daresh, J. C. (2006). *Beginning the principalship: A practical guide for new school leaders* (3rd ed.). Thousand Oaks, CA: Corwin.

Kouzes, J., & Posner, B. (2003). *The leadership challenge workbook.* San Francisco: Jossey-Bass.

Portfolio Development Guides

Campbell, D. M, Cignetti, P. B., Melenyzer, B. J., Nettles, D. H., & Wyman, R. M. (1997). *How to develop a professional portfolio.* Boston: Allyn & Bacon.

Tuttle, H. G. (1997, January/February). Electronic portfolios. *Multimedia Schools,* pp. 33–37.

CHAPTER 3

Blueprints (Mission, Vision, Goals and Objectives)

Web Sites for Developing a School-Based Vision

http://www.leading-learning.co.nz

Quality Learning: Before creating a shared vision, assess your school

http://www.leading-learning.co.nz/school-vision/assess-school.html: The assessment instrument found here may be helpful.

Quality Learning: Creating a vision

http://www.leading-learning.co.nz/creating-vision.html: Visit this Web site to read more about creating a vision for your school. It is instructive for the new principal (step by step).

Teamwork Survey

http://www.leading-learning.co.nz/school-vision/teamwork-survey.html: A team aligned behind shared expectations is the key to a modern organization. This is an activity to introduce before a vision-building process. It is also an ideal School Self-Review questionnaire. The survey is titled "How Good is Your Teamwork?"

http://www.ncrel.org: Web site of the North Central Regional Educational Laboratory

Article

Peterson, K. (1995). Critical issue: Building a collective vision. Retrieved November 26, 2009, from http://www.ncrel.org/sdrs/areas/issues/educa trs/leadrshp/le100.htm.

CHAPTER 4

Organizational Superglue (School Culture)

Books

Daresh, J. C. (2006). Learning your school's culture (p. 125), in *Beginning the principalship: A practical guide for new school leaders* (3rd ed.). Thousand Oaks, CA: Corwin.

Deal, T. E., & Peterson, K. D. (1999). *Shaping school culture: The heart of leadership.* San Francisco: Jossey Bass.

CHAPTER 5

Organizational Conduits (Communication Strategies)

Book

Murphy, C. U., & Lick, W. L. (2005). *Whole-faculty study groups: Creating professional learning communities that target student learning* (3rd ed.). Thousand Oaks, CA: Corwin.

Web Site

http://www.sedl.org/connections/resources/evidence.pdf: Southwest Educational Development Laboratory's Web site, containing the National Center for Family and Community Connections with Schools

CHAPTER 6

Whetstones for Facilitating Professional Development

Books

Dufour, R., & Eaker, R. (1998). *Professional learning communities: Best practices for enhancing student achievement.* Bloomington, IN: Solution Tree.

Fullan, M. (2005). *Leadership and sustainability: System thinkers in action.* Thousand Oaks, CA: Corwin.

Fullan, M. (2008). *What's worth fighting for in the principalship.* New York: Teachers College Press.

Murphy, C. U., & Lick, D.W. (2005). *Whole-faculty study groups: Creating student-based professional development* (2nd ed.). Thousand Oaks, CA: Corwin.

Web Sites

http://www.schlechtycenter.org: The Web site of the Schlechty Center for Leadership in School Reform—a private, nonprofit corporation with headquarters in Louisville, Kentucky, established by Dr. Phillip C. Schlechty in 1988. Its stated purpose is "to provide high-quality and responsive support to public school leaders to transform schools from organizations that produce compliance and attendance to organizations that nurture attention and commitment at all levels in the system."

http://www.nsdc.org: The Web site of the National Staff Development Council, the largest nonprofit professional association committed to ensuring success for all students through staff development and school improvement. Its stated purpose is that "[e]very educator engages in effective professional learning every day so every student achieves."

CHAPTER 7

Lens of Instructional Leadership

Books and Articles

Association for Supervision and Curriculum Development (2004). *The new principal's fieldbook: Strategies for success.* Alexandria, VA: Association for Supervision and Curriculum Development.

Heifetz, R. A., & Laurie, D. L. (1997). The work of leadership. *Harvard Business Review, 75*(1), 124–134.

Reeves, D. B. (2006). *The learning leader: How to focus school improvement for better results.* Alexandria, VA: Association for Supervision and Curriculum Development.

Schmoker, M. (2004). Tipping point: From reckless to substantive instructional improvement. *Phi Delta Kappan, 85,* 424–432.

Web Sites

http://www.ecs.org: Education Commission of the States, a nonpartisan interstate compact created in 1965 by the states and the U.S. Congress to help governors, legislators, state education officials, business leaders, and others identify, develop, and implement public policies to improve student learning at all levels

http://www.gse.harvard.edu/~principals: The Principals' Center at the Harvard Graduate School of Education, dedicated to the personal and professional development of school principals

http://www.nlns.org: New Leaders for New Schools aims to improve education for every child by attracting and preparing the next generation of outstanding leaders for urban public schools.

CHAPTER 8

Tape Measures, Plumb Lines, and Common Sense (Accountability and Testing)

Web Sites

http://www.ecs.org/nclbreauthorization: a database on NCLB issues maintained by the Education Commission of the States

http://www.nea.org/esea/nearesources-esea.html: updates on the federal legislation related to the Elementary and Secondary Education Act and its 2002 version, No Child Left Behind, maintained on the Web site of the National Education Association

http://www.resultsforamerica.org/education/toolkit

http://www.fairtest.org: National Center for Fair and Open Testing (FairTest) works to end the misuses and flaws of standardized testing and to ensure that evaluation of students, teachers, and schools is fair, open, valid, and educationally beneficial.

http://www.bc.edu/research/nbetp: The National Board on Educational Testing and Public Policy, housed in the Lynch School of Education at Boston College, is an independent organization that monitors testing in the United States. The Board provides ongoing information on the uses and outcomes of educational testing for decision-making purposes, paying special attention to groups historically underserved by the educational system

CHAPTER 9

Power Tools (Technology and Data)

Book

Fullan, M. (2005). *Leadership and sustainability: System thinkers in action.* Thousand Oaks, CA: Corwin.

Web Site

http://www.ed.gov.about/office/list/os/technology: the official site of the National Technology Plan for the U.S. Department of Education

CHAPTER 10

Personal Fitness

Books

Covey, S. (2004). *The seven habits of highly effective people: Power lessons in personal change.* New York: Free Press.

Dyer, W. W. (2007). *Change your thoughts—change your life: Living the wisdom of the Tao.* Carlsbad, CA: Hay House.

Workbooks

Bennis, W. G., & Goldsmith, J. (2003). *Learning to lead: A workbook on becoming a leader.* Reading, MA: Perseus.

Brubaker, D., & Coble, L. (2005). *The hidden leader: Leadership lessons on the potential within.* Thousand Oaks, CA: Corwin .

Daresh, J. C. (2006). *Beginning the principalship: A practical guide for new school leaders* (3rd ed.). Thousand Oaks, CA: Corwin .

Kouzes, J., & Posner, B. (2003). *The leadership challenge workbook.* San Francisco: Jossey-Bass.

References

PREFACE

Glickman, C. (1985). *Supervision and instruction: A developmental approach.* Boston: Allyn & Bacon.

Glickman, C. D. (2008). *Leadership for purposeful schools: Fulfilling the promise of a whole education.* Special feature lecture, ASCD annual conference, New Orleans.

CHAPTER 1

Barth, R. (1990). *Improving schools from within: Teachers, parents, and principals can make a difference.* San Francisco: Jossey-Bass.

Bennis, W., & Goldsmith, J. (2003). *Learning to lead: A workbook on becoming a leader.* Reading, MA: Perseus.

Brubaker, D., & Coble, L. (2005). *The hidden leader: Leadership lessons on the potential within.* Thousand Oaks, CA: Corwin.

Covey, S. (1991). *Principle-centered leadership.* New York: Simon & Schuster.

Covey, S. (2004). *The seven habits of highly effective people: Power lessons in personal change.* New York: Free Press.

Daresh, J. C. (2006). *Beginning the principalship: A practical guide for new school leaders* (3rd ed.). Thousand Oaks, CA: Corwin

Fullan, M. (2008). *What's worth fighting for in the principalship: Strategies for taking charge in the elementary school principalship.* New York: Teachers College Press.

Greenfield, W. (1985, June). Instructional leadership: Muddles, puddles, and pioneers. Paper presented at the Dogue M. Smith Lecture, University of Georgia, Athens.

Hersey, P., Blanchard, K., & Johnson, D. (2008). *Management of organizational behavior* (7th ed.). Mahwah, NJ: Prentice-Hall.

Hodgkinson, C. (1991). *Educational leadership: The moral art.* Albany, NY: SUNY Press.

Hoerr, T. (2008). Stop, look, and listen. *Educational Leadership, 65*(8), 88–89.

Interstate School Leader Licensure Consortium (ISLLC). (2008). *Standards for school leaders.* Washington, DC: Council of Chief State School Officers.

Kouzes, J., & Posner, B. (2008). *The student leadership challenge.* San Francisco: Jossey-Bass.

Marzano, Waters, & McNulty with the Mid-Continental Research on Education Laboratory, 2003.

National Association of Elementary School Principals (NAESP). (1991). *Proficiencies for principals: Elementary and middle schools*. Alexandria, VA: NAESP.

National Association of Elementary School Principals (NAESP). (2008). *Leading learning communities: Standards for what principals should know and be able to do*. Alexandria, VA: NAESP.

National Policy Board for Educational Administration (NPBEA). (1993). *Principals for our Changing schools: Knowledge and skill base*. Fairfax, VA: NPBEA.

Razik, T., & Swanson, A. (2001). *Fundamental concepts of educational leadership* (2nd ed.). Upper Saddle River, NJ: Prentice-Hall.

Rooney, J. (2008). What do we believe? *Educational Leadership, 65*(5), 88–90.

Schwahn, C., & Spady, W. (1998). *Total leaders: Applying the best future-focused change strategies to education*. Arlington, VA: American Association of School Administrations.

Sergiovanni, T. (1996). *Moral leadership: Getting to the heart of school improvement*. San Francisco: Jossey-Bass.

Sergiovanni, T. (2006). *The principalship: A reflective practice perspective* (5th ed.). Boston: Allyn & Bacon.

Sergiovanni, T., & Starratt, R. (2007). *Supervision: A redefinition* (8th ed.). New York: McGraw-Hill.

CHAPTER 2

Bennis, W., & Nanus, B. (1985). *Leaders: The strategies for taking charge*. New York: Harper and Row.

Blase, J. R., & Blase, R. R. (2004). *Handbook of instructional leadership: How successful principals promote teaching and learning* (2nd ed.). Thousand Oaks, CA: Corwin.

Cotton, K. (2003). *Principals and student achievement: What the research says*. Alexandria, VA: Association for Supervision and Curriculum Development.

Council of Chief State School Officers (CCSSO). (2008). *Educational Leadership Policy Standards: ISLLC 2008*. Adopted by the National Policy Board for Educational Administration. Washington, DC: CCSSO.

Daresh, J., & Playko, M. (1995). *Supervision as a proactive process: Concepts and cases* (2nd ed.). Prospect Heights, IL: Waveland Press.

Goodlad, J. (1994). *Educational renewal: Better teachers, better schools*. San Francisco: Jossey-Bass.

Hallinger, P., & Heck, R. (1998). Exploring the principal's contribution to school effectiveness: 1980–1995. *School Effectiveness and School Improvement, 9*(2), 157–191.

Jacques, E. (1989). *Requisite organization: The CEO's guide to creative structures of leadership*. London: Cason Hall.

Leiberman, A. (1995). Practices that support teacher development. *Phi Delta Kappan, 76*, 591–596.

Leithwood, K., Jantzi, D., & Steinbach, R. (1999). *Changing leadership for changing times*. Philadelphia, PA: Open University Press.

Leithwood, K., Louis, K., Andersen, S., & Wahlstrom, K. (2004). *How leadership influences student learning: Review of research*. Minneapolis, MN: Center for Applied Research, University of Minnesota.

Leithwood, K., & Riehl, C. (2005). What do we already know about educational leadership? In W. Firestone & C. Riehl (Eds.), *A new agenda for research in educational leadership* (pp. 12–27). New York: Teachers College Press.

Lunenburg, F. C., & Ornstein, A. C. (2008). *Educational administration: Concepts and practices* (5th ed.). Belmont, CA: Wadsworth/Thomson Learning.

Marzano, R., Waters, T., & McNulty, B. (2005). *School leadership that works: From research to results.* Aurora, CO: Mid-continent Research for Education and Learning (McREL).

National Association of Elementary School Principals (NAESP). (1990). *Principals for 21st century schools.* Alexandria, VA: NAESP.

National Association of Elementary School Principals (NAESP). (2008). *Leading learning communities: Standards for what principals should know and be able to do.* Alexandria, VA: NAESP.

National Commission for the Principalship (NCP). (1990). *Principals for our changing schools.* (Scott Thomson, Ed.). Fairfax, VA: NCP.

Peterson, K. (1999, March). The role of principals in successful schools. *Reform Talk:* Comprehensive Regional Assistance Center Consortium-Region, 3.

Razik, T., & Swanson, A. (2008). *Fundamental concepts of educational leadership* (3rd ed.). Upper Saddle River, NJ: Prentice-Hall.

Reeves, D. (2006). *The learning leader: How to focus school improvement for better results.* Alexandria, VA: Association for Supervision and Curriculum Development.

Rooney, J. (2008, February). What do we believe? *Educational Leadership, 65*(5), 88–90.

Schlechty, P. (1990). *Schools for the 21st century: Leadership imperatives for educational reform.* San Francisco: Jossey-Bass.

CHAPTER 3

Allen, L. (2001). From plaques to practice: How schools can breathe life into their guiding beliefs. *Phi Delta Kappan, 83*(4), 289–293.

Beck, L. G. (1994). *Reclaiming educational administration as a caring profession.* New York: Teachers College Press.

Bennis, W. G. (1997). *Managing people is like herding cats.* Provo, UT: Executive Excellence Publishers.

Bennis, W. G., & Goldsmith, J. (1997). *Learning to lead: A workbook on becoming a leader.* Reading, MA: Perseus Books.

Blase, J. R., & Blase, R. R. (1997). *The fire is back! Principals sharing school governance.* Thousand Oaks, CA: Corwin.

Block, P. (1987). *The empowered manager: Positive political skills at work.* San Francisco: Jossey-Bass.

Brown, G., & Irby, B. (2001). *The principal portfolio* (2nd ed.). Thousand Oaks, CA: Corwin.

Covey, S. (1991). *Principle-centered leadership.* New York: Summit Books.

Drucker, P. (1993). *Managing for the future: The 1990s and beyond.* New York: Truman Talley Books/Plume.

Fullan, M. (1997). *What's worth fighting for in the principalship? Strategies for taking charge in the elementary school principalship.* New York: Teachers College Press.

Fullan, M. (2008). *What's worth fighting for in the principalship? Strategies for taking charge in the elementary school principalship* (2nd ed.). New York: Teachers College Press.

Kouzes, J. M., & Posner B. Z. (2007). *The Leadership Challenge* (4th ed.). San Francisco: Jossey-Bass.

Newman, M., & Simmons, W. (2000). Leadership for student learning. *Phi Delta Kappan, 82*(1), 9–12.

Reeves, D. (2006). *The learning leader: How to focus school improvement for better results.* Alexandria, VA: Association for Supervision and Curriculum Development.

Rossow, L. F. (1990). *The principalship: Dimensions in instructional leadership.* Englewood Cliffs, NJ: Prentice-Hall.

Rossow, L. F. (2000). *The principalship: Dimensions in instructional leadership* (2nd ed.). Englewood Cliffs, NJ: Prentice-Hall.

Schwahn C. J., & Spady, W. G. (1998). *Total leaders: Applying the best future-focused change strategies to education.* Arlington, VA: American Association of School Administrators.

Senge, P. M. (1990). *The fifth discipline: The art and practice of the learning organization.* New York: Doubleday Currency.

Senge, P. M. (2006). *The fifth discipline: The art and practice of the learning organization* (2nd ed). New York: Doubleday Currency.

CHAPTER 4

Austin, G., & Holowenzak, S. (1985). *An examination of ten years of research on exemplary schools.* In G. Austin & H. Garber (Eds.), *In search of exemplary schools* (pp. 65–82). Orlando, FL: Academic Press.

Bennis, W. G., & Goldsmith, J. (1997). *Learning to lead: A workbook on becoming a leader.* Reading, MA: Perseus.

Cotton, K. (1995). *Effective schooling practices: A research synthesis: 1995 update.* Portland, OR: Northwest Regional Educational Laboratory.

Daresh, J. C. (2006). *Beginning the principalship: A practical guide for new school leaders* (3rd ed). Thousand Oaks, CA: Corwin.

Deal, T. E., & Peterson, K. D. (1999). *Shaping school culture: The heart of leadership.* San Francisco: Jossey-Bass.

Glatthorn, A. (1993). *Learning twice.* New York: HarperCollins.

Hallinger, P., Bickman, L., & Davis, K. (1990, June). *What makes a difference? School context, principal leadership and student achievement.* The National Center for Educational Leadership, Occasional Paper No. 3 (ED 332 341).

Halpin, A., & Croft, D. (1963). *The organizational climate of schools.* Chicago: University of Chicago Press.

Hoy, W., & Tarter, J. (1997). *The road to open and healthy schools: A handbook for change* (Elementary and middle school ed.). Thousand Oaks, CA: Corwin.

Hoyle, J., English, F., & Steffy, B. (1994). *Skills for successful school leaders* (2nd ed.). Arlington, VA: American Association of School Administrators.

Kouzes, J. M., & Posner B. Z. (2007). *The Leadership Challenge* (4th ed.). San Francisco: Jossey-Bass.

Larsen, T. J. (1987, April). *Identification of instructional leadership behaviors and the impact of their implementation on academic achievement.* University of Colorado (ERIC Document Reproduction Service No. ED 281 286).

Leithwood, K., Louis, K., Andersen, S., & Wahlstrom, K. (2004). *How leadership influences student learning: Review of research.* Minneapolis, MN: Center for Applied Research, University of Minnesota.

Leithwood, K., & Riehl, C. (2003, March). *What do we already know about successful school leaders?* Paper presented at the Annual Meeting of the American Educational Research Association, Chicago, IL.

Lunenburg, F., & Ornstein, A. (2000). *Educational administration: Concepts and practices* (3rd ed.). Belmont, CA: Wadsworth/Thomson Learning.

Lunenburg, F., & Ornstein, A. (2008). *Educational administration: Concepts and practices* (5th ed.). Belmont, CA: Wadsworth/Thomson Learning.

Marzano, R., Waters, T., & McNulty, B. (2005). *School leadership that works: From research to results.* Aurora, CO: Mid-continent Research for Education and Learning (McREL).

National Association of Elementary School Principals (NAESP). (1991). *Proficiencies for principals: Elementary and middle schools.* Alexandria, VA: NAESP.

Peters, T. J., & Waterman, R. H. (2004). *In search of excellence.* New York: HarperCollins.

Sergiovanni, T. (1991). *The principalship: A reflective practice perspective* (2nd ed.). Boston: Allyn & Bacon.

Sergiovanni, T. (2009). *The principalship: A reflective practice perspective* (6th ed.). Boston: Allyn & Bacon.

Snowden, P. E., & Gorton, R. A. (1998). *School leadership and administration: Important concepts, case studies, and simulations.* New York: McGraw-Hill.

Snowden, P. E., Gorton, R. A., & Alston, J. A. (2007). *School leadership and administration: Important concepts, case studies, and simulations* (7th ed.). New York: McGraw-Hill.

Weick, K. (1985). *The significance of culture.* In P. Frost, L. Moore, M. Reis, J. Lundberg, & J. Martin (Eds.), *Organizational culture.* Beverly Hills, CA: Sage.

CHAPTER 5

Association of Supervision and Curriculum Development (ASCD). (1998). *The principal series: Facilitator's guide.* Alexandria, VA: ASCD.

Blase, J. R., & Blase, R. R. (2004). *Handbook of instructional leadership: How successful principals promote teaching and learning* (2nd ed.). Thousand Oaks, CA: Corwin.

Covey, S. (1992). *Principle-centered leadership.* New York: Simon & Schuster.

Daresh, J. (2006). *Beginning the principalship: A practical guide for new school leaders.* (3rd ed.). Thousand Oaks, CA: Corwin.

Dolan, P. (1994). *Restructuring our schools.* Kansas City, MO: Systems and Organizations.

Fullan, M. (1994). *What's worth fighting for in the principalship?* New York: Teachers College Press.

Gallagher, D. R., Bagin, D., & Kindred, L. W. (1996). *The school and community.* Boston: Allyn & Bacon.

Green, R. L. (2001). *Practicing the art of leadership.* Upper Saddle River, NJ: Prentice-Hall.

Henderson, A. T., & Mapp, K. L. (2002). *A new wave of evidence: The impact of school, family, and community connections on student achievement.* National Center for family & Community Connections with Schools—Southwest Educational Development Laboratory: Austin, Texas. Retrieved November 26, 2008, from http://www.sedl.org/connections/resources/evidence.pdf.

Houston, P. (2001). It takes a village to raise achievement. *The School Administrator, 6*(58), 46.

Lunenburg, F. C., & Ornstein, A. C. (2000). *Educational administration: Concepts and practices* (4th ed.). Belmont, CA: Wadsworth/Thomson Learning.

Lunenburg, F. C., & Ornstein, A. C. (2008). *Educational administration: Concepts and practices* (5th ed.). Belmont, CA: Wadsworth/Thomson Learning.

Lysaught, J. P. (1984). Toward a comprehensive theory of communication: A review of selected contributions. *Educational Administration Quarterly, 20*(3), 10–127.

McEwan, E. (2003). *Seven steps to effective instructional leadership* (2nd ed.). Thousand Oaks, CA: Corwin.

National Association of Elementary School Principals (NAESP). (1991). *Proficiencies for principals: Elementary and middle schools.* Alexandria, VA: NAESP.

National Association of Elementary School Principals (NAESP). (2008). *Leading learning communities: Standards for what principals should know and be able to do.* Alexandria, VA: NAESP.

Newman, M., & Simmons, W. (2000). Leadership for student learning. *Phi Delta Kappan, 82*(1), 9–12.

Sashkin, M., & Walberg, H. J. (Eds.). (1993). *Educational leadership and school culture.* Berkeley, CA: McCutchan.

Schwahn, C., & Spady, W. (1998). *Total leaders: Applying the best future-focused change strategies to education.* Arlington, VA: American Association of School Administrators.

Sergiovanni, T. (1992). *Moral leadership: Getting to the heart of school improvement.* San Francisco: Jossey-Bass.

Snowden, P., & Gorton, R. (1998). *School leadership and administration.* New York: McGraw-Hill.

Tanck, M. L. (1994). Celebrating education as a profession. In D. R. Walling (Ed.), *Teachers as leaders* (pp. 83–99). Bloomington, IN: Phi Delta Kappa Educational Foundation.

CHAPTER 6

Beck, L. G. (1994). *Reclaiming educational administration.* New York: Teachers College Press.

Blase, J. R., & Blase, R. R. (2004). *Handbook of instructional leadership: How really good principals promote teaching and learning.* Thousand Oaks, CA: Corwin.

Brown, G., & Irby, B. (2001). *The principal portfolio* (2nd ed.). Thousand Oaks, CA: Corwin.

Cawelti, G. (1993). Foreword. In R. Goldhammer, R. H. Anderson, & R. J. Krajewski (Eds.), *Clinical supervision: Special methods for the supervision of teachers* (3rd ed.). New York: Harcourt Brace Jovanovich.

Daresh, J. C., & Playko, M.A. (1995). *Supervision as a proactive process: Concepts and cases* (2nd ed.). Prospect Heights, IL: Waveland Press.

Ellett, C. (1987). Emerging teacher performance assessment practices: Implications for the instructional supervision role of school principals. In W. Greenfield (Ed.), *Instructional leadership: Concepts, issues, and controversies* (pp. 302–327). Boston: Allyn & Bacon.

Fullan, M. (1994). Teacher leadership: A failure to conceptualize. In D. R. Walling (Ed.), *Teachers as leaders* (pp. 241–253). Bloomington, IN: Phi Delta Kappa Educational Foundation.

Glatthorn, A. A. (1984). *Differentiated supervision.* Alexandria, VA: Association for Supervision and Curriculum Development.

Glickman, C. (1985). *Supervision and instruction: A developmental approach.* Boston: Allyn & Bacon.

Glickman, C., Gordon, S., & Ross-Gordon, J. (2007). *SuperVision and instructional leadership: A developmental approach* (7th ed.). Boston: Pearson, Allyn & Bacon.

Goldhammer, R., Anderson, R. H., & Krajewski, R. J. (1993). *Clinical supervision: Special methods for the supervision of teachers* (3rd ed.). New York: Harcourt Brace Jovanovich.

Hawley, W. D., & Valli, L. (2000). Learner-centered professional development. *News, Notes, & Quotes, 45*(1), 7–9.

Iwanicki, E. F. (2001). Focusing teacher evaluations on student learning. *Educational Leadership, 58*(5), 57–59.

Leiberman, A. (1995). Practices that support teacher development. *Phi Delta Kappan, 76*, 591–596.

Maeroff, G. I. (1994). On matters of body and mind: Overcoming disincentives to a teaching career. In D. R. Walling (Ed.), *Teachers as leaders* (pp. 45–57). Bloomington, IN: Phi Delta Kappa Educational Foundation.

McEwan, E. (2003). *Seven steps to effective instructional leadership.* Thousand Oaks, CA: Corwin.

Mid-continent Research for Education and Learning. (2000). *Leadership for school improvement.* Retrieved February 16, 2001, from http://www.mcrel.org/topics/SchoolImprovement/products/137 and http://www.mcrel.org/topics/SchoolImprovement/products/130.

Murphy, C. U., & Lick, D. W. (2005). *Whole-faculty study groups: Creating student-based professional development* (3rd ed.). Thousand Oaks, CA: Corwin.

Oliva, P. F., & Pawlas, G. E. (1997). *Supervision for today's schools* (5th ed.). White Plains, NY: Longman.

Ornstein, A. C. (1993). How to recognize good teaching. *The American School Board Journal, 180*(1), 24–27.

Razik, T. A., & Swanson, A. D. (1995). *Fundamental concepts of educational leadership.* Upper Saddle River, NJ: Prentice-Hall.

Rogers, C. R., & Freiberg, H. J. (1994). *Freedom to learn* (3rd ed.) New York: Merrill.

Rubin, L. (1975). The case for staff development. In T. J. Sergiovanni (Ed.), *Professional supervision for professional teachers* (pp. 33–49). Washington, DC: Association for Supervision and Curriculum Development.

Sarason, S. B. (1993). *So you are thinking of teaching? Opportunities, problems, realities.* San Francisco: Jossey-Bass.

Sergiovanni, T. J. (1991). *The principalship: A reflective practice perspective* (2nd ed.). Boston: Allyn & Bacon.

Sergiovanni, T. J. (1995). *The principalship: A reflective practice perspective* (3rd ed.). Boston: Allyn & Bacon.

Sparks, D. (2001). Being an informed consumer of electronic learning. *The School Administrator,* (3), 56.

Stiggins, R. J. (1997). *Student-centered classroom assessment* (2nd ed.). Upper Saddle River, NJ: Prentice-Hall.

Sullivan, S., & Glanz, J. (2005). *Supervision that improves teaching: Strategies and techniques* (2nd ed.). Thousand Oaks, CA: Corwin.

Tanck, M. L. (1994). Celebrating education as a profession. In D. R. Walling (Ed.), *Teachers as leaders* (pp. 83–97). Bloomington, IN: Phi Delta Kappa Educational Foundation.

CHAPTER 7

American Psychological Association (1997). *Learner-centered psychological principles: A framework for reform and redesign.* Washington, DC: Center for Psychology in Schools and Education. Retrieved April 13, 2009, from http://www.apa.org/ed/cpse/LCPP.pdf.

Austin, G. R., & Holowenzak, S. (1985). An examination of ten years of research on exemplary schools. In G. A. Austin & H. Garner (Eds.), *In search of exemplary schools* (pp. 65–82). Orlando, FL: Academic Press.

Canter, L., & Canter, M. (1991). *Parents on your side: A comprehensive parent involvement program for teachers.* Santa Monica, CA: Canter & Associates.

Ciliberto, A. (2001). In this issue. *NASSP's Bulletin, 85*(621), 1.

Cohen, D. K., & Ball, D. L. (2001). Making change: Instruction and its improvement. *Phi Delta Kappan, 83*(1), 73–77.

Cotton, K. (1995). *Effective schooling practices: A research synthesis 1995 update.* Portland, OR: Northwest Regional Educational Laboratory.

Epstein, J. L. (1987). Parent involvement: What research says to administrators. *Education and Urban Society, 19*(2), 119–136.

Henderson, A. T., & Mapp, K. L. (2002). *A new wave of evidence: The impact of school, family, and community connections on student achievement.* National Center for Family & Community Connections with Schools—Southwest Educational Development Laboratory, Austin, Texas. Retrieved November 26, 2008, from http://www.sedl.org/connections/resources/evidence.pdf.

Hoyle, J. R., English, F., & Steffy, B. (1994). *Skills for successful school leaders* (2nd ed.). Arlington, VA: American Association of School Administrators.

Keefe, J. M., & Jenkins, J. W. (2002). Two schools: Two approaches to personalized learning. *Phi Delta Kappan, 83*(6), 449–456.

Leithwood, K., Louis, K., Andersen, S., & Wahlstrom, K. (2004). *How leadership influences student learning: Review of research.* Minneapolis, MN: Center for Applied Research, University of Minnesota.

Leithwood, K., & Riehl, C. (2005). What do we already know about educational leadership. In W. Firestone & C. Riehl (Eds.), *A new agenda for research in educational leadership* (pp.12–27). New York: Teachers College Press.

Lewis, A. C. (2001). Toward a nation of "equal kids." *Phi Delta Kappan, 82*(9), 647–648.

McCombs, B., & Whisler, J. S. (1997). *The learner-centered classroom and school: Strategies for increasing student motivation and achievement.* San Francisco: Jossey-Bass.

Ornstein, A. (1993). How to recognize good teaching. *The American School Board Journal, 180*(1), 24–27.

Rossi, R., & Montgomery, A. (Eds.). (1994, January). Educational reforms and students at risk: A review of the current state of the art. *Studies of Education Reform.* Retrieved September 15, 2000, from http://www.ed.gov/pubs/EdReformStudies/EdReforms/title.html.

Shephard, L., & Smith, M. (1990). Synthesis of research on grade retention. *Educational Leadership, 47*(8), 84–88.

Thomas, M., & Bainbridge, W. (2001). The contamination of the effective schools movement. *The School Administrator, 58*(3), 55.

Van Horn, R. (2008). *Bridging the chasm between research and practice: A guide to major educational research.* Lanham, MD: Rowman & Littlefield Education.

CHAPTER 8

Black, P., & Wiliam, D. (1998). Inside the black box: Raising standards through classroom assessment. *Phi Delta Kappan, 80*(2), 139–148.

Bohn, A., & Sleeter, C. (2000). Multicultural education and the standards movement: A report from the field. *Phi Delta Kappan, 82*(2), 156–159.

Ciliberto, A. (2001). In this issue. *NASSP's Bulletin, 85*(621), 1.

Education Commission of the States, NCLB Reauthorization database. (2007). *Education Issues.* Retrieved November 26, 2008, from http://www.ecs .org/html/educationIssues/NCLBreauthorization/NCLB.

Eisner, E. (2001). What does it mean to say a school is doing well? *Phi Delta Kappan, 82*(5), 367–372.

Franklin, J. (2001). Trying too hard? How accountability and testing are affecting constructivist teaching. *ASCD's Education Update, 43*(3), 8.

Glickman, C. D., Gordon, S. P., & Ross-Gordon, J. M. (2007). *Supervision and instructional leadership: A developmental approach* (7th ed.). Boston: Pearson Education.

Houston, P. (2001). It takes a village to raise achievement. *The School Administrator, 6*(58), 46.

Jones, A. (2001). Welcome to standardsville. *Phi Delta Kappan, 82*(6), 462–464.

Kohn, A. (2001). Fighting the tests: A practical guide to rescuing our schools. *Phi Delta Kappan, 82*(5), 348–357.

Knowles, R., & Knowles, T. (2001). Accountability for what? *Phi Delta Kappan, 82*(5), 390–392.

Lewis, A.C. (2008) Washington commentary: Clean up the test mess. *Phi Delta Kappan, 87*(9).

Linn, R. L. (2001, Spring). Reporting school quality in standards-based accountability systems. *CRESST Policy Brief, 3.* Retrieved November 26, 2008, from http://www.cse.ucla.

McCloskey W., & McMunn, N. (2000). Strategies for dealing with high-stakes state tests. *Phi Delta Kappan, 82*(2), 115–120.

Merrow, J. (2001). Undermining standards. *Phi Delta Kappan, 82*(9), 652–659.

National Center for Fair and Open Testing. (2008, January). "No Child Left Behind" after six years: An escalating track record of failure. Retrieved November 26, 2008, from http://www.fairtest.org/NCLB-After-Six-Years.

Mills, R. (2001). Distractions in a season of accountability. *The School Administrator, 6*(58), 40.

Mintzberg, H. (1994). *The rise and fall of strategic planning.* New York: Free Press.

Nave, B., Meich, E., & Mosteller, F. A. (2000). A lapse in standards: Linking standards-based reform with student achievement. *Phi Delta Kappan, 82*(2), 128–132.

Razik, T. A., & Swanson, A. D. (1995). *Fundamental concepts of educational leadership.* Upper Saddle River, NJ: Prentice-Hall.

Reeves, D. (2001). Standards make a difference: The influence of standards on classroom assessment. *NASSP's Bulletin, 85*(621), 5–12.

Schlechty, P. (1990). *Schools for the 21st century: Leadership imperative for educational reform.* San Francisco: Jossey-Bass.

Smith, J. (2001, Spring). Are standards improving teaching and learning? *MASCD's Noteworthy News,* 4–5

Stiggins, R. J. (1997). *Student-centered classroom assessment* (2nd ed.). Upper Saddle River, NJ: Prentice-Hall

Stiggins, R. J. (2001). The principal's leadership role in assessment. *NASSP's Bulletin, 85*(621), 13–26.

Students and accountability. (2001). *ASCD's Education Update, 43,* 6–7.

Thompson, S. (2001). The authentic standards movement and its evil twin. *Phi Delta Kappan, 82*(5), 358–362.

Tirozzi, G. (2001). The artistry of leadership: The evolving role of the secondary school principalship. *Phi Delta Kappan, 82*(6), 434–439.

Van Horn, R. (2008). *Bridging the chasm between research and practice: A guide to major educational research.* Lanham, MD: Rowman & Littlefield Education.

CHAPTER 9

Bennis, W., & Goldsmith, J. (1997). *Learning to lead: A workbook on becoming a leader.* Reading, MA: Perseus.

Bernhardt, V. L. (1998). *Data analysis for comprehensive schoolwide improvement.* Larchmont, NY: Eye on Education.

Burton, G. A. (2001). Success means our graduates give back. *The School Administrator, 58*(4), 42.

Covey, S. (1991). *Principle-centered leadership.* New York: Simon & Schuster.

Creighton, T. B. (2001a). Data analysis in administrators' hands: An oxymoron? *The School Administrator, 58*(4), 6–11.

Creighton, T. B. (2001b). *Schools and data: The educator's guide for using data to improve decision making.* Thousand Oaks, CA: Corwin.

Fitzpatrick, K. A. (Project Director). (1998). *School improvement: Focusing on student performance.* Schaumburg, IL: National Study of School Evaluation.

Fuhrman, S. H. (2003). Is "reform" the answer for urban education? In *Penn GSE: A review of research.* Philadelphia: University of Pennsylvania.

Fullan, M. (1982). *The meaning of educational change.* New York: Teachers College Press.

Fullan, M. (1995). Contexts for leadership and change: Overview and framework. In M. J. O'Hair & S. J. Odell (Eds.), *Educating teachers for leadership and change* (pp. 1–10). Thousand Oaks, CA: Corwin.

Goens, G.A. (2001). Beyond data: The world of scenario planning. *Phi Delta Kappan, 58*(4), 27–32.

Goldberg, M. (2001). Leadership in education. *Phi Delta Kappan, 82*(10), 757–761.

Greenspun, E. (2001). Backtalk. *Phi Delta Kappan, 82*(8), 644.

Hoyle, J. R., English, F., & Steffy, B. (1994). *Skills for successful school leaders* (2nd ed.). Arlington, VA: American Association of School Administrators.

Neuman, M., & Pelchat, J. (2001). The challenge to leadership: Focusing on student achievement. *Phi Delta Kappan, 82*(10), 732–736.

Presidential Task Force on Psychology in Education & American Psychological Association. (1993, January). *Learner-centered psychological principles: Guidelines for school design and reform.* Washington, DC: American Psychological Association/Mid-continent Regional Educational Laboratory.

Razik, T. A., & Swanson, A. D. (2001). *Fundamental concepts of educational leadership* (2nd ed.). Upper Saddle River, NJ: Prentice-Hall.

Reeves, D. (2006). *The learning leader: How to focus school improvement for better results.* Alexandria, VA: Association for Supervision and Curriculum Development.

Schlechty, P. C. (1990). *Schools for the 21st century: Leadership imperatives for educational reform.* San Francisco: Jossey-Bass.

Schwab, R., & Foa, L. (2001). Integrating technologies throughout our schools. *Phi Delta Kappan, 82*(8), 620–624.

Schwahn, C., & Spady, W. (1998). *Total leaders: Applying the best future-focused change strategies to education.* Arlington, VA: American Association of School Administrators.

Southern Regional Education Board. (1998). *Getting results: A fresh look at school accountability.* Atlanta, GA: Southern Regional Education Board.

Streifer, P. A. (2001). The drill-down process. *The School Administrator, 58*(4), 16–19.

Tanck, M. L. (1994). Celebrating education as a profession. In D. R. Walling (Ed.), *Teachers as leaders* (pp. 83–99). Bloomington, IN: Phi Delta Kappa Educational Foundation.

U.S. Department of Education. (2004). *National education technology plan: The future is now.* Retrieved on August 11, 2008, from www.ed.gov/about/offices/list/os/technology/plan/2004/site/theplan/edlite-Recommendations.

U.S. Office of Special Education Programs. (2000). *Promising practices.* Retrieved on September 20, 2000, from http://ericec.org/osep/promprac.htm.

Wells, G. (2001). Software for data use. *The School Administrator, 58*(4), 8.

Yeagley, R. (2001). Data in your hands. *The School Administrator, 58*(4), 12–15.

CHAPTER 10

Covey, S. (2004). *The seven habits of highly effective people: Power lessons in personal change.* New York: Free Press.

Dyer, W. W. (2007). *Change your thoughts—change your life: Living the wisdom of the Tao.* Carlsbad, CA: Hay House.

Index

CORWIN
A SAGE Company

The Corwin logo—a raven striding across an open book—represents the union of courage and learning. Corwin is committed to improving education for all learners by publishing books and other professional development resources for those serving the field of PreK–12 education. By providing practical, hands-on materials, Corwin continues to carry out the promise of its motto: **"Helping Educators Do Their Work Better."**